THE VIOLENCE OF HATE

Understanding Harmful Forms of Bias and Bigotry

FOURTH EDITION

JACK LEVIN

Brudnick Center on Violence and Conflict

Northeastern University

and

JIM NOLAN

West Virginia University

ROWMAN & LITTLEFIELD

Lanham • Boulder • New York • London

Executive Editor: Nancy Roberts
Associate Editor: Molly White
Senior Marketing Manager: Karin Cholak
Marketing Manager: Deborah Hudson
Interior Designer: Ilze Lemesis
Cover Designer: Diana Nuhn

Credits and acknowledgments for material borrowed from other sources, and reproduced with permission, appear on the appropriate page within the text.

Published by Rowman & Littlefield
A wholly owned subsidiary of The Rowman & Littlefield Publishing Group, Inc.
4501 Forbes Boulevard, Suite 200, Lanham, Maryland 20706
www.rowman.com

Unit A, Whitacre Mews, 26-34 Stannary Street, London SE11 4AB, United Kingdom

British Library Cataloguing in Publication Information Available

Library of Congress Cataloging-in-Publication Data

Names: Levin, Jack, 1941– author. | Nolan, Jim (James J.), author.
Title: The violence of hate : understanding harmful forms of bias and bigotry / Jack Levin, Brudnick Center on Violence and Conflict, Northeastern University, Jim Nolan, Department of Sociology and Anthropology, West Virginia University.
Description: Fourth Edition. | Lanham : Rowman & Littlefield, 2016. | Revised edition of The violence of hate, 2011. | Includes bibliographical references and index.
Identifiers: LCCN 2016013460 (print) | LCCN 2016022559 (ebook) | ISBN 9781442260498 (cloth : alk. paper) | ISBN 9781442260504 (pbk. : alk. paper) | ISBN 9781442260511 (electronic)
Subjects: LCSH: Hate crimes. | Racism. | Antisemitism. | Toleration.
Classification: LCC HV6773.5 .L48 2016 (print) | LCC HV6773.5 (ebook) | DDC 305.8--dc23
LC record available at https://lccn.loc.gov/2016013460

Printed in the United States of America

Dedication

From Jack Levin to
> Dan Steven Victoria
> Benjamin Max Bryson
> Jaden Matthew Segal
> Ethan Samuel Segal
> Gavin Finn Segal

From Jim Nolan to
> Darrell Lamar Claybrook
> Dion Del Claybrook
> Reese Carrie Claybrook
> McKenna Nolan Lausch
> Cora Nolan Lausch
> Felicity Spring Thompson

Contents

Preface

The fourth edition of *The Violence of Hate* represents a major revision. Not only have we added a significant number of pages and updated statistics and examples in many places, but we have also expanded our discourse to include a much broader range of victims and perpetrators.

At the same time, we continue to emphasize the commonalities joining rather than the differences separating those in society who have been victimized because they are different in socially significant ways. Under a single conceptual framework emphasizing the power of situations, we explore important, yet perplexing, forms of hate and prejudice, including racism in American society following President Obama's election; the historical and present-day occurrence of anti-Semitism; anti-Muslim sentiment in the aftermath of the 9/11 attacks as well as the recent terrorist attacks in Paris and Brussels; renegade Christians acting as servants of power; disenfranchised Roma—or Gypsies—systematically denied access to basic human essentials such as health care, employment, and education; gay and lesbian youths taunted and teased and victimized by sadistic violence; assaultive behavior directed at immigrants during periods of high unemployment; violence perpetrated against women around the world; and people with disabilities whose rate of violent victimization measures three times that of individuals in the general population.

The new material in this edition includes a chapter dedicated solely to explanations of hate violence and an expanded chapter on hate crimes in which relations between the police and the Black community are explored, beginning with the crisis in Ferguson, Missouri. Along with many new and updated examples, this edition also includes several new sections that pull from the disciplines of sociology, social psychology, and psychology to develop an integrated perspective on the circumstances of hate violence and the reasons we have not always been effective in stopping it.

As in earlier versions of *The Violence of Hate*, we take the position that support for the violence of hate originates not in the ranting and raving of bigoted extremists at the margins of society but in the tacit approval of ordinary, even decent, people who are located squarely in the mainstream. Relatively few Americans actively dabble in bigotry, and even fewer are hardened hatemongers. But millions of individuals who would not dream of committing a hate crime nevertheless contribute to the cause of prejudice by sympathizing with those who do perpetrate violent attacks. In addition, there are countless numbers of otherwise virtuous people in society who remain passive spectators to bigotry because they benefit in either a psychological or socioeconomic sense from the status quo. Although lacking in virulent prejudice, these spectators also lack the courage required to pay the price for doing the right thing. For many, spectatorship is all too comfortable.

Some observers have suggested over the years that blatant acts of bigotry and bias have declined to the point where they no longer threaten the well-being of society's members. From this viewpoint, although prejudice has become harmless or benign, certain environmental or genetic characteristics of marginalized groups continue to play an important role in maintaining group inequalities.

Rejecting this view, we argue that hate is alive, well, and living in our communities where it continues to have a major impact on the access to opportunities and personal safety of millions of Americans. Depending on the circumstances at a particular point in history, hate can remain latent and concealed, making its presence felt in only the most subtle or even unconscious ways until such time as a particular group becomes a challenge or threat. Moreover, even where hate and prejudice have declined, it takes relatively few hate incidents to escalate a situation into a large-scale inter-group conflict. We have certainly witnessed this phenomenon recently with the onset of retaliatory violence in response to acts of terrorism. Since the 9/11 attacks on America, the motivation for hate violence has become more defensive, from the perpetrators' viewpoint.

Unlike those who assert that hate is a result of either culture or self-interest, we suggest that it is a consequence of both. Hate is normal, expected, and, in many cases, quite rational. Respect for differences can be so costly in a psychological and material sense that it may actually require rebellious or deviant behavior. In the final chapter, we suggest strategies for producing rebels, deviants, and other decent people.

From Jack

Speaking of decent people, I take this opportunity to thank a number of my colleagues, students, and family members who have unselfishly donated their ideas, criticisms, and suggestions for improving the form and substance of this book. I am grateful to Kayleen U. Oka, former director of Multicultural Services at Edmonds College, and Stephen L. Wessler, director of the Center for the Prevention of Hate Violence, whose insights and recommendations have been liberally sprinkled throughout this work.

I am indebted to the following colleagues who, over the years, have influenced my thinking about the origins of hate-motivated violence: Arnie Arluke, Chip Berlet, Jo-Anne Bishop, Randy Blazak, Kathleen Blee, Barry Bluestone, William Brustein, Richard Cole, Ed Dunbar, Howard Ehrlich, Amitai Etzioni, Raphael Ezekiel, Luis Falcon, Jamie Fox, Meridith Gould, Bob Hall, David Hall, Mark Hamm, Will Holton, Matt Hunt, Range Hutson, Paul Iganski, Valerie Jenness, Billy Johnston, Tony Jones, Debbie Kaufman, Nancy Kaufman, Tom Koenig, Harlan Lane, Richard Lapchick, Fred Lawrence, Yueh-Ting Lee, David Lennox, Brian Levin (no relation), Michael Lieberman, Larry Lowenthal, Jack McDevitt, Karen McLaughlin, Bill Miles, Petar-Emil Mitev, Marvin Nathan, Kayleen U. Oka, Vincent Parillo, Monte Paulsen, Barbara Perry, Carolyn Petrosino, Mark Potok, Bernard Phillips, Emmett Price, Michel Prum, Gordana Rabrenovic, Debbie Ramirez, Tom Shapiro, Pete Simi, Michael Sutton, Sarah Rine, Andy Tarsy, Robert Trestan, Evelyn Umlas, Steve Vallas, Geoff Ward, Joe Warren, Meredith Watts, Stephen L. Wessler, Julie Wiest, and Darnell Williams.

I am grateful to Scott Wolfman and his outstanding staff at Wolfman Productions for their expert guidance in helping to educate generations of college students about the tragedy of hate and violence.

The following students and former students provided valuable feedback about my ideas concerning prejudice and violence: Arlene Adler, Sarah Bakanosky, Spencer Blakeslee, Kevin Borgeson, Candice Botes, Lorenzo Boyd, Christina Braidotti, Rachel Buff, Katie Conner, Sarah Cope, Tara Doran, Julie Doucette, Anjuli Fahlberg, Vin Ferraro, Janese Free, Maya Genovesi, Trevor Glode, Sandra Hussey, Stephanie Cappadona, David Kay, Colleen Keaney, Daniel Knipp, Adina Koch, Megan Krell, Phil Lamy, Bill Levin (no relation), Eric Madfis, Sam Maron, Jason Mazaik, Liz Mengers, Daniela Methe, Brett Nava-Coulter, Jeff O'Brien, Nelly Oliver, Hanna Page, Ashley Reichelmann, Liz Ridge, Peter Roby, Jeff Sadowsky, Hannah Sattler, Mike Smith, Ben Steiner, and Stas Vysotsky.

I am extremely grateful to Betty Brudnick. She and her late husband Irv (Shim) gave me the inspiration I needed to believe that we can change the world for the better.

The members of my wonderful family—my wife Flea, our children who are now adult children who have children of their own, as well as my sisters and brother—have provided the support and encouragement I needed to move through the stages of a project that demanded both time and energy. I have always appreciated their love, tolerance, and patience.

From Jim

One of the important concepts we explored in this edition of *The Violence of Hate* is "interdependence." Our existence and our fate are the consequence our relations with many other people. Those closest to me who have helped shape my views about human relations belong to my birth family, including my mother and father, Barbara and James Nolan (Jr.), and siblings, Colleen (and Dave) Szaroleta, Patti (and Mike) Rosaio, Kelly (and Glen) DiElieutario, Mary (and Richie) Delitta, and Susan (and Ken) Moss, along with all of their children and grandchildren. I also owe much appreciation to the family I married into, including Delwin Bopp, Annette Rabasca, Deb and Jim Bermingham, and Angie Bopp. In addition, I am forever indebted to my extended family, including William Folger, Jr., William Folger, III, Barbara Ann Folger, Stephanie and Stu Folger Hanford, Jean Lyons, David and Kathy Lyons, the Flynns, and all of their children and grandchildren.

I must also thank my friends and colleagues at West Virginia University who have supported me in numerous ways, including Melissa Latimer, Larry Nichols, Allison Nichols, Ronald Althouse, Corey Colyer, Amy Hirshman, Candace Griffith, Jen Steele, Rachel Stein, Chris Plein, Karen Weiss, Joan Gorham, Fred King, Jeri Kirby, Walter DeKeseredy, Mandy Sanchez, Lynne Sittig Cossman, Adam Dasari, Joshua Woods, Barbara Reiprich, Andy Facemire, Loretta Price, Nancy Feathers, Daniel Brewster, Daniel Renfrew, Genesis Snyder, Rachael Woldoff, Katie Corcoran, Lisa Dilks, Jason Manning, Chris Scheitle,

Jesse Wozniak, Susanna Donaldson, Kirsten Song, Victoria Velding, Cheryl Johnson-Lyons, Maria Altimara, Cynthia Barnett-Ryan, Larisha Campbell, Margie Darrah, Jake Stump, as well as all my students who continue to teach me lessons in sociology.

I have learned a lot about group relations from my very good friends and professional colleagues outside of West Virginia University, including Sarah Trickett, Jim Norton, Jack McDevitt, Yoshio Akiyama, Michael Lieberman, Richard and Diane Iardella, Norman Conti, Randall Kocsis, Don and Beth Copson, J. J. Nuttall and Erin Delano, John and Susan McPheeters, Ken and Peggy Schlezes, Bob Wright, Awilda Borres, Stacia Gilliard-Matthews, Luigi Vitrone, Richard Lamb, Tony Gallo, Paul Goldenberg, Brian Levin, Howard Snyder, Anthony Pinizzotto, Ed Davis, Tony Rispoli, Greg Eckrich, Donald Lemire, Richard Woyden, Samuel Berhanu, Susan and Mark Testman, James Brown, Paul Sheridan, Stephen Haas, Tim Parsons, John Howley, Mark Genatempo, Jo-Anne Bishop, Zsolt Molnar, Susan Pearce, Robert Merrill, Amy Farrell, Shea Cronin, Samuel Berhanu, Susie Bennett, Ron Althouse, Ellen Rodrigues, and Elizabeth Walling.

Finally, I must give special thanks to those who provide me with daily love and support, including my wife Pam; daughter Abigail Lausch, her husband Brandon, and their daughters McKenna and Cora; son Jimmy and his wife Christina, daughter Elizabeth, her partner Darrell and sons Darrell, Dion, and daughter Reese; daughter Christine; daughter Carolyn and her daughter Felicity; and son Michael. I love you all.

About the Cover

Our cover photo depicts clenched fists—Black and White—locked together in a history of ignorance and misunderstanding, a couple of the preconditions necessary for the violence of hate.

Jack Levin
Jim Nolan

About the Authors

Jack Levin is professor emeritus of sociology and criminology and codirector of the Brudnick Center on Violence and Conflict at Northeastern University. He has published more than 30 books and numerous journal articles and newspaper columns, primarily in the areas of hate crimes, sociology of prejudice, school violence, and multiple homicide. Levin was honored by the Massachusetts Council for the Advancement and Support of Education as its "Professor of the Year." He recently received an award from the American Sociological Association for his contributions to the public understanding of sociology and also was the recipient of the Apple Award from the New England Sociological Association and the Lester Ward Award from the Association of Applied and Clinical Sociology. In 2013, he received a Lifetime Achievement Award for his research in criminology from the Society for the Study of Social Problems.

Jim Nolan is professor in the Department of Sociology and Anthropology at West Virginia University where he teaches courses on the topic of crime and social control. His research currently focuses on urban policing, intergroup relations and hate crimes, and the measurement of crime. He has been the recipient of research funding from several U.S. Department of Justice agencies and the National Science Foundation. Dr. Nolan is currently serving on a National Academy of Sciences panel on modernizing the nation's crime statistics. His research publications have appeared in the *American Behavioral Scientist, Journal of Quantitative Criminology, Journal of Contemporary Criminal Justice, Policing & Society, Criminal Justice Studies, Homicide Studies, Journal of Criminal Justice*, and *The American Sociologist*. Dr. Nolan was the 2010 recipient of the Carnegie Foundation for the Advancement of Teaching and Council for Advancement and Support of Education (CASE) West Virginia Professor of the Year.

CHAPTER 1

Perspectives on Hate and Violence

Hate, Prejudice, and Discrimination

At one time, the term "awesome" had to do with awe; now it means "great" or "excellent." The word "cool" formerly referred only to the temperature (e.g., what a cool day for July), and then it also meant "stylish" or "fashionable." Nowadays, "cool" is articulated to indicate that something is acceptable, great, or awesome. Language becomes modified over time in response to changing events and situations. This is almost as true of social science as it is of everyday conversation.

Until recently, the term "hate" referred to any intense dislike or hostility, whatever its object. In everyday conversation, for example, an individual might be said to "hate" his teacher, the taste of liver, communism, or even himself. Thus, in this generic sense of the term, hate could be directed at almost anything—a person, a group, an idea, some other abstraction, or an inanimate object (Levin & Paulsen, 1999).

Transforming the Terms

Beginning in the mid-1980s, in response to a series of racially inspired murders in New York City, the term "hate" became used in a much more restricted sense to characterize an individual's negative beliefs and feelings about the members of some other group of people because of their race, religious identity, ethnic origin, gender, sexual orientation, age, or disability status (Jacobs & Potter, 1998; Jenness & Broad, 1997; Jenness & Grattet, 2004; Lawrence, 1999; Levin, 1992–1993; Levin & McDevitt, 1993). As incorporated into the concept of *hate crime,* this more limited usage overlaps terms such as "prejudice," "bias," "bigotry," "ethnocentrism," and "ethnoviolence" (as in such more specific forms as racism, sexism, ageism, homophobia, and xenophobia—Perry, 2003).

"Hate" is not the only concept in the lexicon of bigotry to have undergone a major shift in meaning. Very much the same sort of transition occurred decades earlier in the original definition of the kindred term "prejudice"—from "any pre-judgment" to "a hostile attitude directed specifically toward the members of an outgroup" (Ehrlich, 1972, 2009; Levin & Levin, 1982; Levin & Rabrenovic, 2009).

In its original usage, the term "prejudice" was used in a legal sense to refer to a prejudgment about the guilt or innocence of a defendant, that is, an evaluation made before all the facts of a case could be properly determined and weighed. This usage was subsequently broadened to include "any unreasonable attitude that is unusually resistant to rational influence" (Rosnow, 1972, p. 53). Thus, a person who was stubbornly committed to a position in the face of overwhelming evidence to the contrary could be characterized as prejudiced, whether about her politics, her religious convictions, her friends, or her children.

After the publication of Gordon Allport's classic work, *The Nature of Prejudice,* in 1954, the term "prejudice" was no longer reserved for characterizing people who jump to conclusions or make dogmatic judgments and instead became associated more narrowly with bigotry, bias, and racism. Thus, a prejudiced individual was someone who stereotyped the members of a particular race as, for example, dirty, lazy, and stupid; despised the people in a particular group for being uncivilized and inferior; or felt sickened by the very thought of those who had a different skin color or religious orientation. The original irrationality was retained in Allport's definition, but he applied it much more narrowly to refer to a negative attitude toward other people because they are in a different race, religion, or ethnic group.

Decades later, the same concept was applied to a wider range of differences including sexual orientation, disability status, gender, gender identity, and age (see Levin, 2009; Levin & Levin, 1982; Levin & McDevitt, 1995a). At this point, the phenomena of hate and prejudice were, for most purposes, treated as interchangeable.[1]

Prejudice versus Discrimination

By the same token, Allport considered discrimination prejudice's behavioral counterpart—as hurtful, harmful, destructive behavior toward others because they are perceived to be members of a particular group. Violence represents an extreme version of discrimination; but other examples include name-calling, vandalizing, threatening, firing, or refusing to have contact with individuals who are different.

The relationship between hate or prejudice on the one hand, and discrimination on the other, has been well documented. There is reason to believe that certain hate offenses *result from* some personal bias or hatred. Perpetrators may act out of prejudicial beliefs (i.e., stereotypes) and/or emotions (e.g., envy, fear, or revulsion) concerning people who are different. In the extreme case, a hatemonger may join an organized group in order to devote his entire life to destroying a group of people he considers "inferior."

---

[1] Although overlapping and used interchangeably in this work, "hate" and "prejudice" also have differences that are important to emphasize. "Hate" tends to focus less on cognition (i.e., stereotyping) and more on the emotional or affective component of bigotry. Indeed, until hate became recently associated with intergroup hostility, researchers focused almost exclusively on the cognitive dimension of prejudice. As a result, sociologists and psychologists have offered many more insights into the nature of stereotypes and other cognitive processes related to prejudice than they have into its affective basis (Pettigrew, 1997).

It is not, however, always necessary for hate to precede the bigoted behavior. In fact, from the literature of social psychology, we know that prejudices often develop or at least become strengthened to justify *previous* discriminatory behavior, including violence (see Blee, 2003; Levin & Levin, 1988).

This is probably true of hate crimes as well as other forms of discrimination. For example, a White teenager may assault someone who is Latino because his friends expect him to comply, not because *initially* he harbors intense hatred toward his victim. If he views the target of his attack as a flesh-and-blood human being with feelings, friends, and a family, the offender may feel guilty. By accepting a dehumanized image of the victim, however, the perpetrator may actually come to believe that his crime is justified. After all, the rules of civilized society apply only to human beings, not to demons or wild animals. Similarly, an individual may commit an act of violence against an individual for economic reasons (e.g., because he believes that the presence of Blacks in his neighborhood reduces property values) and subsequently become totally convinced that all Blacks are rapists and murderers. Who would want a rapist living next door?

Part of the way that we come to understand ourselves is not very different from the way that others come to know us. We observe the manner in which we act over a period of time. If we repeatedly participate in hate crimes or other discriminatory behavior, we might very well gradually modify our self-image and our thinking about the groups we attack so as to be consistent with how we behave. Once again, we see the impact of discriminatory behavior on hate and prejudice (Bem, 1970, 1992).

Most surprisingly, perhaps, individuals who find comfort in joining an organized hate group may not always be so hate-filled as we might believe, at least not at first. In her research into what motivates women who join White supremacist groups, sociologist Kathleen Blee (2003) discovered that many of her respondents became more hateful *after* joining the movement. Their decision to take membership in a hate group was apparently inspired less by prejudice or hate and more by a desire for community; that is, to remain in good standing with their comrades.

The Role of the Individual

During the 1940s and 1950s, the term "prejudice" provided the basis for countless studies of intergroup tension and hostility. One of the most important theories ever developed in the social sciences, the *authoritarian personality structure* (Adorno, Frankel-Brunswick, Levinson, & Sanford, 1950), took a psychoanalytic viewpoint that located the roots of bigotry in early childhood. Authoritarian children were raised by harsh and threatening parents who inculcated a feeling of intense powerlessness in their offspring. Later on, these children began to identify with powerful authority figures. Because they were refugees from Nazi Germany, the authors of the authoritarian personality theory argued that Hitler's appeal came, at least in part, from the desire of some German citizens to again feel the sense of power and control they had lost in the aftermath of World War I. Literally thousands of research projects were initiated to test various aspects of the theory.

At the same time, social psychologists of the day suggested that prejudice or hate derives out of the individual's inability to achieve important objectives. Goal blockage leads to intense frustration, which, in turn, can result in aggression. Under certain circumstances—for example, when the true source of a frustration is very powerful or ambiguous—the aggressive behavior is displaced onto innocent victims. According to Berkowitz (1993), displaced aggression is an important psychological basis for prejudice and hate.

Of course, an individual's beliefs, emotions, and action-tendencies are impacted by the sociocultural environment in which he or she lives. Social scientists have long argued that criminal behavior frequently results from an individual's experience of dealing with the difficulties of everyday living. In 1938, Robert Merton suggested that American culture emphasizes economic success without also emphasizing the requisite opportunities for attaining it. Members of society are urged to pull themselves up by their bootstraps and do what it takes to become wealthy, but many of them lack access to the structural means for improving their socioeconomic status.

As a result, some Americans "innovate," using Merton's terminology. That is, they continue to strive to be financially successful, but they give up on mainstream society and no longer employ the legitimate system (e.g., getting good grades, attending college, working hard in the corporate world, and so on). Instead, they go outside of conventional society and seek to "get ahead" by engaging in criminal behavior (e.g., robbery or fraud or embezzlement).

The profit motive seemed to be at the heart of a horrendous hate crime discovered in 2011 as perpetrated against six mentally and physically challenged adults in North Philadelphia. Over a period of ten years, the ringleader, 55-year-old Linda Weston, and her three associates kept their victims chained in a dark basement boiler room where they were daily sedated with drugs, forced to use a bucket as a toilet, and punished by being punched, kicked, stabbed, or burned. The thieves' purpose was, in Merton's terms, to innovate in order to accumulate wealth—to steal more than $200,000 by cashing their victims' social security checks (Gillman, 2015). The lure of easy money is hardly the one and only basis for frustration or strain. Broadening Merton's conception, Robert Agnew (1992) proposed his General Strain Theory whereby a range of negative experiences or disappointing events in social relationships at home, school, or work, or in the neighborhood, can lead to frustration, anger, depression, anxiety, and ultimately, to criminal behavior. Agnew identified several sources of strain in addition to material success including the failure to achieve positively valued goals, the loss of social status, and the gap between aspirations and achievements.

Racist skinheads come from a broad range of socioeconomic circumstances. The basis of their propensity for hate violence frequently lies not in chronic poverty but in severe domestic conflict or inordinate peer influence. Many come from homes where hostility and conflict run rampant. Not unlike an inner-city gang, an organized skinhead group may serve as a surrogate family, supplying its members with a sense of belonging and acceptance they are unable to secure at home. Instead, they may turn to their delinquent peers for support and encouragement, and grow to view their mother and father as nothing more than obstacles to their rebellious desires.

Certain individual factors may help to determine which youngsters do and do not react to strain by engaging in violent behavior. Some hatemongers may be psychotic; others share a personality disorder (e.g., sociopathy or anti-social personality disorder) in which a strong sense of conscience and empathy are missing. Still others suffer from depression and poor impulse control. At least a few violent hatemongers have been traumatized. They come from broken homes, suffer physical or sexual abuse, or have at least one parent with a criminal history (Langman, 2009). Even where normalcy prevails, family members might pressure a young person to work hard, be politically correct, and study enough to stay in school and get good grades. In a skinhead group, in sharp contrast, the only expectation is to be a loyal member.

In February 1995, two teenaged brothers, Bryan and David Freeman, who belonged to a neo-Nazi skinhead group located in Lehigh Valley, Pennsylvania, brutally bludgeoned and stabbed to death their parents and younger brother in their middle-class Allentown home. For a few months prior to engaging in their killing spree, the two brothers had shaved their heads and began to wear military-style clothing. Schoolmates soon noticed that neo-Nazi tattoos were embedded in their foreheads along with the words "Sieg Heil," a reference to the Nazi salute.

Even though the Freeman brothers' neo-Nazi proclivities became a source of household tension, they apparently did not cause the murders to occur. The hostility in the Freeman home was longstanding and chronic. The parents attempted but failed to interest their offspring in adopting their deeply held religious beliefs. One of the killers later remarked that the murders were a reaction to his mother's intensely strict rules. The second brother had been hospitalized twice for psychiatric difficulties.

Skinhead membership also confers status on those of its members who hold leadership positions. For some reason, these members lack the ability, talent, or sensitivity required for success in mainstream society and are therefore not able to achieve a sense of importance in any middle-class way. Yet their position in a skinhead group makes them feel a sense of power and control that they never felt when they behaved themselves. As a result, it is all but impossible to persuade members of racist skinhead groups to relinquish their memberships and adopt a perspective of tolerance and respect for differences. Why should they give up their sense of belonging and importance to relocate back into mainstream society where they might again feel isolated and obscure, if not obligated to succeed in a middle-class sense?

Justifying Hate Violence

Some hatemongers devote their lives to the objective of cleansing their community, their country, or their world of the dreaded outsiders. Rather than do the things that might help to assure their success in mainstream society, they join hate groups, visit hate websites, communicate with like-minded individuals in chat rooms, listen to white power CDs, and confront their enemies on the streets. They are desperate to feel some sense of their own importance, to feel special and powerful and in charge of things. Not having felt a sense of dominance when they behaved themselves, they instead bash, assault, vandalize, and intimidate.

In the 1960s, Matza and Sykes developed a conceptual framework to explain how certain individuals drift in and out of delinquent behavior. According to Matza and Sykes, delinquents generate a set of techniques of neutralization, which they employ to justify behavior that violates cultural norms. These techniques—for example, believing that their victims deserve their maltreatment—temporarily suspend the perpetrators' attachment to mainstream culture and provide them with the freedom to transgress.

Hate is, in this respect, more powerful than any technique of neutralization. Unlike forms of criminal behavior that violate widely held cultural norms, hate is sanctioned in the dominant culture. As a result, there is no need to suspend commitment. The perpetrator feels supported and encouraged; he sees no need to neutralize his hostilities; his justification is thoroughly accessible.

Hate provides a cultural justication in two ways. First, it identifies the enemy. When they go out looking for a vulnerable victim to bash or assault, groups of youngsters already know—based on accumulated immersion in the culture—exactly which groups are off limits and which groups can be attacked with moral impunity. Second, hate re-emerges after the fact to excuse the victims' pain and suffering. The cultural images again come into play in order to justify criminal behavior. The perpetrator has not attacked human beings; he has targeted subhuman or Satanic forces, thus preventing them from eliminating the finest qualities of our cultural heritage. He has done a favor for his friends and family who despise the members of the group he has chosen to attack but themselves lack the courage to take necessary action. His hate may remain latent, until he has committed an act that begs for justification. Hate, in the short term, is a dependent variable. It follows and is defined by a violent act. But, over time, hate then becomes a contributing factor to allow future acts of violence to be committed with impunity.

The Influence of Significant Others

Many individuals develop a propensity for hate and violence from what they learn during their interaction with other people. Early on, Sutherland and Cressey (1984) proposed that criminal behavior in general derives from *differential association* with a group of intimates—close friends and family members—who reinforce positive attitudes toward criminal behavior. Decades later, Akers (2000) refined and expanded Sutherland and Cressey's original formulation of differential association by recognizing that the impact of interacting with people who commit criminal acts and hold positive attitudes toward criminality varies depending on the frequency, duration, intensity, and priority of the interaction. The same line of reasoning can be applied more specifically to hate-motivated violence. Akers also suggested that close friends and family who are admired and respected tend to be especially influential as role models to be imitated and emulated.

An extreme example of the impact of differential association is provided by the experiences of Lamb and Lynx Gaede, teenaged twin girls from Bakersfield, California, who called their singing duo Prussian Blue and, for several years beginning at the age of nine, performed songs about the superiority of the white race in front of all-white audiences at white supremacist festivals. Almost since birth, the twins were socialized into their racist beliefs by their neo-Nazi stay-at-home mom April, who provided home schooling on a daily basis, and by a rancher grandfather who placed the Nazi swastika on his belt buckle, on the side of his pickup truck, and on his cattle brand. As they grew into adulthood and achieved a degree of independence from their mother, the twins modified their racist views and became much more accepting of diversity. Still, it appears that at least some of their earlier bigotry, learned from an early age, did not totally fall away.

Being socialized by parents, friends, and teachers may be a part of the process whereby hate violence arises, but it is not the entire story. The violence of hate can also grow out of frustrations and strains experienced collectively at the group level. Social scientists have long recognized that hate and bigotry wouldn't last 30 minutes if their consequences were totally costly and harmful to everyone in a society. The question we ask in chapter 5 is the following: "Who benefits from the maintenance of hate and violence? That is, which groups and individuals acquire an advantage in a psychological, political, and economic sense by means of their dangerously hateful behavior?"

Especially during economic bad times, there are certain individuals who suffer with the difficulties of everyday living. As economic inequality has gradually increased since the early 1970s, more and more middle-class Americans are having a hard time making ends meet. Some of them externalize responsibility, blaming an entire category of people considered outsiders—immigrants or African Americans or Latinos or Asians or Jews or Muslims or gays. In European countries, the list includes Roma or Gypsies. In the neo-Nazi version, it is "all of the above."

From Individual to Institutional Discrimination

During the 1960s and later, ripples from the civil rights movement began to make their way through American society. The concept of prejudice fell out of favor with social scientists as vastly more attention became focused on institutionalized rather than individual racism. To a growing extent, the thinking in social science was that racist attitudes (or at least their public expression) were on the decline and that discrimination was more or less independent of hate (see, e.g., Levin & McDevitt, 1995a; Schuman, Steeh, Bobo, & Krysan, 1997).

Thus, rather than focus on individual prejudices, researchers during the past few decades understandably turned more of their attention to investigating institutional and structural forms of discrimination: in large businesses, for example, how union seniority rules assure that people of color do not get promoted, even if individual union representatives oppose the prevailing system; in college applications, the manner in which SATs indirectly favor White applicants, whether or not individual admissions officers hold racist attitudes; in real estate transactions, how real estate associations, as a matter of policy, "steer" Black home buyers away from White neighborhoods, regardless of the racial biases of particular agents (Pearce, 1979; Turner & Mikelsons, 1992).

Because social scientists have enthusiastically examined such structural issues, they may have been surprised when advocacy groups suggested during the 1980s and 1990s that hate violence was dramatically on the rise. The so-called "new" or "modern" racism had emphasized subtle, sophisticated, symbolic, unconscious, and institutionalized forms of bigotry; it had all but failed to recognize the possibility that policies and programs directed at tearing down the barriers separating various racial and religious groups might also provoke increasing numbers of hate crimes committed by members of traditionally advantaged groups in society who felt under attack.

It might be unexpected that two sociologists—the authors of this book—would argue for bringing back the individual into our theorizing about intergroup conflict, but that is exactly what we think is important to do. Just as Allport (1954) long ago suggested, the individual is a silent partner, an active agent, and a gatekeeper in any process of social change. It is important, of course, to recognize the enormous influence of structural and cultural sources of bigotry, but it is just as significant to realize that it takes individual action or lack of action to make hate happen. Individuals still make the decisions; they conform or refuse to conform to group standards; and they decide whether to go along with the dictates of legitimate authority.

Individuals internalize the cultural hate, and many of them also benefit (or they believe that they benefit) from the maintenance of prejudice and discrimination. Based on both company policy as well as on personal preconceptions, real estate agents decide who sees which houses and who doesn't. Based on both school policy and on personal preference, university admissions officers decide who gets into school and who is refused admission. Moreover, while depending on institutionalized practices and policies, the overwhelming majority of hate offenses are committed not by organizations but by individuals. The hate expressed in such crimes is far from indirect or sophisticated or abstract; the discrimination is anything but subtle.

Constructing Group Identity

Group identity has been known to inspire collective pride, guilt, or shame, depending on the circumstances. In theory, there is absolutely nothing wrong with having pride in one's group or heritage, so long as it isn't at the expense of other groups. In reality, however, the stronger the group pride, the more likely it is that outsiders will be treated as inferior.

Several decades ago, when Apartheid was still the reigning system of race relations in the country of South Africa, the first author happened to run across an Associated Press story in the *Boston Globe* concerning an unfortunate White woman in Johannesburg who was being treated for cancer. Through no fault of her own, she had suffered not only a loss of her physical well-being but also a dramatic loss of her social and economic status.

Under the South African system of Apartheid, there were three racial categories: White, Colored, and Black. Actually, the racial identity of South Africans determined almost entirely the range of opportunities they could expect to enjoy over the course of life, including whom they were eligible to date and marry, where they were permitted to live, what sorts of jobs they were qualified to take, the mode of transportation they were permitted to use, and the quantity and quality of their formal education. With respect to such advantages, Whites were always on top, Coloreds were in between, and Blacks were at the very bottom.

Who Controls an Individual's Group Identity?

The cancer-stricken South African woman soon learned—on a deeply personal level—the cold, cruel reality of Apartheid. As an unexpected side-effect of the chemotherapy she had taken, her skin color became progressively darker, so much so that her racial identity appeared to be Colored, not White, and she was no longer permitted to ride the Whites' only bus to work every day. In fact, the bus driver, thinking that any of the woman's offspring must share at least some part of their mother's racial identity, also refused to permit her teenage daughter to ride the bus, even though the girl's skin color was that of a White. But getting to work turned out to be the least of the unfortunate woman's problems. As soon as her skin darkened, she was also shunned by her friends, fired by her boss, and deserted by her husband.

It should not be shocking that a change that was only skin-deep severely restricted the woman's social and economic opportunities. Under the South African version of Apartheid, an individual who was identified as Black or Colored was also considered less than a human being. The dehumanization of South Africans of color was essential to the perpetuation of Apartheid. It permitted both official policy and informal interaction to exclude millions of residents from being treated according to the rules of civilized society. If Blacks are human beings, they must be treated with decency and respect. If they are sub-humans or animals, then they can be enslaved, segregated, brutalized, or even killed with impunity.

One important lesson we learn from the South African example is that we don't always have 100% control over the way we are racially defined by other people. If those who define us have more power and authority than we do, then their definition may be real in its consequences (Thomas & Thomas, 1928). Under such circumstances, theirs—not ours—is the definition that counts, at least in terms of its impact on our economic and social status. It is the definition that determines what bus we are allowed to ride, where we are permitted to live, and which schools we are allowed to attend. We may very well be convinced that we are X, and, psychologically, this may be enough to make us feel very comfortable. Yet, in its ability to influence our status in society, what other people believe us to be may, in a socioeconomic sense, determine that we are Y, not X.

At the extreme, the shared perceptions of race can become grounds for total dehumanization. An appropriate example from the South African experience is provided by the travels of the late Sister Marie Augusta Neal, a professor at Emmanuel College in Boston, who related an episode while visiting her White friends in Johannesburg during its Apartheid era. While picnicking in the countryside, Sister Marie noticed a group of African Blacks across the road engaging in a ritual that she didn't understand. She alerted her South African companions, exclaiming, "Look at those people. Aren't they strange?" Quizzically, her friends replied, "What people?" Under Apartheid custom, Whites refused to refer to Blacks as people.

Yet, as a physical marker of differences between groups, even skin color is not always an important criterion for determining our racial identity. In South Africa during Apartheid, for example, visiting Japanese businessmen were officially classified as White, that is, as honorary Caucasians, as a purely practical matter to spare them the humiliating effects of being categorized as non-Whites. There would have been no Japanese businessmen visiting South Africa at all if they had been forced to live the lives of its Colored citizens.

To the extent that it is *socially constructed,* racial identity varies over time and place. In the United States until recently, anyone found to possess even one drop of "Black blood" was considered Black. Thus, as late as the 1980s, an individual whose ancestry included even a single Black relative but who appeared to be White (had blonde hair, fair complexion, and Caucasoid physiognomy [thin lips and nose]) would still be treated, in law and custom, as belonging to the Black race. Under many state laws, even choice of a marriage partner would have been restricted to someone else defined as Black.

In refusing to relinquish its archaic legal racial categories, the state of Louisiana, as late as 1983, became the only remaining state to have a legally sanctioned formula for determining the racial identity of its residents. By this mathematical method, any citizen who had one thirty-second or less of "Negro blood" was considered to be White under the law (Larson, 2000).

Although such state laws no longer exist, absolute criteria for determining Blackness continue to operate on an informal basis within American culture. Thus, for example, golfer Tiger Woods, who is of mixed ancestry and considers himself multiracial, is often referred to by television and radio commentators as a "Black golfer." Interestingly, individuals defined as Black in the United States could travel to Puerto Rico or Brazil, where, depending entirely on physical appearance instead of genetics, they might very well be considered White. Or they could visit South Africa, where they would almost definitely be thought of as Colored instead of either Black or White.

Changing Group Identity

There is much more wiggle room nowadays for Americans who wish to choose their group identity based on personal criteria rather than genetics. In June 2015, Rachel Dolezal resigned as leader of the NAACP in Spokane, Washington, after being "outed" as a White woman who had presented herself falsely as Black. At the time, Dolezal was severely criticized by both Black and White Americans for pretending to be something that she wasn't. Five months later, however, on national television, Dolezal acknowledged that she had been born biologically White to her White parents, but that she identifies as Black. From an early age, she would draw self-portraits with the brown crayon, not the peach colored one. As an adult, she seemed to have modified her appearance, adopting curly hair and a darker complexion. In Dolezal's view, Blackness is a "state of mind" rather than a biological category (Serico, 2015).

Judging by Senator Elizabeth Warren's appearance, you would probably never guess that she has claimed Cherokee ancestry. But this is exactly what the Senator suggested about herself. And it is highly unlikely that Warren's claim was disingenuous or designed to gain advantage. She grew up hearing "family stories" from her parents and grandparents regarding her Native American ancestry. The credibility of such stories receives additional strength from the fact that Senator Warren grew up in Oklahoma, where the Cherokee constitute the largest minority group in the state. For some observers, the one thirty-second of genetic proportion inherited by Warren, as frequently reported in the press, should be sufficient to support her claim of Cherokee ancestry. As indicated earlier, it was frequently employed throughout the history of the United States to distinguish Black from White Americans.

Racial identity can, in addition to its impact on self-esteem, have a profound political effect. The federal government allocates some $200 billion every year for employment, mortgage lending, housing, health care services, and educational opportunities based on the representation of various racial and ethnic groups in the Census Bureau enumeration. Breaking with past census reports, the 2000 U.S. Census contained 63 racial options. Yet, many Americans refused to categorize themselves racially and opted instead for "other." For the first time in 210 years, the Census Bureau no longer required Americans to identify themselves in only one racial category and permitted them to circle more than one category.

In light of the dramatic recent changes in the way that they are seeing themselves and others, the multiracial alternative has become increasingly appealing to Americans. In the 2010 Census, for example, some 9.0 million Americans identified themselves as multiracial. Over the past 30 years, marriages between Blacks and Whites have increased by some 400%, and marriages between Asians and Whites have increased by 1,000%. By the year 2010, there were 2,340,000 interracial married couples in the United States, nearly 15 times as many as in 1960 (American Academy of Child and Adolescent Psychiatry, 2005; Southern Poverty Law Center, 2001; US Bureau of the Census, 2010).

As we have seen in the case of the South African woman whose skin darkened, the implications of being defined as a member of one race over another can be highly significant on a personal level. The same can be said for an individual's religious preference, especially if it becomes regarded as an ascribed, racial, and therefore permanent status. In their own eyes, for example, former Jews living in Nazi Germany during the 1930s who had converted to Christianity were nothing less than devout Christians. In the eyes of the powerful Nazi regime, however, they were Jewish vermin—subhuman enemies of the state who disguised themselves as Christians, but who deserved to be herded off to death camps and exterminated.

It is not surprising, therefore, that some European Jews whose ancestors suffered profoundly under the Nazis may have given up their Jewish faith in favor of a more conventional and less stigmatizing alternative. The family of thirty-year-old Csanád Szegedi provides an extreme example. He was well known for his anti-Semitic pronouncements. As a leader of Jobbik, a far-right political party in the country of Hungary, Szegedi blamed Jews for a broad range of transgressions. Since 2009, he served in the European Parliament in Brussels as one of Jobbik's EU lawmakers.

Anti-Semitism was widely accepted by representatives of the party, including Szegedi. Many of Jobbik's members believed that the Holocaust and concentration camps never really existed but were Jewish inventions designed to elicit feelings of guilt and to justify the payment of reparations for their victims' pain and suffering.

Then, Szegedi suddenly discovered that his own grandmother was a survivor of Auschwitz and Dachau and his grandfather a former resident of a forced labor camp. Because his grandparents on his mother's side were Jewish, Szegedi would be considered a Jew under Jewish law, yet he was also an anti-Semite.

Things changed dramatically after Szegedi discovered his true ancestry. In a meeting with Orthodox Rabbi Slomo Köves, Szegedi offered apologies to the Jewish community for any of his statements that might have been construed as biased or bigoted. He now referred to himself as Dovid, ate kosher food, was in the process of studying Hebrew, and went to a synagogue in Budapest every Friday evening. He wore an Italian designer suit and a black yarmulke, the brimless cap worn by orthodox Jews to satisfy a cultural requisite that the head be covered at all times.

All of Szegedi's family members, with the exception of his grandmother, have also acknowledged their Jewish identity. As the only member of Szegedi's extended family to survive the concentration camps, she continues to live in the fear that hostility toward Jews will never be eliminated and that the Nazi Holocaust could happen again.

By contrast, Szegedi has gone from being a full-fledged bigot to a full-fledged Jew. Had the leadership of Jobbik been more tolerant, Rabbi Köves speculates, perhaps Csanád would never have become Dovid.

In the same way, the social construction of gayness has often been applied to victims who are bashed because of their presumed sexual orientation. Just as converted German Christians were singled out for discriminatory treatment by anti-Semites, so straight men have been assaulted by homophobic hatemongers. You don't have to be gay to become a victim of a gay hate bashing. Instead, you only have to look gay; that is, you only have to possess some of the characteristics associated in the minds of perpetrators with being gay. Thus, many straight men on college campuses around the country have been threatened or assaulted essentially because they fit the expectations by being "effeminate" in their gestures or expressions (Levin & McDevitt, 2002).

A recent example occurred on the campus of George Washington University where a senior was arrested in March 2015 for assaulting another student whom he believed to be gay. The victim was left unconscious, bleeding in his brain. One observer reported that the attacker had kicked the victim several times in the stomach while he lay on the ground. Another witness claimed that the perpetrator had pushed the victim against a wall and then punched him while repeatedly calling him "motherfucker" and "fag." The attacker and his victim were apparently total strangers to one another. The victim was apparently selected for abuse based on his "gay appearance," but he was actually a straight man (Farrell, 2015).

It has long been recognized that age categories do not exist in nature but are socially determined. Human beings invented the period called childhood and created the stage known as adolescence. In many societies, individuals went straight from infancy to adulthood and to a job working in the fields alongside their older brothers and sisters. Elsewhere, childhood exists but adolescence does not. By a certain age, instead of gradually maturing through a separate and distinct developmental stage, children in such societies go through a rite of passage (e.g., at the age of 12, they are required to kill a lion) that establishes them as adults. Even old age is a construction. In one area of the world, the members of a society are regarded as "old" beginning at 45 or 50; in another, they are regarded as reaching old age at 65 or 70. Aging is a gradual process that begins with birth and ends with death. We divide the life course into categories as though they were part of the natural order. But they are not.

The implications of dividing the life course so arbitrarily were brought home to the first author a number of years ago when he attempted to purchase a ticket for the commuter rail into Boston. When the woman at the ticket counter asked, "Adult or senior citizen?" he recoiled in horror. For the first time ever, he recognized that you couldn't be both. In order to get a small discount based on aging, you are asked to give up your adult status! His response: "One adult ticket, please."

In the same way, many group differences are socially constructed rather than fixed in nature. This is not to say that groups are identical to one another in each and every respect. In fact, groups of human beings obviously differ markedly in terms of almost every conceivable attribute, including skin color, physiognomy, language, culture, socioeconomic status, level of education, political clout, and so on. Some of these differences frequently form the basis for conflict between groups (Lee, Jussim, & McCauley, 1995). It's just that human beings decide which differences are socially significant and which differences deserve to be ignored.

The Privilege of White Identity

Let's face it. Groups vary in terms of their degree of privilege in a society, depending on their history and degree of power and control over the system of social stratification. In the United States, White privilege seems to be a fact of life (Rothenberg, 2015). Indicators are easy to locate:

- Most important figures in our history books are White.
- White Americans almost never attribute their failures to race.
- Most White Americans do not have to think about their race on a daily basis.

White privilege also expresses itself in dramatic differences between White and Black Americans with respect to their accumulation of assets. Over the past few decades, many African American families have seen a steady rise in employment and annual income. But alongside these encouraging signs, sociologist Thomas Shapiro argues in *The Hidden Cost of Being African American*, fundamental levels of racial inequality persist, particularly in the area of asset accumulation—inheritance, savings accounts, stocks, bonds, home equity, and other investments. Shapiro reveals how the lack of these family assets, along with continuing racial discrimination in crucial areas like home ownership, dramatically impact the everyday lives of many Black families, reversing gains earned in schools and on jobs, and perpetuating the cycle of poverty in which far too many find themselves trapped. In 2009, for example, a survey of American households determined that the median wealth of White families was more than $113,000, whereas the median wealth of Latino familes was only $6,325 and of Black families only $5,677 (Shapiro, Meschede, and Charo, 2013).

Shapiro and his colleagues use a combination of in-depth interviews with almost 200 families from Los Angeles, Boston, and St. Louis, and national survey data with 10,000 families, to show how racial inequality is transmitted across the decades. We see how those families with private wealth are able to move up from generation to generation, relocating to safer communities with better schools and passing along the accompanying advantages to their children. At the same time those without significant wealth remain trapped in communities that don't allow them to move up, no matter how hard they work. Shapiro challenges White middle class families to consider how the privileges that wealth brings not only improve their own chances but also hold back people who don't have them. This "wealthfare" is a legacy of inequality that, if unchanged, will project social injustice far into the future. Showing that over half of Black families fall below the asset poverty line at the beginning of the new century, *The Hidden Cost of Being African American* challenges all Americans to reconsider what must be done to end racial inequality.

A cautionary note seems to be in order here. It should be emphasized that White privilege does not assure wealth, prestige, or power. There are many White Americans who are impoverished, downwardly mobile, on welfare, or working at minimum wage. They might have suffered through childhood trauma, lacked important educational opportunities, experienced disabling illnesses, or had terrible economic hardships as adults. Even White privilege cannot save every White person from poverty. Not every White person is in the top 1% with respect to income or assets, just as not every person of color is at the bottom of the economic heirarchy. Racial identity is important, but it is only one of many variables that contribute to an individual's economic standing in society.

When Stereotypes Turn Nasty

Our images of the people in different groups can be molded to fit the occasion for which they are needed, regardless of the way the people in question behave. When the members of another group become too competitive or threatening, they are seen not as industrious and hardworking, but as obsessed workaholics; not as laid-back and mellow, but as lazy; not as courageous, but as bloodthirsty; not as thrifty, but as stingy; not as family oriented, but as clannish; not as assertive, but as aggressive; not as having exceptional athletic ability, but as having all brawn and no brains; not as excelling in math and science, but as having a narrow intellect.

The particular stereotype seems to depend at least somewhat on the forms of discrimination it is meant to encourage or justify. Outsiders who are expected to be submissive and subordinate to the interests of the dominant group are often *infantilized*. Their image is that of children. Yet some stereotypes are more life threatening than others. Those outsiders who are regarded as posing a threat to the advantaged position of the dominant group may be treated not like children but animals or demons (Levin & Levin, 1982).

The derivation of this notion can be traced back to widespread stereotypic thinking among White colonists in which Africans were regarded as apelike heathens and savages controlled almost completely by their senses rather than by their intellect. Their savage behavior was reflected in "primitive" non-Christian religious beliefs and rituals and in reports of their "uncivilized" cultural practices, including polygamy, infanticide, and ritualistic murder (Smith, 1995).

Although predating slavery, such *dehumanizing* ideas about Blacks were quickly rediscovered by European colonists to justify the institution of slavery within the context of an equalitarian ethos. Instead of dealing with the moral consequences of the forced enslavement of an entire group of people based strictly on physiognomy and skin color, the colonists denied the evil of "the peculiar institution" and instead took the moral high ground. Blacks were not people; they were property. From this point of view, they were not victimized or exploited; they were the beneficiaries of a way of life that would ensure their very survival.

Although certainly belittling and degrading, the negative stereotyping of slaves included more infantilization than dehumanization. Blacks who consented to play the role of loyal and lowly slaves were generally regarded as children who needed the wise counsel and guidance of their White masters to survive. The image was that of Little Black Sambo—the musical but ignorant youngster who didn't have the brains to come in out of the rain.

In the years following the end of the Civil War, the infantilized image of Blacks was transformed into a dehumanized stereotype on the basis of which murder and mayhem could be justified. No longer seen as valuable property, Blacks had to fend for themselves. They were unable to rely on their masters to protect them from other racist Whites. Rather than viewed as children, Blacks were now regarded as animals, lacking in human intelligence or spirituality, that needed to be tamed or killed (Levin & Levin, 1982).

Such negative images are often seen in warfare. The underlying causes of a conflict may be economic, but stereotyping has facilitated bloodshed. In Northern Ireland, for example, civil strife seems to have been reinforced by a set of stereotypes of Catholics and Protestants that might be expected to describe racial differences alone; for example, that Catholics have shorter foreheads, larger genitalia, and less space between their eyes than do their taller Protestant neighbors (Levin, 1997b). To this day, the so-called "peace wall" in Belfast provides separation between denominations, and entire towns continue to be populated by either Catholics or Protestants, but hardly ever both.

One joke told in the streets and pubs of Belfast summarizes the incredible strength of sectarianism in Northern Ireland. It is said that a local bartender in Belfast inquired of an American visiting the city as to whether he was Catholic or Protestant. The American replied, "Neither, I am Jewish." The bartender's response: "Yes, but are you a Catholic or a Protestant Jew?" In Northern Ireland during the "troubles," almost everything revolved around the sectarian conflict. Nothing else seemed to matter. Even though the members of conflicting denominations were all Christians, they might as well have been members of different species.

Only the nastiest images of newcomers seem to spread during hard economic times, as the native-born population perceives that its financial position is being eroded. At times, certain prejudices become narrowly targeted. During the 1800s and early 1900s, when they came to the United States and competed for jobs with native-born citizens, Irish American newcomers were stereotyped by political cartoonists of the day as apes and crocodiles (Keen, 1986). During the same period, as soon as they began to compete with native-born landowners and merchants, Italian immigrants settling in New Orleans were widely depicted as dangerous members of organized crime who needed to be controlled (Gambino, 1977; Smith, 2007).

Chinese immigrants to nineteenth-century America tended to be regarded as "honest," "industrious," and "peaceful" so long as jobs remained plentiful. But when the job market tightened and the Chinese began to seek work in mines, farming, domestic service, and factories, a dramatic shift toward anti-Chinese sentiment emerged. They quickly became stereotyped as "dangerous," "deceitful," "vicious," and "clannish." Whites then accused the Chinese immigrants of undermining the American standard of living (Sung, 1961). In a similar way, the depressions of 1893 and 1907 served to solidify the opposition to immigration from Italy, setting the stage for widespread acceptance of stereotypes depicting Italian Americans as "organ-grinders, paupers, slovenly ignoramuses, and so on" (LaGumina, 1973).

On occasion, racial epithets have been voiced by angry Americans to justify injuring or murdering immigrants. In 1994, in a Massachusetts courtroom, 25-year-old Harold Robert Latour was found guilty of second-degree murder and assault and battery with the intent to intimidate based on race. A year earlier, Latour had beaten to death a 21-year-old Cambodian man, Sam Nang Nhem, his neighbor in a Fall River, Massachusetts, housing project. The murder occurred after a family clambake, as Nhem and his friend were walking over to a trash bin to discard some clam shells. Latour shouted, "I'm gonna knock that gook out!" Then he kicked his victim to the ground with his steel-toed Doc Martens (Associated Press, 1994).

The first author played a role in Latour's trial as an expert witness in the area of hate crimes. His task was to inform the jury as to the historical application of the term "gook" as a racial slur. He told the court that the epithet was used by the Allies during World War II to characterize the Japanese enemy, during the Korean conflict to refer to North Koreans, and during the Vietnam War to refer to North Vietnamese and Vietcong. In the mid-1970s, as large numbers of Asian newcomers arrived in the United States, the term "gook" then became a racial slur to discredit all Southeast Asian immigrants. The fact that the defendant had shouted an anti-Asian epithet just prior to beating his Cambodian victim indicated that a hate crime had occurred and may have contributed to lengthening Latour's sentence—a life sentence in Walpole state penitentiary with parole eligibility after 15 years.

Slurs voiced by offenders such as the term "gook" represent the most widely employed evidence for establishing the commission of a hate attack. Racial and religious epithets are widely recognized, even by those individuals who themselves would never use them and are repulsed by those who do. Similarly, anti-gay epithets are frequently employed by homophobic perpetrators who first verbalize their bigotry and then attack with knives, guns, bats, or their fists. In some cases, the evidence for hate motivation is found not in the slurs voiced by hatemongers, but in the graffiti they leave at the crime scene. Not every hatemonger is stupid enough to announce his hate motivation. In the absence of epithets or graffiti, it may be nearly impossible to gather enough evidence to charge a defendant as perpetrating a hate crime.

The nasty labels placed on people with disabilities are just as hurtful as their racial and religious counterparts but are not recognized publicly to the same extent. People with disabilities have been referred to as invalids (i.e., not valid persons), handicapped (capable only of begging, cap in hand), or disabled (incompetent). Other hurtful labels include crippled, deformed, feeble-minded, idiot, moron, imbecile, insane, lunatic, and maniac. Often, people who wouldn't dream of using the N-word or the G-word feel free to say the R-word—they refer to an intellectually challenged individual as a "retard."

War is one important source of dehumanizing racial slurs, but organized hate groups have also offered their members the dehumanizing images they need to feel justified in their efforts to eliminate "the other." For example, the official website of the White supremacist group Aryan Nations recently defined Jews literally as a terminal illness. According to Pastor Jay Faber of Aryan Nations,

> In this world, the races are the parts of the body, and the jew is cancer. When you go to the doctor for cancer treatment, if he tells you that you have almost killed off the cancer, you would never tell the doctor to stop, you would tell him to kill it all. Cancer = jews. Let's join world wide and rid the world of the disease that has inflicted all of us. (http://www. aryan-nations.org)

Is Hate on the Decline?

Many forms of hate have softened significantly since World War II. As determined by large-scale surveys of White racial attitudes from 1942 to 1968, there was a sizable increase in the proportion of White Americans willing to support integration of the public schools. Over the same period of time, the proportion of White Americans who regarded the intelligence of Blacks as equal to that of Whites rose considerably (Bellisfield, 1972–1973; Hyman and Sheatsley, 1956, 1964). Data from a series of surveys of the American population in 1964, 1968, and 1970 suggested that White and Black attitudes during this period of time moved closer together on questions of principle and policy (Campbell, 1971).

Into the 1970s, hate and bigotry, although clearly on the decline, nevertheless continued to hold a tight grip on the thinking of many Americans. Selznick and Steinberg (1969), in their interviews with a representative cross section of the national population in 1964, found that 54% of their respondents thought that Jews always like to be at the head of things, 52% agreed that Jews stick together too much, and 42% felt that Jews are more willing than others to use shady practices to get what they want. Moreover, Petroni (1972) found frequent usage of racial stereotypes among White Midwestern high school students who were highly critical of the prejudices of their parents and yet who failed to recognize they had prejudices of their own.

With reference to stereotypes associated with Blacks, Brink and Harris (1964) reported that a substantial proportion of a nationwide cross section of White Americans taken in 1963—in some cases reaching almost 70% agreement—were willing to agree that Blacks smell different, have looser morals, want to live off the handout, have less native intelligence, breed crime, and are inferior to Whites. In a 1966 survey, Brink and Harris (1967), again conducting a nationwide study of White Americans, found a softening in some of their negativism toward Blacks but still reported about 50% who agreed that Blacks smell different, have looser morals, and want to live off the handout. Campbell's 1968 survey determined that of the Whites living in the 15 cities studied, 67% said that Blacks push too fast for what they want, 51% opposed laws to prevent racial discrimination in housing, and 33% said that if they had small children, they would prefer that their children have only White friends.

At least at an abstract level, hate based on race and religion seems to have plummeted over the last several decades. In 1998, a national poll conducted for the Anti-Defamation League (ADL) found that the number of Americans holding strong anti-Jewish attitudes—agreeing that Jews have too much power and are more loyal to Israel than to America—had declined to only 12% from 20% in 1992 and 29% in 1964. According to a recent ADL study (2015), only 9% of all Americans continued to hold dangerously anti-Semitic beliefs in 2015. This figure compares quite favorably against most other countries—Iraq 92%, Greece and Turkey 69%, Poland 45%, Russia 30%, Spain 29%, Italy and Ireland 20%. Only the United Kingdom at 8%, Netherlands 5%, and Sweden 4% expressed less anti-Semitism than the United States.

In survey after survey, moreover, the majority of Americans now claimed to be accepting of racial integration, at least as a matter of principle. For example, only 7% of all Americans thought that "Blacks and Whites should go to separate schools." Even stereotyped thinking about race seems to have seriously eroded over time. Merely 4% now characterized Blacks as "lazy" (in 1967, that figure was 26%; in 1933, it was 75%) (ADL, 2001).

Not unlike trends in racial and religious bigotry, Americans have grown increasingly more tolerant of homosexuality over the past several decades. According to Gallup pollsters, the percentage of Americans believing that gays should be given equal job opportunities increased from 56% in 1977 to 74% in 1992 and to 89% by 2008. The percentage believing that homosexuality is an acceptable alternative lifestyle grew from only 34% in 1982 to 38% in 1992, to 50% by 1999, and to 60% by 2015 (Saad, 2005; Riffkin, 2014).

Underestimating Bigotry

At the same time, there are certain negative beliefs and feelings about various groups in American society that seem, over the decades, to have persisted and even increased substantially. The August 2014 police shooting of an unarmed Black man and subsequent anti-police demonstrations beginning in Ferguson, Missouri, and spreading to such cities as Baltimore, New York, Cleveland, Chicago, and Minneapolis may have had a profound impact on the nature of American race relations. By the year 2013, attitudes toward race relations had improved substantially. Some 72% of White Americans and 66% of Black Americans had reported to pollsters that "relations between Whites and Blacks" are either "very good" or "somewhat good." By 2015, however, perceptions of racism became vastly more negative. Only 51% of White Americans and 45% of Black Americans described relations between Blacks and Whites as very or somewhat good (http://www.gallup.com/poll/1687/race-relations.aspx).

In the aftermath of the Ferguson police shooting, the state of race relations in the United States took a nosedive. Some 60% of all Whites and 56% of all Blacks told PBS Newshour/Marist pollsters that race relations were worse than a year earlier. More specifically, 87% of Black Americans but only 50% of White Americans reported that African Americans have less of an opportunity to receive equal justice under the law (Myers, 2015).

Recent scandals involving sexual abuse committed by Catholic priests may have caused some backsliding—perhaps temporary—in the acceptance of gays and lesbians. Between 2003 and 2005, Gallup reported decreases in the percentage of Americans saying that gays should be hired as clergy (from 56 to 49%), as elementary school teachers (from 61 to 54%), and as high school teachers (from 67 to 62%). Moreover, the recent debate concerning the legality of gay marriage has not resulted in overwhelming public support for marriages between homosexuals, although public support has recently grown. According to a 2015 Gallup poll, 60% say that such marriages should be legally valid. Though leaving an opposition of some 40%, this is a dramatic increase since

1977, when only 43% supported gay relations being legal (Saad, 2005; Gallup, 2015).

In some areas, stereotyped thinking about racial and religious groups has stalled. In a Harris telephone survey of 3,000 people commissioned by the National Conference for Community and Justice (2000), it was determined that certain stereotypes continue to be accepted not only by Whites but also by Americans of color (Asians, Latinos, and Blacks). In response to the statement that Asian Americans are "unscrupulous, crafty, and devious in business," some 27% of all White Americans registered their agreement, but so did 46% of Latinos and 42% of African Americans. In response to the statement that Latinos "lack ambition and the drive to succeed," 20% of all White Americans agreed, as well as 35% of Asian Americans and 24% of African Americans. In response to the statement that African Americans "want to live on welfare," 21% of all White Americans agreed, but so did 31% of Asian Americans and 26% of Latinos.

These results indicate that hate and prejudice have taken on greater complexity as our society has become increasingly multiracial. To the extent that prejudices are indeed cultural, we shouldn't be surprised that they are shared not only by members of the dominant group but also by minority members. Conflict in Black-White relations continues to hold the attention of the nation, but there are also important hostilities directed toward a range of minorities other than African Americans. In a recent Gallup poll, respondents were asked whether they would vote for a well-qualified candidate for president, in the 2016 election, if the candidate were in a particular minority group. The results revealed a good deal about Americans' preferences for leadership by race, religion, and gender: more than 90% would support someone who was Catholic, Black, Hispanic, Jewish, or a woman; 81% would cast their vote for a Mormon; 74% would vote for a gay or lesbian candidate; and only 60% would vote for a Muslim (Gallup, 2015).

Unconscious Bias

Moreover, arguing that hate and bigotry may be much more widespread than revealed in the typical study, some researchers have called into question the validity of the transparent questionnaire approach for measuring changes in the acceptance of racist stereotypes. Very few Americans, they argue, now want to be known as racists. Therefore, they are unlikely to be honest in answering questions that could make them out to be bigots. Moreover, many respondents may not even be aware of their own racism. In response to straightforward questions about their attitudes, those who hold racist attitudes may give what they see as socially acceptable responses instead of revealing a truth that may be unacceptable even to them (Wachtel, 2001).

In addition to blatant racism, many individuals apparently hold unconscious biases about such characteristics as personal appearance, race, religion, gender, and sexual orientation. Even highly educated and humane individuals, people who sincerely believe that they are entirely free of prejudice or hate, may be totally unaware that they operate from bias or bigotry. For example, one study concluded that White National Basketball Association's (NBA) referees call a larger number of fouls when the players are Black, whereas Black NBA referees call more fouls when the players are White. Another study found that female lab technicians are rated more poorly and less deserving of equal pay in comparison to their male counterparts. In still another study, researchers found that physicians treat their overweight patients differently, while patients treat their overweight doctors in a different manner (Ross, 2014).

In some cases, unconscious bias can take on a life-or-death aspect. Researchers writing in the *New England Journal of Medicine* have reported that physicians were 40% less likely to order sophisticated cardiac tests in response to complaints about chest pain when the patients were women rather than men and Black rather than White. Blatant sexism or racism didn't seem to be at the basis of these differences in doctors' recommendations. Instead, they made decisions—in this case, life-and-death decisions—on the basis of strongly held yet unconscious biases about gender and race. According to U.S. Surgeon General David Satcher, this could be one factor in explaining why Blacks are 40% more likely than Whites to die from heart disease (White, 1999).

Also in support of the notion that we tend to underestimate the presence of prejudice, social psychologists found that Whites' attitudes toward Blacks were reported as substantially more negative when the White subjects believed they had been hooked into an apparatus that monitored their real feelings and beliefs with total accuracy. In this "bogus pipeline" situation, respondents apparently were more willing to reveal the truth about their racist attitudes than risk being caught in a lie (Sigall & Page, 1971).

Research designed to measure concealed prejudice has relied on making inferences about the respondents' attitudes based on their behavior. In one experiment, for example, White Princeton University students who believed they were participating in a study of interviewing techniques were asked to question, on a random basis, either someone Black or someone White. In comparison with students assigned to a White interviewee, their counterparts with a Black interviewee conveyed more negative nonverbal behavior while interacting. More specifically, they chose to sit farther apart, spent a shorter period of time together, and made a larger number of errors in their speech while talking. Apparently, the White students unwittingly expressed a degree of discomfort based on their unconsciously held feelings and beliefs about Black people (Word, Zanna & Cooper, 1974); yet, if you had asked them bluntly to express their attitudes toward Blacks, there is every reason to believe that they would have painted a glowing, or at least an unbiased, picture.

Another factor in the underestimation of bigotry is that at least some hate remains unverbalized beneath the surface, ever ready to strike. In January 2001, almost two years after he was laid to rest at the age of 81, Richard J. Cotter's racism and anti-Semitism first became publicly apparent. The one-time Massachusetts assistant attorney general and long-time bachelor left $750,000 to organized hate groups—more than $500,000 to a church in Louisiana led by a founding member of the American Nazi Party; $100,000 to Andrew Macdonald, the author of a White supremacist novel entitled *The Turner Diaries*; $25,000 to the Confederation of Polish Freedom Fighters; and $100,000 to a Holocaust denier from Toronto. One of his acquaintances of more than 23 years referred to Cotter as "a good and decent man," someone so decent that he couldn't even bring himself to euthanize his sick horses. Neighbors saw Cotter as an eccentric man who wanted to be left alone in the house in which he had lived for 40 years. But inside the front doors of that home, the Harvard law school graduate exhibited a series of wooden trophies from anti-Semitic organizations naming him as their man of the year and stacks of books discussing the virtues of White pride and right-wing patriotism. Choosing to conceal his racist beliefs from public scrutiny, Cotter had long served as a legal advisor to neo-Nazi groups (Belkin, 2001).

The Difference Between Small and Insignificant

Even if subtle and concealed variations of hate continue to exist, it is heartening that at least it has become somewhat uncomfortable for individuals to express their bigotry openly without fear of reprimand or retaliation. At the cultural level, therefore, some progress toward respect for differences seems to have been made. However, when it comes to concrete government efforts to implement equal treatment by race, there is considerably less support. In fact, public support for government intervention to integrate schools and equal treatment in the use of public accommodations actually declined beginning in the 1980s (Schuman, Steeh, Bobo, & Krysan, 1997).

For example, support for affirmative action continues to divide along racial lines. In a 2015 Gallup survey of American adults, 77% of Blacks but only 53% of Whites reported that they favor affirmative action programs. The explanation for affirmative action support also divides racially. The majority of White Americans (72%) but little more than one-third of Black Americans (36%) believe that Blacks in this country have equal job opportunities (Jones, 2005).

The continuing weakness of White support for the implementation of racial integration is indicated by variations in the willingness to participate personally in integrated settings. Very few White Americans object to neighborhood or school integration when it involves only a small number of Blacks. When Blacks promise to become anything like a majority, however, White support dwindles (Schuman, Steeh, Bobo, & Krysan, 1997).

Lack of support for integrating neighborhoods, workplaces, and schools aids in keeping groups separated on a daily basis. Even worse, there are those Americans who feel so threatened by diversity and difference that they translate their anxiety and anger into criminal behavior. Of course, only a relatively small number of Americans ever go this far. There are, for example, many millions of crimes committed every year in the United States, only several thousands of which are officially regarded by the Federal Bureau of Investigation (FBI) to be hate offenses. Considering there are approximately 321 million people in the United States, FBI data suggest that the likelihood is quite small of any given citizen being attacked because of his or her race, religion, or sexual orientation.

Hate Crimes are Vastly Underreported

Quite clearly, however, the FBI figure vastly underestimates the actual incidence of hate episodes. It is really the tip of the iceberg, representing only those incidents that rise to the level of criminal offenses and only those crimes officially recognized as motivated by hate and reported by local police departments as such. Under a voluntary reporting system, some 15,494 police jurisdictions in 49 states and the District of Columbia representing 93% of the total population now report. Still, some states have been more cooperative than others: In 2014, the state of Alabama reported nine hate crimes, Mississippi reported one, and New York reported 572 (FBI, 2014).

Table 1.1 shows the number of law enforcement agencies in each state that participate in the national hate crime reporting program managed by the FBI. It also lists the total population of citizens covered by these agencies. To become a participant in the hate crime program, the law enforcement agency must complete a quarterly reporting packet that includes hate crime incident reports—if hate crimes occurred—or a form that is signed by the chief or sheriff that indicates that no hate crimes occurred in his or her jurisdiction during the reporting period. For example, Table 1.1 shows that 63 police agencies in Wyoming participated in the program but not one reported a hate crime. Compare this with California in which 28% of the participating agencies reported a combined total of 759 hate crimes (FBI, 2014).

Basing an estimate of the prevalence of hate crimes on victims rather than police reports causes a substantial increase in the number of reported cases. According to the Bureau of Justice Statistics, 193,800 hate crime incidents were reported in 2012 by victims in its National Crime Victimization Survey (Wilson, 2014).

But even the reports by victims may under-represent the actual prevalence of hate offenses. It isn't only law enforcement personnel who are reluctant to report hate attacks. Many victims also prefer not to inform anyone—and especially not law enforcement officials—that they have been victimized. Having grown up where residents were distrustful of the police, some simply do not believe that law enforcement will be on their side. Moreover, immigrants may have come from countries where repressive regimes were as likely as individual hatemongers to commit atrocities against them. They see the police as "the enemy of occupation." For certain groups, American institutions may similarly not be trusted. A recent survey found that almost 80% of Shiite Muslims in the United States who were victims of "post 9-11 discrimination" failed to report the incidents to the police (Religion News Service, 2005).

Several years ago, our colleague Jack McDevitt surveyed more than 4,000 students at public high schools across the state of Massachusetts as to how many of them had been victims of hate crimes—vandalism, assault, assault and battery, harassment, or sexual assault. He determined that 30% of the 400 students victimized by a hate offense told no one that they had been attacked. When victims did inform someone, 60% told a friend, 29% told a family

TABLE 1.1   Hate Crime Reporting to the FBI by State, 2014

Participating State	Number of Participating Agencies	Population Covered	Agencies Submitting Incident Reports	Total Number of Incidents Reported
Total	15,494	297,926,030	1,666	5,479
Alabama	39	794,907	4	9
Alaska	33	732,371	1	6
Arizona	99	6,433,584	22	265
Arkansas	270	2,661,818	5	8
California	743	38,802,500	208	759
Colorado	231	5,268,592	40	96
Connecticut	95	3,375,662	54	123
Delaware	60	935,614	9	13
District of Columbia	2	658,893	2	70
Florida	505	19,794,279	37	65
Georgia	479	8,204,655	4	41
Idaho	112	1,634,011	10	25
Illinois	693	12,029,618	48	109
Indiana	348	6,093,574	15	50
Iowa	221	2,974,604	10	11
Kansas	359	2,843,179	37	73
Kentucky	399	4,386,536	84	163
Louisiana	86	2,706,155	6	9
Maine	184	1,330,089	15	28
Maryland	154	5,976,407	9	16
Massachusetts	315	6,485,973	90	375
Michigan	607	9,732,430	119	311
Minnesota	292	5,287,138	27	98
Mississippi	75	1,349,655	1	1
Missouri	630	6,061,406	25	76
Montana	98	992,702	12	30
Nebraska	216	1,763,318	7	47
Nevada	51	2,834,483	4	24
New Hampshire	158	1,238,190	11	14
New Jersey	509	8,936,591	126	336
New Mexico	7	717,010	3	13

New York	572	19,652,379	59	545
North Carolina	524	9,942,854	40	140
North Dakota	111	738,176	16	40
Ohio	606	9,711,237	105	403
Oklahoma	333	3,878,051	18	33
Oregon	92	1,526,458	15	26
Pennsylvania	1,457	12,587,318	22	50
Rhode Island	48	1,054,130	4	4
South Carolina	430	4,813,088	32	49
South Dakota	121	776,484	12	18
Tennessee	465	6,519,911	53	194
Texas	1,033	26,922,758	57	145
Utah	134	2,926,391	23	50
Vermont	91	626,306	10	15
Virginia	414	8,324,943	50	118
Washington	262	7,051,748	67	308
West Virginia	269	1,648,198	16	26
Wisconsin	397	5,610,210	22	51
Wyoming	63	579,446	0	0

Source: Federal Bureau of Investigation, *Hate Crime Statistics 2014*.

member, and 15% told a school employee. Only 3% reported their crime to the police (Rosenwald, 2002).

The problem of people with disabilities reporting hate crimes is especially serious. As shown in Figure 1.1, for the year 2012 alone, only 102 of the more than 6,718 reported hate offenses were directed at people with intellectual, physical, or psychiatric disabilities. But, as displayed in Figure 1.2, when the Justice Department asked persons with disabilities anonymously why they believe they were targeted for violence, some 11%—more than 32,000 people in all—said they believed it was because of their disability (Potok, 2013).

It Takes Only a Few Bad Apples

Aside from the problem of under-reporting, a second difficulty in assessing the impact of hate crimes involves realistically attempting to determine the level of hate incidents that constitutes a menace. Before writing off the threatening influence of a relatively small number of hate offenses, it would be wise to gain some perspective on the relationship of hate to large-scale ethnic conflict. In Northern Ireland, where ethnic warfare seemed, until recently, always to be just around the corner, most violent crimes (robbery, murder, assault, and rape) had

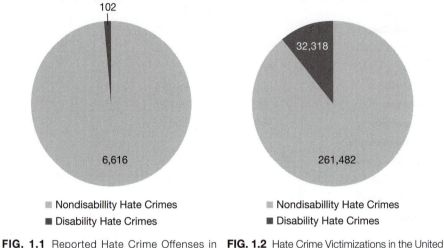

FIG. 1.1 Reported Hate Crime Offenses in United States for the Year 2012.
Source: Federal Bureau of Investigation, *Hate Crime Statistics 2012.*

FIG. 1.2 Hate Crime Victimizations in the United States for the Year 2012.
Source: Bureau of Justice Statistics, *Hate Crime Victimization 2004–2012—Statistical Tables.*

nothing to do with religious differences. Yet, all it took to start a new round of terrorist bombings was one murder of a police officer; all that was necessary to ignite a new round of violence was a single terrorist act. Moreover, middle-class citizens of Northern Ireland who lived in the suburbs and took care not to voice their political views in public may have felt immune from the hate attacks directed against impoverished and working-class residents in cities like Derry and Belfast. A count of the hate incidents in Northern Ireland over the past couple of decades might have led one *incorrectly* to conclude that ethnic conflict was no longer a problem there, and that Northern Ireland's Protestants and Catholics were living in peace and tranquility, when they were actually engaged in something approaching civil war.

Conclusion

Notwithstanding a decline in its public expression since World War II, hate continues to dictate the terms of intergroup conflict in the United States. In certain circles, prejudice has become more subtle and sophisticated. Among some, it may exist only on an unconscious level. In others, it remains dormant until such time as the advantaged status of the group is challenged. At this point, the stereotyped image of "outsiders" is brought forth to justify doing them harm.

Rather than focus on individual acts of bigotry, researchers during the past few decades have turned more of their attention to studying institutional and structural forms of discrimination. Although perfectly understandable, it is also true that acts of hate violence have formed the response of some Americans in dealing with the frustration and strain that seriously erode the quality of their lives. They might employ negative stereotypes in order to justify doing harm to those they consider outsiders. They might displace their aggression to vulnerable targets. Policies and programs designed to tear down the barriers separating racial and religious groups might have also provoked increasing numbers of hate crimes committed by members of traditionally advantaged groups in society who felt under attack.

The term "hate crime" has become entrenched in our vocabulary, yet there is still much ambiguity as to its prevalence in society. The moral acceptability of various minorities may have grown over the decades, but the extent of hate-motivated crime continues to be vastly under-estimated in official statistics. At the same time, recent events remind us, all too clearly, that racial antagonism continues to be alive and well in American society as well as countries around the world.

CHAPTER 2

Explaining the Violence of Hate

Environment, Heredity, and the Power of the Situation

Social scientists have long sought to increase their understanding of the nature of hate—its origins, maintenance, and consequences. Many have expressed their concern about the debilitating impact of prejudice on the life chances of minority group members; on such attendant factors as confused self-identity, poor self-esteem, and serious sex-role conflicts (Pettigrew, 1964), and on what Smith (1995) has labeled "internal inferiorization." Others have focused their attention on what influence prejudice has on the quality of moral life for all Americans, majority and minority alike. In his classic work, *An American Dilemma,* Myrdal (1944) depicts American race relations as posing a major moral struggle for White America that is the result of a deeply rooted cultural conflict between the democratic values of the "American creed" and the social, political, and economic inequities experienced by Black Americans.

Social scientists have traditionally regarded prejudice and hate as destructive to society and to the individual. Directly or indirectly, prejudice causes innocent people to suffer, commits society's resources to antidemocratic if not unproductive ends, and does irreparable harm to the personality of the prejudiced individual. In the American experience alone, prejudice has been linked to a civil war, urban decay, crime and delinquency, and international tension.

The Environmental View—Blaming the Victim

Appealing for its simplicity, a conception of prejudice, the *benign prejudice* viewpoint, has been advanced throughout history to explain the problems experienced by minority members of society. Instead of seeing hate and bigotry as causing poverty, unemployment, lack of education, and related social problems, the benign prejudice viewpoint locates the responsibility for inequality in characteristics of the minority group itself. From this standpoint, hate and prejudice are regarded as relatively harmless, secondary, or entirely irrelevant.

Some historians have suggested, for example, that throughout history, Jews have been at least partially responsible for their own ills. In his early writings, Lazare (1894/1995) argued that throughout history (in ancient Alexandria, Rome, Persia, Turkey, the countries of Europe, or wherever else they settled),

Jews remained apart, refusing to give up their beliefs and rituals or to assimilate into the mainstream of society. Instead, in whatever land to which they were deported, they sought to remain Jews by insisting on being able to practice their religion, to receive exemption from the customs of the majority, to remain separated from other inhabitants, and to govern themselves by their own laws. In ancient Rome and Alexandria, Jews were not required to appear in court or to market grain on a Saturday. In ancient Alexandria, they were permitted total self-governance, constituting a state within a state. In some countries, they were even exempted from paying taxes.

Such privileges as well as the bond they shared as a separate religious community combined to give Jewish residents special opportunities for engaging in trade and accumulating wealth. But such opportunities also engendered widespread jealousy and envy that in turn created large-scale animosity toward them among the local inhabitants. Ancient Greeks and Romans were already covetous of the advantages that permitted Jews to carry on trade under favorable economic circumstances. The wealth of the Jew, it was said, was gained by deception, fraud, and oppression at the expense of the Christians (Lazare, 1894/1995).

Over the course of his career, Lazare's benign prejudice view of anti-Semitism was gradually modified to take into account the historical impact of victimization on the Jewish experience. For one thing, he came to understand that much of the separateness of Jewish life was not self-imposed but originated in discrimination from the wider society. However they behaved in relation to the dominant inhabitants, Jews were treated as slaves and pariahs. During the Crusades, the presence of Jewish citizens who refused to convert to Catholicism was regarded as a symbolic threat by religious zealots who sought to spread their theology across the continent. Jews who refused to convert were massacred.

During the Middle Ages, Jews were systematically excluded from many respectable ways of making a living such as owning land, farming, or being craftspeople. Because of its importance to society, however, the dreaded role of usurer, a role despised on religious grounds by the Catholic majority, was granted to Jews by default. In Spain, Jews were forced at the threat of death or exile to practice their religion secretly, masquerading in public places as converted Christians. In seventeenth- and eighteenth-century Germany, Jews were at best second-class citizens who lacked many of the rights afforded to other inhabitants. In Polish cities, Jews were prohibited from living among the Christian population and were forced to live in ghettos. By mid-twentieth century, long after the death of historian Bernard Lazare, German anti-Semitism had turned decidedly racist, so much so that even total conversion to Christianity would not have protected a Jew from paying the ultimate price.

Despite compelling evidence to indicate the malignancy of racism, some social scientists have implied, if not explicitly stated, that prejudice can no longer be held accountable for the poverty, miseducation, or underemployment presently experienced by members of certain groups in our society. Their argument usually runs as follows: Although initially responsible for the problems of a group (e.g., back in the days of slavery), prejudice or racism of the majority is no longer to blame. Current prejudice is regarded as benign. The minority group is viewed as trapped in a self-feeding vicious circle of deprivation that is difficult if not impossible to reverse. Ryan (1971) regarded this view in the most negative sense possible as blaming the victim; others see it as a refreshing change from a viewpoint that has led us nowhere fast in our efforts to reduce various inequalities.

According to Ryan, the most common form of blaming the victim involves the cultural deprivations to which a minority group member is presumably exposed. As a case in point, Ryan considers an inner-city child who is blamed for his own miseducation. The focus here is on the alleged defects of the child: his lack of exposure to books and magazines, the absence of encouragement or support from his parents, and his own impulsiveness. By confining attention to the child and to deficiencies in his home environment, it is possible to overlook the

> collapsing buildings and torn textbooks, the frightened, insensitive teachers, the six additional desks in the room, the blustering, frightened principals, the relentless segregation, the callous administrator, the irrelevant curriculum, the bigoted or cowardly members of the school board, the insulting history books, the stingy taxpayers, the fairy-tale readers, or the self-serving faculty of the local teachers' college. (Ryan, 1971, p. 4)

To explain the persistence of socioeconomic inequalities between groups, certain social scientists have concentrated on the individual characteristics of victims to explain the persistence of poverty and inequality (Wright, 2005). Others have posited the existence of a culture of poverty (Lewis, 1968), a way of life that includes shared views about desirable and undesirable behavior as well as adaptational techniques and institutions for coping with the problems of a lower-class existence. But such a conception of a culture of poverty depicts more than just a way of adapting to a set of conditions imposed by the dominant group. Once it becomes widely accepted, the culture of poverty, because of its influence on children, tends to maintain itself from one generation to the next. By the age of six or seven, children have usually internalized the values and norms of their subculture, making them incapable of taking full advantage of the opportunities that may become available to them during their lifetime (Lewis, 1968, p. 188).

Since Lewis's analysis in the 1960s, the notion of a vicious circle of cultural deprivation to account for inequalities between dominant and minority groups has gained rather wide acceptance among social scientists and laypersons alike. The late Daniel Patrick Moynihan gave it official recognition when as U.S. assistant secretary of labor (long before he became a senator from New York) he asserted in his so-called Moynihan Report that it was not hate or racism but the deterioration of the Black family that was the fundamental source of the economic weaknesses in the Black community (1965).

More recently, the benign prejudice view has been articulated forcefully by both Blacks and Whites in an attempt to explain the perpetuation of racial inequality into the twenty-first century. During the summer of 2004, comedian Bill Cosby, who himself is Black, told an audience of Black activists in Chicago that Black teenagers are the "dirty laundry" in the Black community because of their "poor grammar, foul language, and rude manners" (Harris & Farhi, 2004, p. A1). Rather than focus on racist practices and policies in the wider society, Cosby pointed the finger squarely at the high rates of teen pregnancy and illiteracy characterizing impoverished Black teenagers.

In 2007, comedian Cosby—in collaboration with psychiatrist Alvin F. Poussaint—repeated his benign prejudice argument. Not that Cosby and Poussaint deny the continuing existence of racism. It is only that they emphasize what they believe Black Americans must do in order to improve their own socioeconomic condition in American society. Some would argue that their book is full of racial stereotypes and that they demoralize impoverished Blacks who are doing the best they can to keep their children out of harm's way. Moreover, Cosby and Poussaint arguably discourage government and business leaders from providing greater resources and opportunities to assist those Blacks who are in need of aid (see, for example, Hutchinson, 2007).

Larry Elder (2000), an attorney who hosts a courtroom series on national television and writes a syndicated newspaper column, similarly blamed the continuation of disproportionate poverty in the Black community on the fact that 70% of all Black children are born out of wedlock, a figure that is almost three times larger than the level decried in the Moynihan Report. Elder suggested that scholarships and other forms of financial aid to impoverished students will be wasted if the recipients lack the "discipline" and "character" to work hard when they don't want to. And these, he said, are values that are instilled in the home, especially in a home in which both mother and father are present and capable of raising their children in an effective manner.

John McWhorter (2000, 2005), professor of linguistics at the University of California, Berkeley, similarly claims to locate the source of Black academic underachievement in certain themes running through Black subculture rather than in White racism. The first theme he calls the *cult of victimology*, whereby Black Americans focus on their victimhood as an identity to be nurtured and preserved instead of a problem to be solved. The second he refers to as *separatism*, which encourages Black Americans to see themselves as a distinct and separate group whose members are morally exempt from the rules of behavior governing the lives of others. The third theme McWhorter identifies as *anti-intellectualism*, whereby Black youngsters associate academic success and learning for learning's sake as being characteristic of White America and therefore as not appropriate to their lives. According to McWhorter, these three cultural themes represent a form of collective "self-sabotage." Together, they assure that Black Americans will continue to perform badly both in and out of the classroom, even in the absence of large-scale racial discrimination.

Criminologist James Q. Wilson (1992) takes a benign prejudice viewpoint by blaming racism on the high crime rate among Black Americans and Latinos. In light of the elevated rate of crime committed by Black Americans, he argues, it only makes sense that White Americans would be fearful of Black Americans.

According to Wilson, White racism will come down to the extent that Black crime also comes down.

Taking a contrary point of view, Russell (1998) takes Wilson to task for the narrowness of his view of the relationship between Black crime and White racism. Russell suggests that Whites' fear of Blacks and Latinos has a basis in more than just a high crime rate. Whites are also fearful that Blacks will take their jobs, contaminate White popular culture (its music, dress, and language), overpopulate the country, and exact a measure of revenge for their treatment by White America. Russell also argues that Wilson's view of the relationship between Black crime and White racism is simplistic and ahistorical, ignoring the interrelationships of crime, poverty, and education, as well as the impact of slavery. In other words, Wilson's view has reversed the order of cause and effect: Crime does not cause racism; racism causes a high crime rate. This viewpoint—that a disproportionate level of Black crime is a result of economic and social disadvantage and discrimination—is shared by most criminologists, although not those who take a benign prejudice position.

Wilson's viewpoint fails to receive support in the explanation for hostility toward immigrants from Latin American countries who are widely stereotyped as murderers, terrorists, and rapists. Actually, newcomers to America have a disproportionately low rate of violent crime and incarceration (Sampson, 2008). Cities like El Paso, Laredo, and San Diego, where the majority population consists of immigrants—both legal and illegal—from Latin America, have some of the lowest murder rates in the country. Yet, anti-immigrant sentiment continues unabated, as more and more native-born Americans—especially those who lack job skills—become fearful of being laid off in a bad economy and replaced by cheap labor from Mexico.

Some versions of benign prejudice form the basis of a policy of "benign neglect." If the responsibility for Black and Latino poverty can be located in the one-parent family or the minority subculture, then why bother enacting policies and programs designed to eradicate poverty? If the blame for White racism can be located in a high crime rate among Blacks, then why enact policies to reduce discrimination and prejudice?

At the same time, the benign prejudice perspective can instead be employed to justify policies of affirmative action and preferential treatment designed to level the playing field for minorities who have suffered from past discrimination. Such policies do not necessarily aim to reduce current racism; they try to make up for previous inequities. For example, court-ordered busing during the 1970s in Boston schools was meant to make up for a history of decisions made by the Boston school committee purposely meant to keep the city's schools segregated by race. Similarly recognizing the inequalities in the educational experiences of Blacks and Whites (not to mention the educational value of a diverse student body), affirmative action policies in colleges and universities sought to encourage growth in the enrollment of students of color.

It should also be noted that efforts to improve school dropout rates and rates of teen pregnancy do not necessarily preclude efforts to reduce discriminatory policies in the wider society. The most effective response to group inequities, it might be argued, would be to do both.

The benign prejudice viewpoint continues to provide an easy explanation for racial inequality. In 2013, Gallup asked a representative sample of Americans whether discrimination against Blacks can be blamed for the fact that their jobs, income, and housing tend to be worse than those of Whites. The response of "mostly discrimination" to account for these racial inequalities was chosen by only 15% of all White Americans, 21% of all Hispanic Americans, and 37% of all African Americans.

Eduardo Bonilla-Silva (2014) argues that racism has become "color-blind." Rather than subscribe to traditional versions of racist beliefs, it has become socially acceptable to accuse Blacks and other minorities of "playing the race card," of supporting racially divisive programs and policies such as affirmative action, and of charging "racism" whenever they are criticized by someone who is White. The benign prejudice view for explaining racial inequality continues unabated. Rather than accept the genetic explanation for group differences, some social scientists regard people of color as not working hard enough to improve their socioeconomic position relative to Whites. The blame for group inequality is focused squarely in the environment of society's most vulnerable members.

The Hereditary View—Blaming the Victim

Another version of benign prejudice developed from the work of those who assume a genetic basis of group differences in intelligence. The idea that heredity plays a major role in determining human intelligence has been around for more than a century. In 1883, Galton, who made a study of family eminence, suggested that "the instincts and faculties of different men differ almost as profoundly as animals in different cages of the zoological gardens."

During the early part of the twentieth century, psychologists found that immigrants coming from Poland, Russia, Greece, Turkey, and Italy tended to score lower on intelligence tests than immigrants coming from northwestern Europe. Because of group differences, these psychologists argued that "Mediterranean-Latin-Slavic people" must be genetically stupid and that admitting them to the United States in large numbers would pollute the stream of national intelligence. This finding became a basis for the restrictive immigration laws of the 1920s (Kamin, 1973).

The argument that minority group members are genetically inferior is by no means a new one, but over the past few decades there has been renewed interest in it in the United States. For many, the re-emergence of this view in social science is associated with Arthur Jensen, an educational psychologist who revised the hypothesis that "genetic factors are strongly implicated in the average Negro-White intelligence difference" (1969, p. 82). In a subsequent article, Richard Herrnstein (1971) similarly suggested that socioeconomic status may be based on inherited differences in intelligence, permitting the development of an *hereditary meritocracy* for American society in which intellectually superior individuals will rule.

In a particularly distressing version of the benign prejudice viewpoint, the late J. Philippe Rushton (2001), an evolutionary psychologist from the University of Western Ontario who died in 2012, suggested that racial differences in such advantageous traits as family stability, ability to postpone gratification, sexual restraint, and law-abiding behavior are actually a result of differences in brain size and weight. Rushton argued that Asians are at the top of the positive trait scale and also have larger and heavier brains, Caucasians are in the middle on advantageous traits and brain size, and Africans are at the bottom on both counts.

Rushton's viewpoint has never had great impact on popular culture, although abridged versions of his books have been circulated to a wide range of social scientists. A best-selling book titled *The Bell Curve* by Richard Herrnstein and Charles Murray (1994) focused the attention of the nation once again on racial differences in intelligence. In particular, these behavioral scientists reported, among other things, that the average Black American has a lower intelligent quotient (IQ) than the average White or Asian American, and that this IQ gap is largely inherited.

The title of Murray and Herrnstein's book, *The Bell Curve,* evokes an image of scientific impartiality and precise neutrality. Yet, given the present stage of our knowledge about human behavior, it remains all but impossible to draw unbiased conclusions about racial differences in intelligence. There is simply no evidence of any significance to support the contention that the members of one race are inherently smarter than the members of another race.

One thing seems certain: Americans need guidance in how to wipe out the really important problems that divide us as a people—lack of opportunity, educational inequality, hopelessness, and bigotry. Only when these vital differences have been held constant will racial differences in intelligence be made clear. In some future society in which equality of opportunity is truly a reality, we may not need social scientists to justify selfishness. In the meantime, we might turn our attention to do what is possible to make our social environment conducive to maximizing the potential of all citizens, regardless of race, religion, sexual orientation, gender, disability status, or ethnic origin.

Common-sense observations highlight the absurdity of claims as to the immutability of IQ. In 1923, psychologist Carl Brigham, using the results of IQ tests, concluded that 83% of Jews, 80% of Hungarians, and 70% of Italians were feeble minded and should consequently be excluded from citizenship in the United States. Notwithstanding the current widespread belief that Jews are an intelligent (perhaps too intelligent, according to the stereotype) people overall, Brigham argued then that Jews have the color, stature, mental abilities, and head form of their Alpine neighbors, what he referred to as a "race of peasants" who make perfect slaves and serfs.

Ironically, the Jewish experience in America provides us with one of the most compelling arguments for the environmental instead of the hereditary basis for intelligence. During the 1920s, when Brigham singled out Jews for scoring relatively low on IQ tests, Jews were also concentrated in the lower classes along with other impoverished newcomers to America. By contrast, today's Jewish Americans tend to score among the very highest groups on various tests of intelligence, not coincidentally at the same time that their wealth, power, and status have also seen major improvement. This leaves the unmistakable impression that changes in socioeconomic status are responsible for changes in the way that Jews and, of course, other groups score on IQ tests (Smith, 1995).

Any scientific conclusion, or even hypothesis, concerning genetically determined racial differences in ability or potential is also a political statement with potentially serious political consequences. Scientists who proclaim the inequality of the races have been cited by attorneys in desegregation cases and by legislators with respect to appropriations bills. During economic hard times, such ideas seem to gain in credibility.

Members of the dominant group seek to justify cutting back government-spending programs to minority Americans in the areas of education and welfare. If the overrepresentation of inner-city Blacks in poverty can be traced to some problem in their environment or heredity (rather than to centuries of discrimination), there is no reason to throw additional government resources at such programs. As Smith (1995) correctly notes, many policy makers and academics enjoy good reputations although they have adopted this benign prejudice viewpoint.

But one must wonder what impact the bell curve crowd has had on the self-concept of Black Americans who repeatedly hear from at least a few members of the so-called scientific community that in relation to Whites and Asians they are stupid, incompetent, and lacking intellectually. Even more insidious, the bell curve debate has had its analogue in the racial images outside the academy where people of color struggle on a daily basis with the unflattering messages they receive from members of the dominant group. Thus, some White cab drivers won't stop for a Black man and some White women won't share an elevator ride with a Black woman. When some Black men drive through a White neighborhood, they are prepared to be stopped by a suspicious police officer who uses some sort of racial profile that treats all Blacks as drug dealers and smugglers; when they go shopping downtown, Blacks are followed through stores by security guards who see them as potential shoplifters. According to a recent study, Blacks and Latinos are twice as likely as Whites to report that the police used or threatened force against them. Moreover, Black drivers are more likely to be pulled over and Black and Latino drivers are more likely to be searched, handcuffed, or ticketed (Gullo, 2001). More than 4 of every 10 Black Americans report having been the victims of racial profiling, including almost three-quarters of young Black males (Newport, 1999).

This is one of the reasons why so many Black Americans cringed in horror when in 1995 they saw O. J. Simpson's courtroom appearances in his murder trial being telecast daily to a national audience. It isn't only that Blacks mistrust the criminal justice system (in cities like Philadelphia and Los Angeles, police officers have been charged with planting evidence on Black suspects), Blacks were also concerned that the publicity surrounding the Simpson murder trial would reinforce the afrophobic stereotype by which they were being personally judged, on an everyday basis, to be thugs and rapists. Even if the environmental version of benign prejudice has a degree of validity, and it probably does, there is reason to believe that hate and prejudice continue to feed the vicious circle in which many Black Americans have been trapped.

Stereotyping has more than a material effect on its victims. Especially in situations in which little or nothing is known, on a first-hand basis, about an individual—in shops and stores, elevators, real-estate offices, cabs, college campuses, factories, restaurants, large companies, and the criminal justice system—minority members may be treated stereotypically as a matter of routine (Lee, Jussim, and McCauley, 1995).

Having endured a lifetime as victims of stereotyping, many Black Americans—even those who have achieved inordinate success in economic and prestige terms—become sensitized to slights, indignities, or biases in their dealings with White Americans. When recognized for their individual achievements, certain Black Americans may be treated with dignity and respect. But when anonymous, they may come to feel, rightly or not, as though they are the victims of racial profiling.

On July 16, 2009, shortly after noon, famed African American scholar Henry Louis Gates, Jr., returned to his residence in Cambridge, Massachusetts, from a trip to China only to discover that his front door was stuck, and he could not gain entry. The 59-year-old Harvard professor, along with a companion who also was African American, put their shoulders to the door, forcing it open to get inside.

A 911 call from a passerby who didn't recognize Gates and suspected a break-in brought police officer James Crowley to the scene. The details of the encounter between officer Crowley and professor Gates were never really made clear. But we do know that they engaged in a heated exchange of words. Moreover, Gates was then arrested for disorderly conduct and handcuffed, even though it was obvious that he was a resident of the house and not an intruder.

Initial reactions to the Cambridge incident were based more on emotion and personal experience than on the evidence. President Obama, Massachusetts governor Patrick, and Cambridge mayor Simmons—all of whom are African American—were critical of the Cambridge police response and not of the professor. It is not outrageous to speculate that all three had experienced countless numbers of racial slights and indignities over their own lifetimes, and that they empathized with Professor Gates, who seemed to have suffered the same experiences.

Whatever the actual circumstances involving Gates and Crowley, the racial gap in evaluating the treatment of Gates was wide and deep. Sadly, few White Americans sided with the Black professor. Few were even willing to acknowledge that he might have been victimized by ugly stereotyping in the past and that his reaction to Officer Crowley might have been colored by such previous experiences.

The size of the racial divide was made clear by the results of a *Wall Street Journal*/NBC poll (*Wall Street Journal*, July 29, 2009) taken days after the Cambridge incident. Among African Americans, just 4% said Professor Gates was more to blame versus 30% who identified Officer Crowley as being at fault. In contrast, 32% of White respondents said Gates was more at fault while only 7% blamed Crowley. It should be noted as well that the majority of Americans, both Black and White, refused to place the blame on either Gates or Crowley.

Though the charges against Gates were quickly dropped, the controversy surrounding the incident in Cambridge continued for some time. Professor Gates argued that his arrest was racially motivated; Officer Crowley claimed that he acted by the book. Days later, both men met with President Obama at the White House to have a beer (and a friendly conversation) together. As for other Americans, it is doubtful that this single experience was capable of modifying their preconceived ideas about race.

A more recent incident involving police reaction to a Black suspect occurred on a February evening 2012 in a Sanford, Florida, gated community. An unarmed Black teenager, Trayvon Martin, was shot to death in an altercation with the neighborhood watch coordinator, George Zimmerman, while the 17-year-old walked home from a nearby shop. Six weeks after the shooting occurred, 28-year-old Zimmerman was charged with second-degree murder by a special prosecutor. After a trial lasting more than one month, a jury acquitted Zimmerman of all charges, but many Americans continued to regard him as guilty.

According to a Gallup poll, the accuracy of Zimmerman's guilty verdict was an issue of sharp dispute between Black and White Americans. When asked, "Do you think the verdict was right or wrong?" 54% of White respondents but only 7% of Black respondents said, "Right." The Hispanic responses fell between their White and Black counterparts at 25%, perhaps being influenced in part by the defendant's Hispanic background.

Note that the fear of confirming negative stereotypes about their own group can seriously erode the ability of minority group members to achieve their potential. In one series of studies, Black students who were given a difficult test of their verbal abilities performed well except when they were asked to report their race and they were made to believe that doing poorly would confirm the stereotypic belief that Blacks are intellectually inferior to Whites (Steele & Aronson, 1995). Not only can the threat of being stereotyped reduce an individual's performance, but it can also cause an individual to avoid those areas of life in which she is expected to fail (Crocker & Major, 1989; Steele, 1992). Concerned about confirming the stereotype that they are less intelligent than Whites, some Black children over time tend to disconnect academic achievement with self-image. They come to associate learning for learning's sake and academic achievement as within the province of White America and not within their own. In the long run, the acceptance of this anti-intellectual attitude profoundly reduces Black children's ability to compete in any arena where the ability to learn is essential (Osborne, 1995).

It should be noted that some psychologists have shown certain stereotypes to have a degree of accuracy (Lee, Jussim, & McCauley, 1995). For example, it is indeed true that 53% of all homicides are committed by Black Americans, who represent only 13% of the population of the United States. Knowing of the overrepresentation of Blacks in violent crime does not, however, answer the important question as to *why* Black Americans are overrepresented among violent criminals. To explain this phenomenon, one might examine the impact of poverty, discrimination, social disorganization, racism, strain, and other factors that have been demonstrated to serve as direct causes of criminal behavior found disproportionately among Black Americans. Even more than Hispanics who also were victimized by discrimination, Black Americans had long suffered fewer opportunities for regular employment in the private sector. Companies in cities like Los Angeles had for generations expressed a preference to hire Hispanics rather than Blacks (Leovy, 2015).

For those who are eager to apply a genetic explanation to Black violent crime, it should be emphasized that the rate of serious violence committed by Black Americans has not remained constant. It has risen and fallen dramatically over many decades. The same is true of other groups in society whose crime rates have varied significantly over the years. In the nineteenth century, impoverished Irish immigrants were overrepresented among street criminals; during the 1920s, it was impoverished Italian and Jewish Americans who became identified with gangland killings.

Some White Americans, concerned about their personal safety, might argue that knowing that 53% of all murders are perpetrated by Blacks is important information in order to avoid their own victimization. From this viewpoint, the argument might be that they should avoid Blacks to reduce their chances of being killed. The problem with this kind of thinking is that it ignores a couple of important points. First, that murder tends to be intraracial—Black perpetrators kill Blacks; Asian perpetrators kill Asians; Latino perpetrators kill Latinos; and White perpetrators kill Whites.

Second, and even more important, although it is true that more than half of all murders are committed by Blacks, this does not mean that more than half of all Blacks commit murder. In fact, only 25 in every 100,000 Black Americans have killed anyone, leaving 99,975 in every 100,000 who have not. Just to put the predictability issue in comparative perspective, we might use the same logic to suggest that any individual would be far safer if he were totally to avoid all men. After all, not 53% but a truly shocking 90% of all murders are committed by men rather than women. Once again, however, the logic of this approach to predictability leads us astray. Only 12 in every 100,000 men ever kill anyone. Like the overwhelming majority of Blacks, most men are law-abiding citizens, not murderers.

Acting on the anti-Black stereotype is therefore not at all an effective predictor and is tantamount to treating most Blacks as murderers for the sins of a few. Most people do not like to be stereotyped; instead, they seek to be treated as unique individuals with their own sets of strengths and weaknesses and of accomplishments and failures. It would make vastly more sense for the purposes of reducing the likelihood of being harmed to avoid any man or woman who has a history of being dangerous and violent, whether they are Black, White, Latino, or Asian.

Not that particular characteristics of groups don't have some bearing on the way they are treated by members of the dominant group. It's just that these characteristics may themselves still be a result of their treatment. The vicious circle of deprivation is no closed system. It often begins with discrimination and exploitation and ends with more of the same (Patterson, 1998).

In his role as the president of Harvard University and prior to becoming Obama's economic advisor, Lawrence Summers inspired a major controversy when he suggested that innate differences between men and women might explain, in part, why fewer women succeed in math and science. Taking a benign prejudice position, Summers also questioned to what extent discrimination was a factor in the small number of female professors of engineering and science at elite universities.

Some argued that Summers used his benign prejudice position in order to justify substantial declines in the percentage of tenured faculty positions offered to women in Harvard's College of Arts and Sciences since he took office. Others viewed Summers's remarks as "hate speech" that would keep larger numbers of young women from entering fields related to science and mathematics in the future.

Trend statistics tell a different story. Rather than demonstrate the influence of innate gender differences, they suggest that women have excelled in fields of science and math when they are given an opportunity to do so. For example, the percentage of medical school graduates who are female increased dramatically from less than 7% in 1965–1966 to almost 50% in 2007–2008 (Association of American Medical Colleges, 2007–2008).

Many women teaching at medical schools perceive that they are discriminated against and sexually harassed, according to a study from Massachusetts General Hospital (MGH) and Boston University School of Medicine. Men seem to be relatively unaware of the problems and much less affected by them (Carr, 2000). This may explain why in 2008, 20% of male medical school faculty but only 4% of female faculty were full professors (Association of American Medical Colleges, 2007–2008).

During the Middle Ages, Jews were systematically excluded from respectable occupations and restricted to the role of money lending. Their consequent overrepresentation in fields of finance and banking was later used to confirm the stereotype that Jews are money grubbing and mercenary as well as to justify efforts to grant them only second-class citizenship or to expel them from the countries in which they lived since birth. Similarly, when their land was deemed important for White Americans to possess, American Indians were forcibly expelled from their homes to be transplanted to impoverished reservations where their opportunities for economic progress became almost nonexistent. Any armed resistance on their part was then used to prove that Indians were barbaric savages who deserved whatever fate they were given. Black Americans were initially enslaved and subsequently became the recipients of Jim Crow laws that until the 1960s kept them separated from Whites in most areas of public life. The Black subculture that arose out of their legal and *de facto* segregation over many generations has been thought by some White Americans to be the primary source of Black economic disadvantage. It is easy enough to put blinders on and ignore the historical role of hate and prejudice in determining the life chances of an entire people.

A Situationist View of Hate Violence

When people act in ways that stray from local norms or cultural standards, their behaviors are generally attributed to dispositional or psychological factors. This is true for groups of people too, such as racial or ethnic groups. Sometimes these odd or repulsive behaviors conform to stereotypes about the group, serving to confirm and reinforce the negative images. From the benign prejudice view, individuals and groups are to blame for their own failings rather than the stresses and strains present in their daily *situations* or social contexts.

This viewpoint prevents law-abiding citizens from seeing and acknowledging their own culpability for creating and maintaining these negative situations. The victims of hate and prejudice are now regarded as the villains. Zimbardo (2004, p. 25) explains this phenomenon as follows: "Locating evil within selected individuals or groups carries with it the 'social virtue' of taking 'society off the hook' as blameworthy; societal structures and political decision making are exonerated from bearing any burden of the more fundamental circumstances that create racism, sexism, elitism, poverty, and the marginal existence for some citizens."

The situationist perspective provides a framework for understanding why certain groups of people are overrepresented in the disadvantaged and disenfranchised margins of society, and why they are likely targets of hate and discrimination. In addition, this viewpoint helps us see why "good people" participate in discriminatory practices, and why otherwise very caring people won't step in to stop it. The situationist perspective is informed by research in social psychology and sociology, some of which is highlighted in the final chapter of this book (Zimbardo, 2004).

The local situation plays an important role with regard to facilitating hate and violence. Still, it cannot be denied that *social structure*—the patterned arrangements between the members of a society—also has a major impact on the course of bigotry, determining whether it remains dormant, spreads like wildfire, or is transformed into violence. Social structure consists of collective norms that shape the behavior of individuals, a system of socioeconomic stratification, and several major institutions including family, work, education, law enforcement, and the courts.

In order to demonstrate the situationist perspective to his course in the sociology of deviance, the second author often begins the class in a way that is, at first, very disorienting to students, and which later produces widespread "bad" behavior. It goes like this: On the very first day of class, he says nothing to the students for about a half an hour or so. Some students become fidgety; others disengage and begin talking on their cell phones or reading the newspaper. At this point he asks students to arrange their desks in a circle. When this task is accomplished he introduces himself as the instructor and informs students that we "will meet weekly for the next several months in order 'to explore the topic of deviance.'" Then he doesn't say anything more; he just sits back, looks, and listens.[1] At first students become anxious, then annoyed. Friendly smiles and nervous giggles give way to outbursts of frustration after about an hour. Some students have actually warned him that if he didn't "begin class soon," they would get up and leave the room. Some have threatened to report him to the university administration. About a year ago a young male student stood by his desk looking down at him in a threatening manner with clenched fists and said, "I'd be less pissed off at you if you told me the truth; that you forgot to prepare the f—ing syllabus." Other students have tried to ease the tension by suggesting that they (the students) introduce themselves to each other. Some have even tried to begin a discussion on the topic of the course—deviant behavior. These attempts by students to return the class to "normal" are rarely accepted by their peers, which results in increased conflict between students and rising anxiety within the classroom. By the end of the second hour (of a three-hour class), students are frazzled. Some have stormed out of class. Others have insulted Jim openly as being "lazy" and "incompetent." On some occasions students have even cried out, "Please stop this and tell us what we should do."

The class has never gone the entire three hours. Jim generally ends the session when he sees that students have had enough, before violence erupts, or emotional harm is done. At the end of this exercise he tells students that the next class, the following week, will be the "real first class" and that this class was an exercise in the study of deviance. Jim then gives students an assignment, to describe in writing exactly how they were feeling and what they were thinking during this exercise. In addition, he asks them to be prepared to discuss this exercise at the next class the following week.

During the debriefing in the following class session, students almost always confirm their feelings of frustration, boredom, anger, and confusion. They often admit that their own behavior in this class was not "typical" for them. Many have said that they were embarrassed by their behavior, while others have defended their actions as being "normal under abnormal conditions." Jim often suggests to them that had a sociologist been studying "deviance in the class room" *that day* and decided to visit each classroom at the university to count the number of deviant acts that were being committed, our classroom would easily have been the most deviant at the university.

So, then he asks, who is ultimately responsible for the outbursts and disorderly behavior in the classroom? Is it the person or persons who commit the acts? Clearly, not everybody is disorderly, so why do some people act this way and not others? Is the classroom environment to blame? To what extent is the formal authority figure (the teacher in this case) to blame? He is simply doing what he is paid to do: teaching students about deviance. But, how do his teaching methods appear to the students? Or is it the combination of factors

---

[1] This exercise is adapted from the training group model known as T groups. See Bradford, L. P., Gibb, J. R., & Benne, K. D. (1964). *T-group theory and laboratory method: Innovation in re-education.* New York: John Wiley & Sons, Inc.

including the temperament of the students *and* the anomic classroom environment? These are questions posed for the students to reflect on and discuss, but they are also questions that have been addressed over the years with great success within the fields of social psychology and sociology.

Kurt Lewin (1890–1947), one of the most influential figures in modern social psychology, claimed that behavior (*B*) is always a function of the person (P) and the environment (*E*). He presented this idea mathematically as $B = f(P, E)$ (Lewin, 1951). Lewin's conceptual approach is useful to us as we reflect on the classroom experience. We modify Lewin's equation a bit, separating the environment into two parts, the immediate (most local) situation (E_{ls}) and the larger (global) sociocultural environment (E_{sc}).

In Figure 2.1 we depict person (P) in the middle of the figure enveloped by two circles. The inner circle closest to person (P) represents the immediate local situation (E_{ls}), such as when person (P) is "hanging out" with friends in his neighborhood at night or when he is at work on an assembly line or at a meeting with coworkers. The outer circle farthest from person (P) represents the larger sociocultural environment (E_{sc}) in which the local situation (E_{ls}) exists. This area includes the broader social structure, including cultural norms, social institutions, and national ideologies.

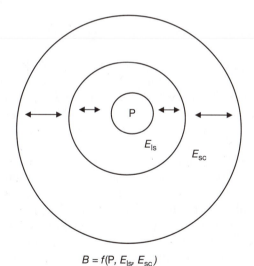

$$B = f(P, E_{ls}, E_{sc})$$

Key

P = Dispositional and psychological forces affecting the person's behavior.
E_{ls} = The most local situation, e.g., the neighborhood, workplace, the family home, as examples.
E_{sc} = The larger sociocultural environment. This includes social institutions, mainstream culture, and political and economic ideology, among others.

FIG. 2.1 The Situationist Perspective.
Source: This figure presents a modified version of a model used by Kurt Lewin to express the interdependent relationship between the person and his or her environment. See Lewin, K. (1940). Formalization and progress in psychology. *University of Iowa Studies in Child Welfare, 16*(3), 9–42.

Each of us, including hypothetical person (P), has a disposition or temperament that we carry with us into each local situation (E_{ls}). Norms, values, expectations, and environmental conditions in the local situation (E_{ls}) may conform to or conflict with the larger environmental conditions (E_{sc}). In the classroom experiment the local situation (E_{ls}) conflicts with the normative behaviors of teachers at state universities in the United States (E_{sc}). This conflict produces an atmosphere of confusion in the local situation (E_{ls}). When this happens, students don't know how to act appropriately because they can't rely on past experiences or social norms to inform them. They have tried behaviors that they *thought* would return the classroom to "normal," such as asking others to "introduce themselves."

But, when they don't get the responses they expect, some students become angry and frustrated. This condition produces a high frequency of disorderly behavior from students. However, not everybody participates in antagonistic and disorderly ways. Perhaps it is only those individuals with certain internal dispositions who become angry and visibly aggressive. As shown in Figure 2.1, individual responses to deviance in the classroom may also depend on students' definitions of the situation. Some may regard their instructor's unresponsive demeanor as a failure in carrying out his professional role, while others might see the chaotic situation as a welcome break from listening to lectures and taking notes.

During the discussion that follows the class exercise, students easily recognize the many ways the classroom "experiment" paralleled the dynamics of the "real" world. For example, it is often true that individuals who live in neighborhoods with high rates of unemployment have a higher risk of becoming involved with illegal drugs and crime. When this occurs in minority neighborhoods it reinforces negative stereotypes about these groups. From the situationist view, however, crime in disadvantaged neighborhoods can be explained as the result of the frustration and sense of injustice that many residents feel when "the authorities" funnel resources such as good schools or high-paying jobs to other places. Racist attitudes among the majority and among the most powerful members of the society can serve to create situations of hopelessness, frustration, anger, and helplessness, which then can lead good people to do bad things. The criminal acts and other "bad behavior" committed disproportionately by minority group members prove to the majority that these groups have innate criminogenic dispositions or live in a "culture of violence" that mark them for surveillance and state-sponsored control, thus making a bad situation even worse.

The situationist view helps us to think more deeply about the causes and effects of hate, discrimination, and intergroup violence by making us look beyond the actor(s) and toward the situations—both immediate and sociocultural—that give rise to these negative conditions and behaviors. In reality we all share some blame for creating and maintaining situations, both locally (E_{ls}) and globally (E_{sc}), that antagonize people with particular dispositions to behave in counterproductive ways and then to suffer unnecessarily because of it. The situationist perspective enables us to see the actual root causes of hate and violence, allowing us to develop more effective ways to respond and prevent them from occurring in the first place.

Threatening Situations Can Inspire Hate

Rather than search for trends in hate and prejudice over time, it might be more useful to examine situations, some of which are totally unpredictable, that threaten a group of people and therefore inspire bigotry and hate-motivated violence. Just when you are convinced that stereotyped thinking and hurtful bigotry have substantially declined, you may be forced to recognize that respect for differences continues to be an elusive dream. Indeed, hate can remain dormant in a culture, emerging without warning from the darkness in response to some threatening but enlightening episode or situation.

In 1958, sociologist Herbert Blumer suggested that racial prejudice had its roots in a collective perception of group positioning relative to one another. He argued that members of the dominant group in a society tend to remain unconcerned with the status of subordinate groups unless they become regarded as threatening the distribution of power and privilege between majority and minority. Prejudice develops as members of the dominant group search for a justification for continuing to hold a position of superiority even as minority members attempt to alter the socioeconomic hierarchy.

More recently, Quillian (1995) demonstrated that the connection between prejudice and perceived threat posed by a subordinate group depends in part on characteristics of the economic situation facing members of the dominant group and the relative size of the subordinate group's membership. Also relevant is a theory proposed by Green, Strolovitch, and Wong (1998), according to which rates of racial violence are higher in "defended neighborhoods"—that is, in locations that have been historically dominated by Whites but have also experienced a surge in the minority population. According to the defended neighborhood explanation, an increase in inter-group violence is a result of the threat to a historically dominant group posed by a sudden growth in the number of minority group residents. Group threat is a factor that can be applied to explain not only inter-group violence in neighborhoods but also in classrooms, college dormitories, and workplaces (Levin and Reichelmann, 2015).

Hate Crimes Against Muslims

In the week following the 1995 Oklahoma City bombing in which 168 people lost their lives, many Americans assumed that Middle-Eastern terrorists had been responsible. Before the real killer, Timothy McVeigh, could be arrested, news commentators and politicians had already implicated Middle-Eastern militants in the deadly attack. In response, there was an outbreak of anti-Muslim incidents—some 216 episodes of harassment, discrimination, and violence. But even when it was clear later on that the Oklahoma City attack was carried out by a White Christian lacking any ties to Muslim extremists, bigotry continued to make life miserable for Muslim Americans. In the workplace, some were fired for refusing to remove their head scarves ("hijabs") or taking breaks to pray. In schools, Muslim girls reported having their scarves yanked from their heads and being taunted by their classmates. In their neighborhoods, Muslims claimed to have been denied service at gas stations and grocery stores (Goodstein, 1996).

Similarly, during the tense months following the September 11 attack on America in 2001, Muslims and Arabs were the targets of violence perpetrated by angry Americans who looked in vain for the terrorists responsible for orchestrating 3,000 deaths at the World Trade Center in New York City and at the Pentagon in Washington, DC.

Not surprisingly, 9/11 brought with it an unprecedented number of hate offenses against Muslims. Specifically, in 2001, there was a 1,600% increase in anti-Muslim, anti-Middle Eastern, and anti-South Asian hate crimes reported to local police departments. In 2000, Americans committed 28 hate offenses against their Muslim neighbors; in 2001, the number of such hate incidents rose to 481. Most (296 incidents) were acts of intimidation, but there were also 185 aggravated and simple assaults (Schevitz, 2002).

At least during the first weeks following 9/11, none of the hate-motivated offenses resulted in the murder of Muslim Americans, though many of them were vandalized, intimidated, or assaulted. Ironically, however, Sikh Indians—who are neither Islamic nor Middle Eastern—became mistakenly targeted for death. Days after the attack on America, 49-year-old Balbir Singh Sodhi from Punjab, India, was fatally shot as he did landscaping outside of his Mesa, Arizona, gas station. Sodhi's turban and long beard apparently reminded the killer of Osama bin Laden. As stated by a friend of the victim, Sikh Indians "are different people from Muslim people. We have different beliefs, a different religion" (CNN, 2001).

Within a few days of the 9/11 attack, more than 1,200 people were arrested, but only a few were proven to be linked to terrorism. In the eyes of American law enforcement, Pakistan was considered to be a "terrorist feeder state" that exported terrorists to other countries. Almost 40% of the detainees could be regarded as Pakistani nationals.

After September 11, 2001, the Asian-American community suffered a dramatic decline in everyday acceptance. Rather than being viewed as a "model minority," Asian Americans—and especially South Asian Americans—were now regarded with suspicion and distrust as potential terrorists. In response, some South Asians decided to avoid the American backlash by leaving the country. By 2003, more than 2,100 Pakistani-Americans had applied for political asylum in Canada. During the 10-year period following the 9/11 attacks, more than 100,000 Pakistanis have been estimated to have left the United States to return to their homeland in Asia (Lee, 2015).

Of course, it was not only Pakistanis whose public image among Americans became associated with terrorism. For the same reason that the number of anti-Muslim hate crimes soared, stereotyped attitudes toward Muslims also turned especially nasty following September 11, 2001. Opinion polls conducted by the *Washington Post* and ABC News indicated that some 33% of Americans regarded Islam in a negative light. Fourteen percent reported believing that Islam helps to inspire violence (Deane & Fears, 2006).

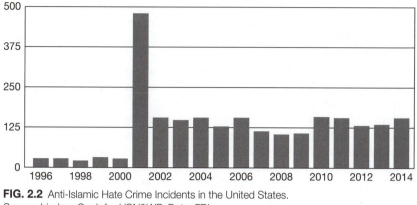

FIG. 2.2 Anti-Islamic Hate Crime Incidents in the United States.
Source: Lindsey Cook for *USN&WR*; Data: FBI.

But more than five years later, in March 2006, the same pollsters found only a hardening in the attitudes of Americans toward Muslims. The unpopularity of the war in Iraq as well as major acts of terrorism against civilians in Spain and England linked to Islamic extremists apparently contributed to a growing distrust of Muslims in general. Forty-six percent of adult Americans told the pollsters that they now viewed Islam negatively; some 33% said that Islam helps to inspire violent behavior. As shown in Figure 2.2, the prevalence of anti-Islamic hate crimes in the United States similarly rose at least slightly in 2006 and then fell again for a couple of years. More recently, in the aftermath of the November 2015 terrorist massacre of 130 civilians in Paris, attributed to the radical Islamic group known as ISIS, American Muslims experienced a backlash of hateful phone calls and online messages, issuing threats of violence to mosques and Islamic centers (Cook, 2015). Similarly, after terror attacks in Brussels killed at least 35 people in March 2016, Muslims in the United States reported experiencing an increasing level of discrimination and suspicion around the country.

Hate Crimes Against Immigrants

Xenophobia is nothing new. Even in the late nineteenth and early twentieth centuries, when most newcomers to America were European, some part of anti-immigrant sentiment reflected widespread fear of job loss. Whenever the jobless rate soared, so did the forces of nativism.

Outside of the United States, newcomers have often been attacked by racist members of society. As East Germany struggled to make the transition from Communism to a free-market economy, its high unemployment inspired violent attacks on refugees and workers from Eastern European and developing countries. During the 1990s, there were thousands of attacks against foreigners, especially Turks, Africans, and Vietnamese. In September 1991, for example, 600 right-wing German youths firebombed a home for foreigners and then attacked 200 Vietnamese and Mozambicans in the streets of Hoyerswerde.

In 1992, hundreds of angry youngsters attacked the apartments housing Asian targets with gasoline bombs and rocks in the Lichtenhagen district of Rostock.

A decade later, a group of young Germans firebombed the same block of high-rise apartments and a nearby Asian grocery store in the city of Rostock. The more than 100 residents of the building—all immigrants from Vietnam and other Asian countries—fled in panic across the rooftop to safety (*Deutsche Presse-Agentur*, 2003).

We must be careful not to view anti-immigrant sentiment as an exclusively "German problem." In reality, violence against foreigners has recently increased in countries around the world, mainly in response to a burgeoning presence of immigrant workers and refugees at a time when economic circumstances are less than optimal and native-born residents feel threatened by the possibility of terrorism.

Across the globe, millions have left their homelands for the sake of a better life—and they have not always received a friendly welcome from the citizens of their host countries. Many English citizens equate foreigners with terrorists (Cracknell and Gadher, 2003). In France, resentment against its 6 million Muslim immigrants has provoked the government to tighten controls against illegal immigration. Even Scandinavian nations have been affected by the recent arrival of unprecedented numbers of immigrants. In Sweden, for example, racist youth movements have been more active, using White power rock music to spread their xenophobic propaganda and violence to target their enemies.

The United States has never been a stranger to strangers. Indeed, it would not be much of an exaggeration to characterize America as a nation of immigrants. In 1830, the largest number of our newcomers were Irish; in 1890, they were German. In 1900, they were Italian; then, they were Canadian. During the 1980s, four out of five immigrants came from Asia, Latin America, or the Caribbean. Beginning in 1990, the newcomers were coming in great numbers from Mexico, the Philippines, Vietnam, China and Taiwan, South Korea, and India. Smaller quantities also entered from the Dominican Republic, El Salvador, Jamaica, and Iran.

The September 11 assault on the United States also inspired a growing disdain for immigrants, especially those coming from Latin America, Asia, and the Middle East. Since the 9/11 terrorist attack, as Americans became increasingly anxious about the threat of international terrorism, stereotyped images of immigrants have turned decidedly more negative. Myths and misconceptions about newcomers have assumed the status of cultural truisms. Anxious advocates of nativism envision huddled masses of impoverished, uneducated, disease-ridden criminals and terrorists who sneak across our porous border with Mexico or traverse an ocean to steal jobs and murder our citizens (Levin & Rabrenovic, 2006).

In response, White supremacists and racist skinheads have committed a growing number of hate crimes against Latinos, both illegal and legal, both foreigners and American citizens. Masquerading as immigration reform groups, these fringe elements of the anti-immigrant movement have contributed to a climate of hate and violence (ADL, 2006). Moreover, when asked whether "you, a family member, or a close friend ever experienced discrimination because of your Latino or racial background," 47% of a national sample of Latinos responded in the affirmative (Time/Schulman, Ronca, & Bucuvalas, 2005).

Discrimination against minority Americans tends to increase as the size of a minority population increases (Quillian, 1995). For newcomers to the United States, this relationship has produced an especially ominous result. As the number of Latino newcomers has grown to unprecedented proportions, so has the perception that immigrants represent a major threat to the economic viability of native-born Americans. Because so many recent immigrants have come from Latin American countries, Latinos have become the primary targets of hate-motivated assaults on newcomers and their families.

The year 2010 was a particularly problematic period of time for Latinos. Both the number of immigrants living in the United States (37.8 million) as well as the national unemployment rate (10%) peaked at the same time, causing a sharp rise in hate-motivated assaults targeting Latinos. In 2002, merely 1% of all such attacks were perpetrated against Latinos; by 2010, as immigration reform became a major focal point of political debate and work-related anxiety, fully 40% of all hate-motivated assaults targeted the Latino population (Levin and Reichelmann, 2015).

The New Anti-Semitism

Situations have also affected the level of anti-Semitism in the United States and in nations around the globe. Beginning especially in 2000, as the conflict in the Middle East between Israelis and Palestinians became increasingly more violent and intractable, the character of anti-Semitism in countries around the world was observed to change in ever more destructive and harmful ways. In what has come to be labeled the *new anti-Semitism,* Jews everywhere—even those who supported the establishment of a Palestinian state and had never even visited the Middle East—were now being held responsible for Israeli military policies (Chesler, 2003; Iganski & Kosman, 2003).

The second intifada or uprising of Palestinians began at the end of September 2000, in response to Israeli opposition leader Ariel Sharon's visit to a disputed area of Jerusalem in which both the Temple Mount and the Al-Aqsa Mosque are located. By October 7, as conflict between Israelis and Palestinians began to reach a fever pitch, Jews around the world became targets of anger and violence. In the United States alone, the number of anti-Semitic acts reached a peak, with some 259 incidents occurring during a 30-day period (Radler, 2001).

Unlike traditional forms of anti-Jewish bigotry associated with the White power movement and Nazi ideology, the new anti-Semitism was espoused not only by right-wing extremists but by proponents of progressive politics who voiced their opposition to all varieties of colonialism and racism. Many right-wingers in France and Germany regarded Jews, along with immigrants from Africa and the Middle East, as one element of the "foreign" influence in their countries responsible for the demise of European culture and an increase in the national unemployment rate. Many American and British left-wingers saw Palestinians as victims and Israel as an oppressor state. When Middle-Eastern tensions rose—during the second Palestinian intifada in September 2000 and again in the spring of 2002 after the Israeli military occupied West Bank towns—the number of anti-Semitic attacks also increased (Chesler, 2003; Iganski & Kosmin, 2003). By 2003, there were more anti-Jewish hate attacks in European countries than at any time since World War II (Rosenblum, 2003). According to the Israeli government, more than 2,500 French Jews had decided in 2002 to immigrate to Israel—the largest number since the 1967 war, and double the number who left France in 2001 (Frankel, 2003).

In the United States, the level of anti-Semitism never escalated to the same degree as in European cities. Still, the Anti-Defamation League (ADL, 2005) determined anti-Jewish incidents as being at their highest level in nine years. The league reported a total of 1,821 incidents in 2004, representing a 17% rise over the 1,557 incidents reported for 2003. Similarly, in both 2006 and 2008, while Israel was involved in warfare with Hamas and Hezbollah, the percentage of hate-motivated assaults against Jewish Americans grew again (Levin & Reichelmann, 2015).

While the new anti-Semitism was spreading through both Europe and North America as well as the Islamic world, old-fashioned forms of anti-Semitism also managed to find a niche in the thinking of Americans. In the immediate aftermath of presidential candidate Al Gore's selection of Senator Joseph Lieberman as his running mate in the 2000 election campaign, anti-Semitic messages appeared in chat rooms and online message boards around the Internet. On racist websites there were messages about Zionist occupied government (ZOG), slurs about Lieberman's religion, and warnings about having a Jew in the White House (FNC, 2000).

Matthew Hale, then the 27-year-old leader of World Church of the Creator, in a press release e-mailed to his protégés, said the following about the selection of Lieberman: "While undoubtedly some will be surprised by this, I am very happy that the Jew Joseph Lieberman has been chosen by Al Gore to be his running mate, for it brings the pervasive Jewish influence of the federal government out in the open so that people can see what we anti-Semites are talking about" (ADL, 2000).

Tom Metzger, who heads the White Aryan Resistance from his home in Falbrook, California, sent the following message to a mailing list of American Nazi Party members:

> The lusting for power and total control by the jew [sic] knows no limits and I can only pray that when the Jewish masters find a way to remove gore (if elected) and install the first jew [sic] president of the most powerful and bloodthirsty corporate empire in world history, that Lieberman and his controllers will institute every oppression that their twisted imaginations can invent, and aim them directly and solely at White MEN! (As quoted by ADL, 2000)

White extremists were not the only ones who reacted with anti-Semitism to the choice of a Jewish vice-presidential candidate. Lee Alcorn, president of the National Association for the Advancement of Colored People (NAACP) in Dallas, Texas, told a radio audience that Black voters "need to be suspicious of any kind of partnerships between the Jews at that kind of level because we know that their interest primarily has to do with, you know, money and these kinds of things" (National Journal Group, Inc., 2000). Nation of Islam leader Louis Farrakhan warned that Lieberman's Jewish identity gives him "dual loyalty" to both the United States and the state of Israel.

Such anti-Semitic remarks about Lieberman are not the first (nor the last) expressions of hate and prejudice articulated by well-known and not-so-well-known Americans about specific individuals who are different with respect to religion or race. In June 2015, as Vermont Senator Bernie Sanders made his bid to succeed Obama as the president of the United States, Diane Rehm, a syndicated talk show host on National Public Radio, accused the Jewish candidate of holding dual Israeli citizenship. According to Politifact.com, the exchange went as follows:

Rehm: Senator, you have dual citizenship with Israel.

Sanders: No, I do not have dual citizenship with Israel, I'm an American. Don't know where that question came from. I'm an American citizen. I have visited Israel on a couple of occasions. No, I'm an American citizen, period.

Rehm: I understand from a list we have gotten that you were on that list. Forgive me if that . . .

Sanders: No, that's some of the nonsense that goes on in the Internet. But that is absolutely not true.

Rehm: Interesting. Are there members of Congress who do have dual citizenship or is that part of the fable?

Sanders: I honestly don't know. But I have read that on the Internet. You know, my dad came to this country from Poland at the age of 17 without a nickel in his pocket. He loved this country. I am, you know, I got offended a little bit by that comment, and I know it's been on the Internet. I am, obviously, an American citizen and I do not have any dual citizenship.

Rehm later apologized for making a false accusation on air, and evidence of Sanders's dual citizenship was never forthcoming. Yet this did not stop White supremacist groups on the Internet from treating the unfounded accusation as gospel and using the occasion to spew anti-Semitic rhetoric. Infostormer (June 11, 2015), which claims to be dedicated to destroying "Jewish tyranny," published the following commentary on the home page of its website:

A group of Jewish vermin are in tears after an NPR interviewer asked Bernie Sanders if he had dual Israeli citizenship on air.

The National Kike Democratic Council called the question indefensible and cried anti-Semitism.

The fact is that this is a legitimate question. Having dual citizenship in another country raises questions about one's allegiances. I would go even further that being a Jew raises questions about one's allegiances. They are a people who feed and leech off of other societies and cultures. They do not belong in any position of power within America or any other nation.

Over the past few decades, beginning especially during the 1980s, Americans have been forced by circumstances to deal with people who are different, whether they liked it or not. During this period and continuing into the present, almost unprecedented numbers of newcomers have arrived from Asia and Latin America. More people of color began to participate in workplaces, neighborhoods, schools, and college dormitories, where they had been almost totally absent just a few decades earlier. Gays and lesbians increased their demands for equality. Gender identity became a basis for acceptance in venues and under conditions not previously viewed as appropriate or even possible.

In everyday life, we created more points of contact between groups whose members are different with respect to race, sexual orientation, gender identity, and religion, forcing more Americans to give some thought to the possibility of retaliation and reprimand when they verbalized hateful remarks. Some might call it being politically correct, but it is really a result of the presence of groups whose members previously hadn't been around to object.

A Continuing Racial Gap

The continuing influence of hate in the lives of Americans is illustrated by the wide, perhaps widening, gap between Black and White Americans with respect to their worldviews. On both sides of the racial ledger, there are Americans who tend to be pessimistic about our future as a multicultural nation. Some even predict civil war. Before blowing up the federal building in Oklahoma City, Timothy McVeigh had secured the "blueprint" for his mass murder from a bigoted novel, *The Turner Diaries* (Macdonald, 1978), in which Americans battle the forces of evil represented by Jews, Blacks, and a communist-inspired federal government. White supremacists characterize Jews as "children of Satan" and Blacks and Latinos as "mud people" who exist at the spiritual and intellectual level of animals (Levin & McDevitt, 2002).

The cultural gap between Whites and Blacks can be seen in survey data that examine racial differences in Americans' explanations for inequality. Respondents from both racial groups tend to reject the idea that Blacks have less innate ability than Whites; both Whites and Blacks stress the need to equalize educational opportunities. But when asked to account for continuing Black disadvantage, the majority of Whites blame lack of motivation. In other words, Blacks don't make enough of an effort on their own behalf "to crawl out of the gutters of America."

In sharp contrast, the majority of Blacks explain their own economic disadvantage as a result of persistent White discrimination or racism (Schuman, Steeh, Bobo, & Krysan, 1997), something that many White Americans deny. Indeed, regarding whether opportunities for Blacks exist in their local communities, the gap between Black and White opinions is large and persistent. For example, only 10% of all Whites report that Blacks are treated less fairly than Whites on the job; yet, 47% of all Blacks feel that way. Only 15% of all Whites say that Blacks are treated less fairly in stores downtown or in shopping malls; yet, 46% of all Blacks feel that way. Only 11% of Whites report that Blacks are treated less fairly in restaurants, bars, and theaters; yet, 39% of all Blacks feel that way. Only 30% of all Whites say that Blacks are treated less fairly by the police; yet, 64% of Blacks feel that way (Ludwig, 2000).

According to Patricia Turner (1993), the collective thinking of many Black Americans assumes the status of urban legends in which White Americans are seen as conspiring against them. Whereas most White Americans saw O. J. Simpson as his wife's murderer, the majority of Black Americans believed Simpson was not a perpetrator but an innocent victim of racist police officers who conspired to plant incriminating evidence against him. When years later Simpson was again tried, this time for perpetrating an armed robbery in Las Vegas, the majority of Whites—59%—but far fewer Blacks—only 24%—reported believing that he was guilty as charged. Even more indicative of conspiratorial thinking was the Fox News/Opinion Dynamics survey finding that 45% of Black Americans compared with only 13% of their White counterparts believed that Simpson was an innocent man who had been "set up." Similarly, many Blacks believe that nationwide restaurant chains add a secret ingredient to sterilize Black men, that soft drink companies are owned by the Ku Klux Klan, that the U.S. government's so-called war against drugs was actually waged as an excuse to incarcerate large numbers of young Black men, and that the U.S. military conspired to infect Africans with AIDS (Blanton, 2007; Turner, 1993).

Unfortunately, the actions of our institutions too often give reason for Americans to be cynical and provide the evidence they need to maintain their conspiratorial beliefs. The fiascos at Ruby Ridge and Waco suggested to members of marginal groups that the FBI was just as evil as they had suspected. The disproportionately heavy sentences for possessing and dealing crack cocaine predictably assured that the war against drugs would bring under the control of the criminal justice system incredibly large numbers of Black men (Tonry, 1995). The widely held belief that law enforcement continues to discriminate against Black men was confirmed by several incidents of police brutality, profiling, and corruption in police departments around the country. In Philadelphia, for example, 300 cases were overturned or dismissed because police officers were thought to have planted evidence on Black suspects and lied at the trials of Black defendants (Janofsky, 1997). Moreover, Washington, DC, law enforcement officials were caught sending hundreds of e-mail messages on their squad car computers that contained vulgar racist and homophobic references (Santana & Lengel, 2001).

Some of the racial skepticism of Black Americans has been translated into hate directed toward Whites, especially toward Catholics and Jews. A rally of thousands of Black youngsters in New York City was organized by Nation of Islam members who repeatedly referred to Jews as "bloodsuckers" and to the Pope as "a cracker." The hostility of Americans of color toward Whites is by no means restricted to a relatively few radicals or professional discontents. A Harris survey of 3,000 Americans sponsored by the National Conference for Community and Justice (2000) found that people of color and especially Black Americans have adopted a largely unflattering view of White Americans. More than 75% of all Black Americans reported believing that Whites are bigoted and prejudiced, bossy, and unwilling to share their inordinate wealth and power. More than 50% of all Latino Americans also share this view of White Americans.

In 2008, a Harris nationwide survey determined that most Black Americans—fully 86%—continue to believe that discrimination prevents them from achieving full equality. A large majority of Black respondents reported being discriminated against in terms of getting white-collar jobs, decent housing, skilled labor jobs, higher wages, quality education in public schools, and proper treatment by the federal government as well as the police. In 2015, a Gallup national poll reported that 80% of all Black Americans believe that racism against them continues to be widespread in the United States. Some 55% of all Whites and 64% of all Hispanics voice their agreement.

At the same time, about one-third of all Blacks, Whites, and Hispanics concur that racism against Whites is also widespread. A smaller but still important minority of Hispanics see hate and prejudice as impacting their lives. A 2015 Gallup poll determined that approximately 25% of Hispanics feel they have been treated unfairly because of their ethnic identity in the last 30 days—at their place of work, in a store, in a restaurant or bar, in dealing with the police, or while obtaining health care.

The Obama Factor

The election of Barack Obama may have reduced the number of Black Americans who felt that the federal government failed to represent their interests as a group, but the impact of the election among White Americans was anything but uniform. It is true that early in his first term as president, Barack Obama enjoyed broad public support. According to an Associated Press (2009) poll taken during the first weeks of his administration, 67% of Americans reported feeling "proud" because Obama was elected. On January 24, moreover, the Gallup Organization reported that 68% of Americans approved of his performance in office (2009).

At the same time, the election of the first African American to the highest political office provoked some White Americans to feel as though their racial well-being was being wrested from them. During the first weeks following Obama's victory, there were hundreds of hate crimes against African Americans committed by individuals who felt profoundly threatened by recent progress in racial equality. Even before his election, moreover, Obama's life was threatened by alleged White supremacist plots in Colorado, Tennessee, and New Jersey (Southern Poverty Law Center, 2009).

In the early morning of November 5, just a few hours after Obama's victory, three White men burned down the predominantly Black Macedonia Church of God in Christ in Springfield, Massachusetts. The defendants were subsequently convicted of conspiring to deprive the church congregation of their civil rights. As stated in an affidavit by an FBI special agent, the men were angry over Obama's victory.

On the day after Obama was inaugurated, a 22-year-old man allegedly carried out a racially motivated double-homicide and rape in Brockton, Massachusetts. In order to fight against "the demise of the White race," Keith Luke had planned to kill as many "non-Whites" as possible. He then intended to shoot up Wednesday's bingo night at a local synagogue.

How was Luke inspired to transform his racist views into murderous behavior? As far as we know, he was not an official member of any White supremacist group, but he told the police that he had been inspired by White supremacist websites in which "the demise of the White race" was frequently discussed.

Luke told detectives he spent most of his free time searching the Internet for racist websites. He also confessed to engaging in cyber conversations with other people who addressed the issue of "nonWhites" in the United States.

According to the ADL (2009), there are hundreds of hate websites in which all of the traditional anti-Black, anti-Latino, anti-Asian, and anti-Jewish stereotypes are dredged up and reinforced. Men and women who feel down and out, who have been victimized by a terrible economy, and who blame minorities for all of their personal miseries can log on and tune in to the chat rooms, bulletin boards, and blogs that comprise the hate movement online. All of a sudden, they find not only exciting propaganda but also vast social support for their hatemongering.

In their own communities, racist youngsters may be outcasts among their peers. But over the Internet, they easily locate hundreds, perhaps thousands, of similarly distraught and stigmatized individuals who hold the same stereotyped beliefs. Rather than being isolated, they now have plenty of company.

Most White supremacist groups have dwindling membership rolls and little money. But the Internet gives them influence far beyond their small numbers and poor economic resources. In response, the ADL has produced a hate-filtering software program enabling concerned parents to censor their children's Internet activities including their access to hate sites.

Of course, Keith Luke was no child. He had a constitutionally protected right to visit as many hate websites as he wished. There are many dangers, just as there are many valuable opportunities, on the Internet; but it is highly unlikely that censorship of the Internet will ever pass constitutional muster.

Still, according to the Southern Poverty Law Center (2009), certain hate websites go beyond spewing bigotry and hate; they also give instructions for making Molotov cocktails, constructing other explosive devices, and using handguns in combat. In addition, they explicitly encourage and celebrate "lone wolf" terrorism including the murder of non-Whites and Jews, as represented in the alleged crimes of Keith Luke in Brockton. Some inspire the attempted assassination of public figures like Barack Obama.

Bashing Gays and Lesbians

Hate-motivated assaults targeting gays and lesbians similarly peaked at a time when public pressure for the passage of same-sex marriage laws became a focal point of national controversy and concern. At the state level, the first legal sanction for gay marriage occurred in the year 2004, when the state of Massachusetts became the first of many to enact and implement its equal marriage law. During this period in the mid-2000s, assaultive hate crimes against gay and lesbian Americans soared from only two violent incidents in 2002 to a total of 20 in 2003. By the year 2004, hate-motivated assaults targeting the gay community had peaked at 24 episodes and continued to be a threat to gays and lesbians so long as the gay marriage issue remained front and center (Levin and Reichelmann, 2015).

Gay bashing can give some homophobic hatemongers a sadistic thrill. In September 2014, two men and a woman were arrested for their violent attack against a same-sex couple—two gay men—in downtown Philadelphia. One of the victims had to be hospitalized, suffering from a broken jaw and cheekbones. The two male defendants plea-bargained to avoid serving time behind bars. Instead they received a probationary sentence that included 200 hours of community service at a gay and lesbian facility. The female defendant opted to go to trial and has not yet been convicted or cleared (Peacock, 2015).

Across the country, gay students as well as students thought to be gay have been cruelly bashed by their schoolmates. In March 2007, for example, a 24-year-old student at the University of Massachusetts was arrested for assaulting another student and member of the school's swim team he believed to be gay. While attacking, the perpetrator allegedly shouted homophobic remarks. According to a friend of the victim, it is a widespread belief on campus that members of the men's swim team are gay. The victim suffered a fractured eye socket and a concussion (Towle, 2007).

Those who commit homophobic hate offenses target the offices or meeting rooms of gay and lesbian groups on campus, simply because the identification of an individual's sexual orientation is vastly more difficult than the identification of his or her property. For the same reason, anti-Semitic hate crimes often target temples and community centers, where the perpetrator can be fairly certain to find Jewish victims. Misidentification can still take place, as we saw in the April 2014 case of a White supremacist who—thinking his victims must be Jewish—shot to death three Christians at a Jewish community center outside of Kansas City.

Hate Crimes Against Women

Unlike hate-motivated offenses based on race, religion, and sexual orientation, violence against women is a truly global phenomenon. Of course, individuals of varying racial and religious identities are accorded better or worse treatment depending on the particular countries in which they reside. In certain places, Muslims are victimized. In other countries, it is Jews or Blacks who are targeted. In still other countries, the victims tend to be Asian or Christian. Yet gender bias is global: it is women, not men, who receive discriminatory treatment almost everywhere.

Still, gender-based maltreatment of women varies in its intensity from place to place. Among a group of twenty major economies known as the G20—Argentia, Australia, Brazil, Canada, China, France, Germany, India, Indonesia, Italy, Japan, South Korea, Mexico, Russia, Saudi Arabia, South Africa, Turkey, the United Kingdom, and the United States—along with the European Union (EU)—certain countries were particularly guilty of tolerating physical and sexual gender violence. Specifically, Canada turned out to be the best G20 country to be a woman, and India was the worst, given its prevalence of sexual violence, female infanticide, child marriage, and slavery. The United States was in sixth place, behind Canada, Germany, Britain, Australia, and France (Iganski & Levin, 2015).

The American version of gender bias may be more subtle than in certain other countries, but nevertheless results in considerable harm to women. For example, according to the U.S. Department of Labor, the median weekly earnings of American women continue to be only 77% of the male median. Just 20 of our United States senators are women. Female inmates at state women's prisons around the nation continue to be subjected to psychological, physical, and sexual abuse. And almost three out of every four of the victims of intimate partner homicide are women.

Since the September 11 attack on America, we have become vastly more aware of women's human rights issues around the world. Our military action against the Taliban regime in Afghanistan focused our attention on the plight of Afghan women. We learned they had been systematically prohibited from working in most occupations and banned from formal education beyond primary school. Less publicized was gender inequality in Saudi Arabia, where women are systematically denied access to jobs, forced to comply with restrictive dress codes enforced by the threat of public beatings, and segregated in public life; or the treatment of Kuwaiti women, who are denied the right to vote and segregated in public areas.

The list of discriminatory practices by country goes on and on. In Nigeria, Kenya, and Zambia, women are denied equal inheritance and property rights. In Thailand, women who marry non-nationals are not permitted the right to buy and own property in their own names. In Venezuela, women are prevented from marrying until ten months after a divorce or an annulment. In Chile, husbands are legally granted control over household decisions and their wives' property.

Discriminatory practices often prevent women from escaping lives of abject poverty. In South Africa, female farm workers are far more likely than men to be seasonal or temporary workers who perform menial and low-paying jobs. In the Ukraine, women work longer hours and are paid less than men. Kenyan women do most of the work, when the land is first cleared for subsistence farming. Yet women in Kenya rarely own the property and are therefore denied access to the loans and extension services available to male landowners.

In Eastern European nations such as Bulgaria, Ukraine, Russia, Lithuania, and Armenia, pervasive hardships in the aftermath of the breakdown of national economic and political systems have resulted in a growing problem of trafficking in migrant women. Many of these women have turned to prostitution out of desperation, having lost their jobs at home and lacking the basic means to survive. A number had hoped to escape the poverty of their homelands, thinking that they would find legitimate work as maids, dancers, or waitresses in their host countries.

Instead, as soon as they arrive in the new land—in such countries as Poland, Bosnia, and Herzegovina—their immigration documents are stolen. Then, they are threatened and harassed and are kept as prisoners in a room, where they are forced to have sex with clients. Many are beaten, raped, tortured, and starved.

Eastern Europe is not alone in failing to discourage trafficking. In Japan, women trafficked into the sex industry account for a large proportion of the hundreds of thousands of undocumented migrants, many of whom have fled the deplorable economic conditions in Thailand for the sake of a better life. Israel has failed to provide human rights protections for trafficked women who serve as domestics, farm laborers, construction workers, and enslaved prostitutes. In Colombia, women trafficked to European countries as forced laborers and prostitutes is an everyday occurrence, yet this is largely ignored by government authorities.

Violence against women is also pervasive. In Turkey and Jordan, under the assumption that the female victim had dishonored a male family member by committing immoral behavior, hundreds girls and women have been murdered. In Zimbabwe, many women on farms and in rural areas are raped with impunity. In Uzbekistan, local officials have limited the number of divorces, coercing women into remaining with their abusive partners. In the Ukraine, one in every three women suffers domestic violence.

In the former Yugoslavia, the Democratic Republic of the Congo, Indonesia, Guinea, and Tanzania, women—especially young women— have suffered large-scale episodes of rape and other forms of sexual and physical violence during periods of armed conflict and civil agitation.

Though recognized internationally as war crimes and offenses against humanity, such acts of abuse experienced by women have seldom been treated seriously by government officials. Perpetrators are rarely brought to justice.

There is a particularly brutal form of revenge against "an uppity woman" in which a husband, boyfriend, or suitor throws sulfuric acid into her face, scarring her for life. Many victims of acid attacks are forced to quit school and work, and the recovery is long and expensive. Such attacks, motivated by a woman's rejection of a man's advances, have been reported in Bangladesh, Egypt, England, India, Italy, Jamaica, Malaysia, Nigeria, and Vietnam (Welch, 1999). In 2014 alone, according to the Acid Survivors Foundation of India (ASFI), 349 people in India, mostly women, had acid thrown on them in deliberate assaults. Many were seriously injured; some victims lost their lives. The number of acid attacks was three times higher in 2014 than in 2013, and more than four times higher than in 2010.

Mexican authorities have revealed that a total of 370 women have been brutally murdered since 1993 in the city of Juarez, across the border from El Paso, Texas. Journalists have suggested that the number of women murdered is closer to 500. In any case, about half of the homicides were precipitated by such motives as robbery and gang wars, while a third involved sexual assault. In other cases, the motive is suspected to have been organ trafficking—that is, they were killed for their body parts. In addition, some federal agents have examined the possibility that violent religious groups or pornography dealers were involved in the killings. In a number of cases of missing women, the victims have apparently become sex slaves (Tuckman, 2003; Flannery, 2015).

Conclusion

There is a large and apparently growing number of citizens and social scientists alike who believe that hate or prejudice is no longer responsible for racial inequalities. Instead, they blame some characteristic of the victims' culture or heredity. Although the benign prejudice viewpoint alerts us to the possibility of environmental sources of inequality, there is every reason to believe that hate continues to play an important role in causing cultural changes that contribute to the disadvantages experienced by a minority group. The hereditary view of racial inferiority may have an impact of its own in sending a message to people of color, especially to Black Americans, suggesting that they cannot possibly improve their ability to achieve educational or economic parity no matter how hard they try. Unfortunately, this seems to be the same message that many Black Americans get every day from ordinary White Americans who sincerely believe that they are not prejudiced. The situationist perspective helps us recognize the conditions in both the local situation and the larger social context that affect our perceptions, attitudes, and behaviors regarding other races and other groups. From this perspective perhaps we can see our own culpability for creating and maintaining situations that give rise to hate violence in our society. It is from this viewpoint that we are also most likely to see solutions to the thorny problem of intergroup relations.

CHAPTER 3

Hate Crimes

Motive Matters

Well before the evening of April 15, 1989, Tom Gibison, a 17-year-old high school student from Wilmington, Delaware, had already decided he wanted a spider-web tattoo on his elbow. He also wanted to be entitled to wear red shoelaces and red suspenders that were symbols of honor in the Eastern Hammerskins skinhead organization to which he belonged. The real problem was this: Gibison wanted to earn the tattoo, the suspenders, and the shoelaces the *right way*, by killing a "black person" and "spilling blood for the cause."

Gibison told his friend Craig Peterson, also a racist skinhead, about his idea and invited him along. So the two of them took off in Peterson's mother's car—armed with a .38 caliber Colt revolver—to find a "suitable target." They started out in the Riverside projects on the city's east side and then drove to a city park on the west side. But after several hours of driving around, they were becoming increasingly frustrated by their inability to find a Black person to kill. At one point while they were driving through Rockford Park on the city's west side, they spotted a jogger who they thought was Black. But, as Peterson pulled closer to the jogger and Gibison prepared to pull the trigger, the lights from their car hit the side of the jogger's face, revealing that he was actually White. Surprised and further frustrated by this, they quickly abandoned the plan to kill him and continued their hunt.

As midnight approached the two decided to make the 30-minute drive north to Philadelphia in hopes of having better luck. Forty minutes later, Gibison spotted Aaron Wood, a 33-year-old Black man, standing between two parked cars in a North Philadelphia neighborhood. Wood was handing out fliers for an upcoming Mother's Day event when Gibison motioned for him to come over to the car. As Wood leaned into the car to see what the men wanted, Gibison very calmly raised his weapon and shot Wood in the forehead "right between the eyes," killing him instantly. Peterson later told police investigators that Gibison would openly laugh and mock the sound of Wood's head hitting the concrete. Within days both Gibison and Peterson got the tattoos they earned and boldly displayed them. In fact, at his girlfriend's high school prom that year, Gibison showed off his new tattoo and told fellow students that he "killed a black man to get it."

This case went unsolved for nearly 20 years. It wasn't until 2006 when a confidential informant came forward with details of Gibison's involvement in the skinhead organization, including the murder of Wood, that an investigation was launched and an arrest eventually made. Wood was sentenced to 12½ to 25 years in the state prison for his crimes.[1]

Between the time Tom Gibison pulled the trigger killing Aaron Wood and the time he was convicted by a Philadelphia jury and sent to prison, nearly two decades had passed. During this time many other hate crimes were committed throughout the United States. We know about many of these other offenses because it was during these two decades that many of the federal, state, and local hate crime laws were enacted. On April 23, 1990, exactly one year and one week after Tom Gibison and Craig Peterson killed Aaron Wood, the U.S. Congress passed the Hate Crime Statistics Act (HCSA), which set into motion the development of a law-enforcement-based data collection system aimed at learning more about "hate crimes."

The Hate Crime Statistics Act

The Hate Crime Statistics Act (HCSA) requires the attorney general to establish guidelines and collect data "about crimes that manifest evidence of prejudice based on race, religion, sexual orientation, or ethnicity, including, where appropriate, the crimes of murder, non-negligent manslaughter; forcible rape; aggravated assault, simple assault, intimidation; arson; and destruction, damage, or vandalism of property" (Public Law 101–275).[2] The attorney general appointed the director of the FBI with the responsibility for developing a national data collection program for hate crimes. Working with other law enforcement officials, criminologists, nongovernmental organizations (NGOs), and a myriad of other supporters, the FBI developed the current national hate crime program as an adjunct to the existing—and well-established—Uniform Crime Reporting (UCR) program (FBI, 2004).

The FBI's Uniform Crime Reporting Program

The Uniform Crime Reporting (UCR) program is a national crime data collection system in which state and local law enforcement agencies send their crime statistics to the FBI. It is probably the best known and most used source of national crime statistics in the United States (Regoli & Hewitt, 2000; Schmalleger, 1999, among many others).

---

[1] Interview with Richard Iardella, a Wilmington police detective who participated in this investigation, July 2009.

[2] The Violent Crime and Law Enforcement Act of 1994 amended the Hate Crime Statistics Act to include crimes against persons with disabilities. Also, the Church Arson Prevention Act of 1996 removed the five-year sunset provision from the original Hate Crime Statistics Act ensuring that hate crime data collection will continue for some time to come. The Matthew Shepard and James Byrd Act of 2009 added "disability status," "gender," and "gender identity" to the list of bias categories in the Hate Crime Statistics Act.

Existing since the late 1920s, the FBI's UCR program now has more than 18,000 federal, state, and local law enforcement agencies contributing nationwide. The law enforcement agencies that participate in the UCR program cover nearly 95% of the U.S. population (FBI, 2008a). In order to better understand how the national hate crime data collection fits into UCR, it is important to know that there are two subprograms under the umbrella named UCR: Summary UCR and the National Incident-Based Reporting System (NIBRS). Although the data for each of these subprograms come from the same source—law enforcement—they offer very different information about crime in general and hate crimes specifically. A very brief description of these subprograms is provided below.

Summary UCR provides an annual report with aggregate counts of certain recognized offenses known as "index crimes," including criminal homicide, forcible rape, robbery, aggravated assault, burglary, larceny-theft, motor vehicle theft, and arson. For each police agency that participates in the UCR program, the FBI publishes its crime totals, along with arrest statistics. FBI statisticians also compile regional and national totals in an annual report titled *Crime in the United States* (FBI, 2008b).

The National Incident-Based Reporting System was designed in the mid-1980s to collect detailed information about *each criminal incident* reported to the police. The technological advances in computer systems and databases in the late twentieth century have enabled this shift from a simple counting of crimes to the storage and analysis of information of each incident that gets reported to the police. Once stripped of unique identifiers such as name and address, these incident-level data are made available to anyone interested. It is public information that is formatted and stored online at the National Archive of Criminal Justice Data at the University of Michigan. The FBI anticipates that NIBRS reporting will one day replace Summary UCR altogether. At the present time, however, only about one-quarter of the nation's crime data comes to the UCR Program in NIBRS format (see Table 3.1).

NIBRS Hate Crime Data

The collection of hate crime data is built into the NIBRS program, but not into Summary UCR. Police departments that have not yet converted to the NIBRS format must complete an additional set of forms in order for their hate crimes to be included in the FBI database. In NIBRS reporting agencies, on the other hand, police officers must decide whether a crime is bias motivated each time they take a report. Therefore, hate crime information is part of the actual reporting structure. About 93% of the United States is covered by law enforcement agencies that participate in the FBI hate crime program; 38% of agencies submit their data in NIBRS format (see Table 3.1).

This is important because although hate crimes are vastly underreported to police, NIBRS still enables researchers to treat the data as a sample and examine the relationships between and among the variables collected in each incident. There are 57 pieces of information collected about each incident that

TABLE 3.1   U.S. Population Covered by NIBRS and Hate Crime Participants by Year

Year	U.S. Population	Population Covered by NIBRS Reporters	Population Covered by Hate Crime Reporters	Percent of Police Agencies Reporting Hate Crime via NIBRS
1995	262,755,000	4%	75%	5.4%
1996	265,284,000	6%	84%	7.1%
1997	267,637,000	8%	83%	9.6%
1998	270,296,000	10%	80%	12.5%
1999	272,691,000	13%	85%	15.2%
2000	281,421,906	14%	84%	16.6%
2001	284,796,887	15%	85%	17.7%
2002	288,368,698	17%	86%	19.8%
2003	290,809,777	20%	83%	ND[a]
2004	293,656,842	22%	87%	ND[a]
2005	296,507,061	24%	83%	37.8%
2006	299,398,484	24%	85%	31.4%
2007	301,621,157	25%	86%	32.0%
2008	304,059,724	26%	89%	32.4%
2009	307,006,550	26%	91%	35.3%
2010	309,330,219	28%	92%	35.6%
2011	311,587,816	28%	92%	36.1%
2012	313,873,685	30%	79%	37.1%
2013	316,497,531	30%	93%	37.3%
2014	318,857,056	31%	93%	38.0%

[a]Data not available.
Source: Federal Bureau of Investigation publications *Hate Crime Statistics and Crime in the United States.*

is reported through NIBRS. This information can be used to examine the nature of hate crimes that come to the attention of police and also to test theories related to these crimes. For example, in 2005 there were 768,003 crimes of assault reported to the FBI through NIBRS. Of these crimes, 21% were listed as "aggravated assault" and 79% were listed as simple (or minor) assault. Only 763 of these assault reports were labeled as hate crimes.

In analyzing the NIBRS data from these reported assaults, the second author found that hate-motivated assaults were 1.8 times more likely to result in serious injury to the victim. Serious injury means that the victim sustained broken bones, missing teeth, severe laceration, or internal bleeding, or was rendered unconscious. The hate-motivated assaults were nearly 3 times more likely to involve multiple offenders on one victim than non-hate-motivated assaults. In addition, bias-motivated assaults were nearly 2 times more likely to involve juveniles (under the age of 18) as both victims and offenders than they were to involve adults, or individuals 18 years of age or older. And, although hate assaults had more serious consequences, they had a 22% lower risk of resulting in an arrest.

In addition to this type of information, NIBRS data enable us to see unique differences in types of hate crimes, such as in Figures 3.1 and 3.2. Figure 3.1 depicts the time of day hate crimes occur either when the offenders are juveniles or adults. For juveniles, the peak occurrences of hate crimes are from noon to 5:00 p.m. while students are at school and at the end of the school day (see Figure 3.1). For adult offenders the peak hours are from 6:00 p.m. to 1:00 a.m.

Figure 3.2 compares the time of occurrence for sexual orientation and ethnicity hate crimes. As shown, these two types of hate crimes are most likely to occur at particular times of the day: sexual orientation hate crimes in the early morning hours, perhaps as bars are closing, and ethnicity hate crimes at 12:00 noon perhaps reflecting the presence of idle time, such as during daily lunch breaks.

In addition to providing a rich source of new information on hate crimes, the Hate Crime Statistics Act, and the programs developed because of it, helped move the term "hate crime" into contemporary public discourse. It is much more commonplace now to hear about hate crimes on television and in the print media than it was in the years before passage of the act. For instance, in an eight-year period before passage of the HCSA (1980 through 1987), the

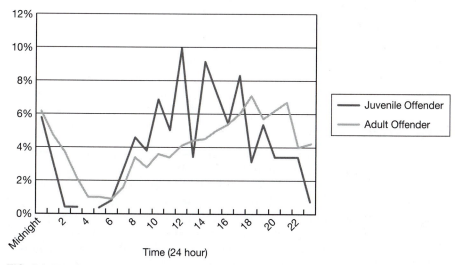

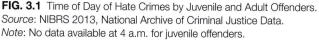

FIG. 3.1 Time of Day of Hate Crimes by Juvenile and Adult Offenders.
Source: NIBRS 2013, National Archive of Criminal Justice Data.
Note: No data available at 4 a.m. for juvenile offenders.

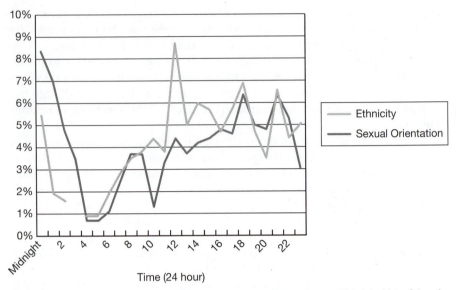

FIG. 3.2 Time of Day of Hate Crimes by Bias Type (Sexual Orientation and Ethnicity Hate Crimes). *Source*: NIBRS 2013, National Archive of Criminal Justice Data. *Note*: No data available at 3 a.m. for ethnicity.

New York Times printed 178 articles that contained the terms "hate crime" or "bias crime"; only four news stories had headlines that included these terms. However, in an eight-year period after passage of the Act (1992 through 1999), the same paper published 1,440 news stories about "hate crimes" or "bias crimes"; 148 of these stories used these terms in the headlines (second author's search via *Lexis Nexis*). Clearly, by 1999, the term had become so widely used and recognizable that when news broke of the murder of Matthew Shepard, a University of Wyoming student who was brutally murdered because he was gay, and James L. Byrd, a Black man with a disability who was savagely murdered because of his race, the media understandably labeled these acts as "hate crimes."

Why Now?

One may wonder why it is that hate crimes—as a new category of criminal offenses—came onto the social and political landscape in the late twentieth century and not before. Sociologists explain the emergence of "hate crimes" as a consequence of the civil rights movement, the crime victims' movement, the women's movement, and the gay and lesbian movement (Grattet & Jenness, 2001). The term itself is attributed to early efforts by the Anti-Defamation League (ADL), an interest group founded in 1913 to fight bigotry, anti-Semitism, and racism (Gerstenfeld, 2004).

Justifications for adding hate crimes as a new and distinct crime category are well documented and include their more serious nature, more harmful aftermath, more threatening contribution to civil disorder, and their creation of fissures in the social fabric (Dunbar, 2006; Herek, Gillis, Cogan, & Glunt, 1997; Levin, 1999; McDevitt, Balboni, Garcia, & Gu, 2001). Hate crimes are considered more harmful as the original act permeates from the victim to the victim's family, group, and society at large (Boeckmann, Turpin-Petrosino, & Levin, 2002; Sullaway, 2004).

For many, the passage of hate crime laws was seen as a breakthrough for combating bias-related violence and intimidation. However, others criticized these laws as being nothing more than symbolic gestures at best and identity politics at worst (Grattet & Jenness, 2008; Jacobs & Potter, 1998). To say the least, the concept of hate crimes—as a special category of criminal offenses—has been controversial. This is interesting since laws for other crime categories such as domestic and intimate partner violence, carjacking, and stalking had been implemented during the same general time period without much fanfare.

Pros and Cons of Hate Crime Laws

Proponents of hate crime laws argue that hate crime offenders want to send a clear message to the victim and others who share the victim's group status that they are not welcome in the neighborhood, community, office, school, dormitory, or the like. Hate crime laws, therefore, should send a message back to the offenders that their behaviors will not be tolerated by society. Proponents also say that hate crime laws are not new. They are analogous to antidiscrimination civil rights laws, which are, for the most part, accepted by both the courts and the general public. For example, a business owner cannot fire or refuse to hire a person simply because he is Black. Prohibiting a crime that is based on a similar bias is seen as being consistent with the spirit of these workplace civil rights laws. Supporters of hate crime laws also argue that such laws are comparable to statutes covering other status crimes, such as when enhanced penalties are imposed for an assault on a teacher in the classroom or a police officer acting in the performance of his or her duties. Finally, they argue that law enforcement and punishment have a deterrent effect, and that legislators (and judges) should recognize, by way of more substantial punishment, the uniquely serious impact of hate crimes on victims and communities (Lieberman & Freeman, 2009).

On the other side of the issue, some people argue that hate crime laws don't really protect anyone; they are merely symbolic statutes that have no real impact. They also suggest that hate crime laws can make things worse because, in practice, they are more likely to be enforced by the police when the offender is Black and the victim is White (Franklin, 2002). In addition, they argue that hate crime laws punish biased thoughts and hate speech, which are protected by the First Amendment. Finally, those who oppose hate crime laws assert that these laws protect only certain groups, the unintentional consequence of which is that they pit groups against each other and actually weaken intergroup relations and harmony in our society (Jacobs & Potter, 1998).

The truth is there are relative merits to both sides of the argument. Hate crime laws, like all laws, are symbols of what our society will not tolerate. But, these specific laws have increased the *recognition and reporting* of hate crimes by state and local law enforcement, which is an example of their instrumental effect (Grattet & Jenness, 2008). Recognizing that an underlying crime is a hate crime, when the facts bear this out, is what these laws are meant to do even if the perpetrators don't get prosecuted.

Opponents of hate crime laws also argue that institutional racism exists within the criminal justice system in the United States, as evidenced by the fact that African Americans tend to get longer sentences for similar crimes than do Whites. Blacks are also disproportionately represented on death row. So, why count on the criminal justice system to fix a culture of racism through the enforcement of hate crime laws when the institution itself is racist? This is a good question. Fred Lawrence, the former dean of George Washington University's School of Law as well as former president of Brandeis University, answers this question, in part, in this way:

> The punishment of hate crimes alone will not end the bigotry in our society. That great goal requires the work not only of the criminal justice system but of all aspects of civil life, public and private. Criminal punishment is indeed a crude tool and a blunt instrument. But our inability to solve the entire problem should not dissuade us from dealing with parts of the problem [i.e., through the criminal justice system]. If we are staunch defenders of the right to be the same or different in a diverse society, we cannot desist from this task. (Lawrence as quoted in Lieberman & Freeman, 2009, p. 12)

In addition, we assume that with the increased training of law enforcement officers to recognize and investigate hate crimes (resulting in large part because of passage of the HCSA), along with increased exposure to minority groups that feel the impact of these crimes, police officers (particularly White police officers) will become more sensitive over time to the nuanced ways that these offenses affect victims and whole communities. This type of training and exposure would probably not have happened (at least not as quickly as it did) had it not been for the passage of the Hate Crime Statistics Act.

Hate Crime Laws Today

In most cases hate crimes are investigated and prosecuted by state and local authorities. Until recently there were no federal hate crime statutes that gave federal agents the jurisdiction to investigate local crimes motivated by bias. However, there are several federal statutes that provide FBI agents with jurisdiction to investigate violations of civil rights laws. These laws are necessary so that federal agents can work *with* local law enforcement on task-force operations and so that they can initiate investigations *against* state and local authorities when they become the perpetrators of hate. The murder of three civil rights workers just outside Philadelphia, Mississippi, in June 1964 provides a good example of the need for these federal laws.

In 1964 Mississippi was considered by many to be the front line for civil rights activism. Mickey Schwerner, a 24-year-old Jewish man from New York, had moved to Meridian, Mississippi, with his wife Rita in January 1964 to become a field worker for the Congress for Racial Equality (CORE), a civil rights organization. In his first few months on the job he successfully organized a boycott of a White-owned variety store that sold items to Black customers but had no Black employees. He also was very active in voter registration drives that had been started in many Black communities in the state. In addition, Schwerner was active in coordinating the Mississippi Summer Project (also known as Freedom Summer), a plan that would bring more than 600 volunteer college students—mostly White and from the north—to Mississippi to register new Black voters.

To put it mildly, the White Knights of the Ku Klux Klan, led by Sam Bowers, *hated* Schwerner and the fact that civil rights workers were coming to Mississippi that summer. By May 1964, Bowers had given the order for Schwerner to be killed. Cecil Price, a deputy sheriff in Neshoba County and a member of the Klan, was an outspoken opponent of the civil rights movement. He conspired with Bowers and others inside and outside of law enforcement to carry out the ordered killing.

The first attempt to murder Schwerner was on June 16, 1964, when Klan members received false information the he was attending a business meeting at Mount Zion Church, a Black church that was slated to participate in the summer project. When the meeting ended and the participants were leaving the church, they were greeted by approximately 30 Klansmen armed with rifles and shotguns. When they learned Schwerner was not at the meeting, the Klansmen assaulted the church members and burned the church to the ground. The reason for the arson was to bait Schwerner into coming back to inspect the damage.

Schwerner was not at the Mount Zion Church meeting that night, because he was in Ohio attending the training for student volunteers who had joined the Mississippi Summer Project. Among these volunteers was another New Yorker, Andrew Goodman, a 20-year-old college student from Queens College. After hearing of the church fire and assaults, Schwerner was anxious to return to Mississippi. He asked Goodman to join him on the return trip. In addition, James Chaney, an African American CORE worker from Meridian, Mississippi, and Schwerner's chief assistant accompanied Schwerner on the return trip.

Schwerner, Goodman, and Chaney drove back to Mississippi on June 20, arriving late in the evening. In the morning of June 21, 1964, they drove to Mount Zion Church to inspect the remains of the burned-out building and to visit with some members of the congregation. By 3:00 p.m. the three civil rights workers were ready to return to their Meridian office. On the way back they were stopped by Deputy Sheriff Price in a marked police cruiser. Price arrested Chaney, who was driving, for speeding, and took all three men into custody. Schwerner and Goodman were taken into custody for "investigative purposes" related to the Mount Zion Church arson.

Once the three were placed in jail cells, Deputy Price notified Klansmen of the capture. Price then met with about 17 other Klansmen, including Neshoba County Sheriff Lawrence Rainey, so that they would all "be ready" once the trio was released later that night. About 10:30 p.m. on June 21, 1964, Sheriff

Price released the three civil rights workers from jail. According to investigative reports and trial transcripts, the Klan had appointed certain of its members to carry out the execution while others destroyed the car the three had occupied. The Klan had also arranged to have a backhoe operator standing by to do the digging for the late night burial.

Shortly after their release from custody, Deputy Sheriff Price, followed by two carloads of Klansmen, stopped the vehicle occupied by Schwerner, Chaney, and Goodman one more time and demanded that they get out of their car and into the back of his police cruiser. While he was following orders and stepping into the rear seat of the police car, Chaney, who had offered no resistance, was struck by Deputy Price on the back of the head with a blackjack. Price then drove the three to a deserted rural road where they were removed from the police car and systematically executed one by one. Schwerner was shot one time in the torso at point-blank range by Wayne Roberts, who also shot Goodman in the back while Chaney and the others looked on. After Roberts had executed Goodman and Schwerner, a second individual, Jim Jordan, emerged from the group and urged his companions to "Save one for me." Chaney was shot three times, twice in the torso and once in the head. It is believed that Deputy Price fired at least one of these shots. After Chaney was killed, Jordan exclaimed, "You didn't leave me anything but a nigger, but at least I killed me a nigger." The three civil rights workers were buried under an earthen dam on the property of another Klansman. The vehicle they drove, belonging to CORE, was set on fire by other members of the Klan so that no evidence of the crime could be obtained.

Given the pervasive hatred of minorities and civil rights workers in Mississippi at the time, it took months of investigative efforts on the part of the FBI to obtain enough information to make arrests in this case. Many people held negative beliefs about African Americans, so the Klan was seen by some as an organization that was doing what others were afraid to do alone.

White southerners both admired and feared the Klan, which had permeated many of the traditional institutions in Mississippi, such as the legal and criminal justice systems. It was impossible to seek justice in this case at the state and local level, so the federal government became actively involved, finding jurisdiction in federal civil rights laws rather than in Mississippi state statutes.

In his closing argument at the federal civil rights conspiracy trial for the 18 codefendants, the prosecutor, John Doar, from the U.S. Department of Justice (USDOJ) stated the following: "If there is to be any hope for this land of ours the Federal Government has a duty to eliminate the evil forces that seize local law enforcement. . . . When local law enforcement officials become involved as participants in violent crime and use their position, power and authority to accomplish this, there is very little hope to be hoped for, except with assistance of the Federal Government."

The trial ended with the conviction of Deputy Sheriff Price and seven other Klansmen. The Neshoba county sheriff, Lawrence Rainey, along with six codefendants, was acquitted. No verdict was reached in the case of Edgar Ray Killen, who coordinated the entire conspiracy at the request of Bowers. Not one of the men convicted on federal charges served more than six years in jail. Judge William Cox, the trial judge—from Mississippi—was reported to have said of his sentencing: "They killed one nigger, one Jew, and a white man—I gave them all what I thought they deserved."[3]

The case provides a good example of the importance of post–Civil War anti-Klan federal laws that work to protect the civil rights of individuals and groups even when the state laws do not protect them. This is really the purpose of federal hate crime statutes, to step in as needed so that local discriminatory practices are not tolerated. But, as noted at the beginning of this section, the enforcement of *hate crime* laws is mostly the exclusive jurisdiction of state and local law enforcement. In the next sections we will review federal and state hate crime statutes and examine what the latest rulings by the U.S. Supreme Court have to say about them.

Federal Civil Rights Statutes

One of the federal civil rights laws that was applied in the Schwerner, Chaney, and Goodman murders was 18 U.S. Code, Section 241, Conspiracy Against Rights. This statute makes it unlawful for "two or more persons to conspire to injure, oppress, threaten, or intimidate any person in any State, Territory, commonwealth, Possession, or District in the free exercise or enjoyment of any right or privilege secured to him by the Constitution or laws of the United States . . . or go in disguise on the highway, or in the premises of another, with intent to prevent or hinder his free exercise or enjoyment of any right or privilege so secured."[4]

First and foremost this is a conspiracy statute. This is why John Doar, in his closing statement at the trial of Deputy Cecil Price and his co-conspirators, stressed to the jury that "this is not a murder case. The question is *was there a conspiracy in which the law was involved*. . . . It was our duty, the Federal Government's duty, to do its best to bring to light the perpetrators in the conspiracy and to make it understandable to you to show you that this crime did occur, and who did it."[5] When a death occurs because of a conspiracy, the penalty under this statute can extend up to life in prison or even the death penalty. As mentioned above, none of the defendants in the 1964 murder of Schwerner, Chaney, and Goodman, all White males, received more than six years in prison for their crimes.

A federal statute enacted in 1968 in response to the inadequate state response to the Schwerner, Chaney, and Goodman murder was 18 U.S.C. Section 245, Bias Motivated Interference with Federally Protected Rights.

---

[3] The information about the murder of Schwerner, Chaney, and Goodman is taken from multiple sources including: *Freedom Summer* by Doug McAdam and *God's Long Summer* by Charles Marsh. Information was also obtained at http://www.law.umkc.edu/faculty/projects/ftrials/price&bowers/barnetteconfession.html; http://www.law.umkc.edu/faculty/projects/ftrials/price&bowers/Cox.htm.

[4] 18 U.S.C. Section 241, retrieved on July 26, 2009, at http://caselaw.lp.findlaw.com/casecode/uscodes/18/parts/i/chapters/13/sections/241.html.

[5] Transcript of John Doar's closing argument, retrieved on July 27, 2009, at http://www.law.umkc.edu/faculty/projects/ftrials/price&bowers/doarclose.htm.

This statute makes it unlawful to interfere with the enjoyment of any federal right, such as voting or going to school, on the basis of race, color, religion, or national origin. However, the law has limited utility because of a dual motivation requirement, that is, that the person is intimidated, injured, or interfered with because of his or her race, color, religion, or national origin *and* because he or she was engaged in a federally protected activity (Lieberman & Freeman, 2009).

Other federal statutes that have been enacted relating to hate crimes are those pertaining to the destruction of religious property and the interference with the free exercise of religion (18 U.S.C. 247) and the interference with the right to fair housing (42 U.S.C. 3631). Between 1995 and 2000, the USDOJ launched nearly 1,000 investigations related to the burning of churches and other houses of worship, mostly in the South. During this five-year period, more than 400 people were arrested in connection with 225 church arsons or bombings (Lieberman & Freeman, 2009). The fair housing statute prohibits interference in the process of obtaining housing, including purchasing or renting or obtaining a loan, based on race, color, religion, sex, handicap, family status, or national origin.

In addition, the Hate Crime Sentencing Enhancement Act (28 U.S.C. Section 994) required the U.S. Sentencing Commission to increase penalties for crimes in which the victim was selected because of his or her actual or perceived race, color, religion, national origin, ethnicity, gender, disability, or sexual orientation (Lieberman & Freeman, 2009).

The Matthew Shepard and James Byrd Jr. Hate Crimes Prevention Act

On October 28, 2009, President Barack Obama signed into law the Matthew Shepard and James Byrd Jr. Hate Crimes Prevention Act, as part of the larger National Defense Authorization Act of Fiscal Year 2010. The law creates a new federal criminal code provision, 18 U.S.C. Section 249. This new statute fixes some of the loopholes and impediments in existing federal legislation and offers federal assistance to state and local law enforcement in the investigation and prosecution of hate crimes. Specifically, it provides authority for the USDOJ to provide technical assistance, such as forensic identification, to state and local law enforcement to aid in the investigation and prosecution of crimes that are violations of state and local hate crime laws. In addition, the act also provides grant funding to help defray the cost of hate crime investigations and prosecutions (Lieberman & Freeman, 2009). The Matthew Shepard and James Byrd Jr. Hate Crimes Prevention Act is attached as Appendix B.

State Hate Crime Statutes

State hate crime laws do not typically cover separate and distinct criminal offenses, but apply to a range of existing crimes, like assault and destruction of property, that are intentionally directed at individuals or groups, either in whole or in part, because of the victim's actual or perceived race, religion, national origin, gender, gender identity, sexual orientation, or disability (Lieberman & Freeman, 2009).

Generally, there are three types of state hate crime statutes: (1) penalty enhancement laws, (2) institutional vandalism statutes, and (3) data collection and law enforcement training mandates. In addition to these laws some states have enacted anti-mask or -hood statutes in order to prevent Ku Klux Klan criminal activities.

According to the ADL, a group that monitors state and federal hate crime laws, 45 states and the District of Columbia have penalty enhancement laws. However, not every state statute covers the same categories of bias. For example, only 31 states include sexual orientation bias, 26 states include gender bias, and only nine states include gender identity bias (Lieberman & Freeman, 2009).

Delaware's hate crime statute provides an example of a penalty-enhancement law.

a. Any person who commits, or attempts to commit, any crime as defined by the laws of this State, and who intentionally:
1. Commits said crime for the purpose of interfering with the victim's free exercise or enjoyment of any right, privilege or immunity protected by the First Amendment to the United States Constitution, or commits said crime because the victim has exercised or enjoyed said rights; or
2. Selects the victim because of the victim's race, religion, color, disability, sexual orientation, national origin or ancestry, shall be guilty of a hate crime. For purposes of this section, the term "sexual orientation" means heterosexuality, bisexuality, or homosexuality.
b. Hate crimes shall be punished as follows:
1. If the underlying offense is a violation or unclassified misdemeanor, the hate crime shall be a class A misdemeanor;
2. If the underlying offense is a class A, B, or C misdemeanor, the hate crime shall be a class G felony;
3. If the underlying offense is a class C, D, E, F, or G felony, the hate crime shall be one grade higher than the underlying offense;
4. If the underlying offense is a class A or B felony, the hate crime shall be the same grade as the underlying offense, and the minimum sentence of imprisonment required for the underlying offense shall be doubled.[6]

Institutional vandalism refers to the destruction, defacement, or desecration of houses of worship, such as churches, mosques, and synagogues, and other religious institutions, including cemeteries. Currently 43 states and the District of Columbia have passed institutional vandalism statutes. Below is an example of an institutional vandalism statute from the state of Mississippi.

If any person, by any means whatever, shall willfully or mischievously injure or destroy any of the burial vaults, urns, memorials, vases, foundations,

---

[6] Delaware State Code, 11, § 1304. Retrieved on July 27, 2009, at http://delcode.delaware.gov/title11/c005/sc07/index.shtml#1304.

bases or other similar items in a cemetery, or injure or destroy any of the work, materials, or furniture of any courthouse or jail, or other public building, or schoolhouse or church, or deface any of the walls or other parts thereof, or shall write, or make any drawings or character, or do any other act, either on or in said building or the walls thereof, or shall deface or injure the trees, fences, pavements, or soil, on the grounds belonging thereto, or an ornamental or shade tree on any public road or street leading thereto, such person, upon conviction, for such offense, shall be punished as follows:

a. If the damage caused by the destruction or defacement of such property has a value of less than Three Hundred Dollars ($300.00), any person who is convicted of such offense shall be fined not more than One Thousand Dollars ($1,000.00) or be imprisoned in the county jail for not more than 1 year, or both.

b. If the damage caused by the destruction or defacement of such property has a value equal to or exceeding Three Hundred Dollars ($300.00), any person who is convicted of such offense shall be fined not more than Five Thousand Dollars ($5,000.00) or be imprisoned in the State Penitentiary for up to 5 years, or both.[7]

Data collection and police training mandates are specific laws that require police to report crimes either to the state UCR program or directly to the FBI's UCR program. The UCR program is typically mischaracterized in part as a "voluntary" program, meaning that police departments could opt out of reporting if they wanted to. It is true that there are no federal laws that require state and local police agencies to report hate crimes. Moreover, in 23 states, there is no statutory requirement of reporting on the books. According to the ADL, however, 27 states and the District of Columbia do require local departments to report hate crimes and other UCR offenses usually in a manner and format prescribed by the federal UCR program. In addition, colleges and universities are required by law to report hate crimes on their campuses. Below is an example of a data collection law passed in the State of West Virginia.

(i) All state, county and municipal law-enforcement agencies shall submit to the bureau uniform crime reports setting forth their activities in connection with law enforcement. It shall be the duty of the bureau to adopt and promulgate rules and regulations prescribing the form, general content, time and manner of submission of such uniform crime reports. Willful or repeated failure by any state, county or municipal law-enforcement official to submit the uniform crime reports required by this article shall constitute neglect of duty in public office. The bureau shall correlate the reports submitted to it and shall compile and submit to the governor and the Legislature semiannual reports based on such reports. A copy of such reports shall be furnished to all prosecuting attorneys and law-enforcement agencies.

(ii) Neglect or refusal of any person mentioned in this section to make the report required herein, or to do or perform any act on his or her part to be done or

---

[7] Mississippi State Code, § 97-17-39. Retrieved on July 27, 2009, at http://www.lexisnexis.com/hottopics/mscode/.

performed in connection with the operation of this section, shall constitute a misdemeanor, and such person shall, upon conviction thereof, be punished by a fine of not less than $25 nor more than $200, or by imprisonment in the county jail for a period of not more than 60 days, or both. Such neglect shall constitute misfeasance in office and subject such persons to removal from office. Any person who willfully removes, destroys or mutilates any of the fingerprints, photographs, records or other information of the department of public safety, shall be guilty of a misdemeanor, and such person shall, upon conviction thereof, be punished by a fine of not more than one hundred dollars, or by imprisonment in the county jail for a period of not more than 6 months, or both.[8]

The state of Connecticut's requirement for police training on hate crimes reads as follows:

> Basic or review training programs conducted or administered by the State Police, Police Officer Standards and Training Council, or municipal police departments must include training on bigotry and bias crimes.[9]

In addition to these three main types of state statutes, 20 states have "anti-Klan" statutes that prohibit cross burning and mask wearing under certain conditions. For example, in the state of Connecticut it is a violation of the state's criminal code to place a burning cross or simulation of one on public or private property without the written consent of the owner. This is a class A misdemeanor, but it is a class D felony if there is more than $1,000 of property damage.[10] This penalty also increases to a class D felony if the person commits the crime "while wearing a mask, hood, or other device designed to conceal his identity and (2) intends to deprive another person of any legally guaranteed right because of his religion, national origin, lineage, color, race, sex, sexual orientation, blindness, or physical disability.[11]

Hate Crime Laws and the U.S. Constitution

Arguments about the constitutionality of hate crime laws usually focus on one of three main points: That hate crime laws punish thoughts and speech, which are protected by the First Amendment; that they violate the equal protection clause of the Fourteenth Amendment; or that they violate the due process clause of the Fourteenth Amendment. That hate crime laws violate First Amendment protections is by far the most frequent criticism. Opponents of hate crime laws claim that when two identical crimes occur, but one is considered more egregious, and therefore elicits a more severe penalty, because of the offender bias against

---

[8] West Virginia State Code § 15-2-24(i).

[9] Connecticut State Code CGS § 7-249n. Retrieved on July 27, 2009, at http://www.cga.ct.gov/2008/rpt/2008-R-0276.htm.

[10] Connecticut State Code CGS § 46a-58. Retrieved on July 27, 2009, at http://www.cga.ct.gov/2008/rpt/2008-R-0276.htm.

[11] Connecticut State Code CGS § 53-37a. Retrieved on July 27, 2009, at http://www.cga.ct.gov/2008/rpt/2008-R-0276.htm.

the victim's race, this amounts to the punishment of "thoughts," not behaviors, which are protected by the First Amendment. On the other hand, supporters of hate crime laws argue that it is the behavior, not the thought, which violates the law and is, therefore, not protected by the First Amendment. Until an offender assaults a victim, no crime has been committed. He was free to have all the hateful thoughts he wanted until he acted on them in a criminal way.

Hateful speech is considered an extension of hateful thoughts. The U.S. Supreme Court in *R.A.V. v. City of St. Paul* made it clear that hate speech laws are unconstitutional. In 1990 several teenagers burned a cross inside the fenced yard of a Black family that lived across the street from one of the defendants. The police charged the defendant with the St. Paul Bias-Motivated Crime Ordinance, which reads, in part, as follows:

> Whoever places on public or private property a symbol, object, appellation, characterization or graffiti, including, but not limited to, a burning cross or Nazi swastika, which one knows or has reasonable grounds to know arouses anger, alarm or resentment in others on the basis of race, color, creed, religion or gender commits disorderly conduct and should be guilty of a misdemeanor.

The U.S. Supreme Court held that the city of St. Paul ordinance was unconstitutional. The behavior of the defendants clearly broke some state or local laws, but police and prosecutors chose to charge them with this particular hate crime statute, which was viewed by the court as a violation of the First Amendment. In the opinion of the court, the late Justice Scalia wrote, "Let there be no mistake about our belief that burning a cross in someone's front yard is reprehensible. But, St. Paul has sufficient means at its disposal to prevent such behavior without adding the First Amendment to the fire" (Gerstenfeld, 2004, p. 31). At the time of the *R.A.V. v. St. Paul* decision in 1992, it appeared as if hate crime statutes would have a hard time standing up to constitutional challenges. This changed the following year with the *Wisconsin v. Mitchell* decision.

The *Wisconsin v. Mitchell* case involved a group of young African American males who attacked a lone White male after discussing a scene from the motion picture *Mississippi Burning* in which a White man beat a young Black boy who was praying. In the late Justice Rehnquist's opinion, writing for a unanimous Court, he described the incident that led to the arrest of Todd Mitchell. The group moved outside and Mitchell asked them: "Do you feel hyped up to move on some white people?" Shortly thereafter, a young White boy approached the group on the opposite side of the street from where they were standing. As the boy walked by, Mitchell said: "You all want to fuck somebody up? There goes a white boy; go get him." Mitchell counted to three and pointed in the boy's direction. The group ran to the boy, beat him severely, and stole his tennis shoes. The boy was rendered unconscious and remained in a coma for four days (*Wisconsin v. Mitchell*, 1993).

Mitchell was arrested and prosecuted in Kenosha County, Wisconsin, for aggravated battery, which carries a maximum sentence of two years' imprisonment. However, because Mitchell intentionally selected the victim by his race, the maximum penalty was increased to seven years' imprisonment. Mitchell actually was sentenced to four years in prison for his role in the assault. Mitchell's arguments before the U.S. Supreme Court included that his thoughts and speech should be protected by the First Amendment, and that enhanced penalty statutes are invalid because they punish discriminatory motive, or reason, for acting. In regard to the First Amendment, Justice Rehnquist wrote:

> The First Amendment . . . does not prohibit the evidentiary use of speech to establish elements of a crime or to prove motive or intent. Evidence of a defendant's previous declarations or statements is commonly admitted in criminal trials subject to evidentiary rules dealing with relevancy, reliability, and the like. (*Wisconsin v. Mitchell*, 1993)

In regard to the enhanced penalty argument, Justice Rehnquist wrote for the Court:

> [T]he Wisconsin statute singles out for enhancement bias-inspired conduct because this conduct is thought to inflict greater individual and societal harm. . . . [B]ias motivated crimes are more likely to provoke retaliatory crimes, inflict distinct emotional harm on their victims, and incite community unrest. The State's desire to redress these perceived harms provides an adequate explanation for its penalty-enhancement provision over and above mere disagreement with offenders' beliefs or biases. As Blackstone said long ago, "it is but reasonable that among crimes of different natures those should be most severely punished which are the most destructive of the public safety and happiness." (*Wisconsin v. Mitchell*, 1993)

For these reasons, among others, the *Wisconsin v. Mitchell* decision provides the final say, to date, on the matter of the constitutional merits of hate crime statutes.

Policing Hatred

The topic of policing hatred is complex. It assumes on the one hand that the role of the police is to protect innocent victims of hate violence by enforcing just laws, including hate crime laws. But the history of American policing is rife with hate-motivated violence committed by the police and against the police. It also includes many examples of the police enforcing discriminatory laws, such as slavery and Jim Crow (Williams & Murphy, 1990). Before we discuss problems associated with the investigation and reporting of hate crime, we want to focus on these related issues.

When the Police Are Viewed as Perpetrators of Hate Violence

As indicated in Figures 3.3 and 3.4, most of the residents of Ferguson, Missouri—a city of more than 21,000 located in St. Louis county—are African American. At the same time, the police force in Ferguson is overwhelmingly White. It is not surprising, therefore, that most criminal encounters in the city consist of White police officers arresting Black suspects.

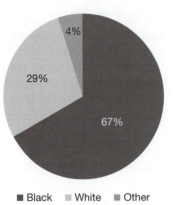

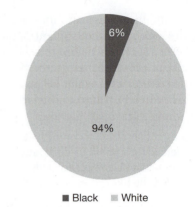

■ Black   ▨ White   ■ Other   ■ Black   ▨ White

FIG. 3.3 Race/Ethnicity of Community Members in Ferguson, MO.
Source: Based on Paulina Firozi, "5 Things to Know About Ferguson Police Department." *USA Today*, August 19, 2014.

FIG. 3.4 Race/Ethnicity of Law Enforcement in Ferguson, MO.
Source: Based on Paulina Firozi, "5 Things to Know About Ferguson Police Department." *USA Today*, August 19, 2014.

In August 2014, Darren Wilson, a 28-year-old White Ferguson police officer, shot and killed Michael Brown, an unarmed 18-year-old African American man. Brown, a recent high school graduate, reportedly had stolen several packages of cigarillos from a convenience store in Ferguson when Wilson, in uniform and driving a marked police vehicle, responded to assist in an investigation. On his way to the area where the crime occurred, Wilson saw Brown and his accomplice Dorian Johnson, also African American, walking down the center of the road. Initially, Officer Wilson, not connecting the two with the reported theft, asked them to get out of the road. Brown and Johnson refused to immediately comply and so Wilson stopped them for questioning. When Wilson attempted to get out of his vehicle, Brown held his door closed. A struggle ensued between Brown and Wilson, and Wilson claimed to have feared for his life when Brown began punching him. Officer Wilson fired his weapon at Brown 12 times, hitting him six of those times and killing him (Clark & Lett, 2014).

The disputed facts about the killing sparked widespread protest in Ferguson and throughout the country about police abuse of force, particularly against African Americans. Witness testimony varied widely in the Ferguson case, but one version of events recounted that Michael Brown was shot as he was giving up, holding his hands in the air, saying, "I am unarmed." This version of events sparked widespread rage and popularized a "hands up" gesture as a statement of protest against the police. In the photo below, several members of the NFL's St. Louis Rams football team entered the field at a nationally televised game with their hands up, protesting police actions and supporting Michael Brown.

A grand jury failed to indict Wilson and the U.S. Department of Justice (USDOJ) decided not to charge him with criminal wrongdoing in the killing of Brown. But USDOJ did launch an investigation into biased policing in the Ferguson Police Department. The findings of the investigation were released in

Members of the St. Louis Rams walk onto the field during introductions before an NFL football game against the Oakland Raiders, Sunday, November 30, 2014, in St. Louis. The players said after the game that they raised their arms in a "hands up" gesture to acknowledge the events in Ferguson, Missouri.
Source: AP Photo/L.G. Patterson.

a March 4, 2015, report, which is available online at http://www.justice.gov/sites/default/files/opa/press-releases/attachments/2015/03/04/ferguson_police_department_report.pdf.

The USDOJ report found that the Ferguson Police Department (FPD) had been heavily focused on "aggressive enforcement" of Ferguson's municipal code. Rewards and recognitions in the department were centered on "productivity," meaning the number of citations issued. Ferguson police officers tended to see residents of African American neighborhoods as potential offenders and sources of revenue rather than "constituents to be protected."

Investigators found the culture within FPD supported the detaining of citizens without reasonable suspicion or probable cause in violation of Fourth Amendment protections. Officers were found to demand compliance and use excessive force. The investigators provided the following as an example:

> In the summer of 2012, a 32-year-old African-American man sat in his car cooling off after playing basketball in a Ferguson public park. An officer pulled up behind the man's car, blocking him in, and demanded the man's Social Security number and identification. Without any cause, the officer accused the man of being a pedophile, referring to the presence of children in the park, and ordered the man out of his car for a pat-down, although the officer had no reason to believe the man was armed. The officer also asked to search the man's car. The man objected, citing his constitutional rights. In response, the officer arrested the man, reportedly at gunpoint,

charging him with eight violations of Ferguson's municipal code. One charge, Making a False Declaration, was for initially providing the short form of his first name (e.g., "Mike" instead of "Michael"), and an address which, although legitimate, was different from the one on his driver's license. Another charge was for not wearing a seat belt, even though he was seated in a parked car. The officer also charged the man both with having an expired operator's license, and with having no operator's license in his possession. The man told us (DOJ investigators) that, because of these charges he lost his job as a contractor with the federal government that he had held for years. (USDOJ, 2015, p. 3.)

The USDOJ report further claims that FPD's practices "reflect and reinforce racial bias, including stereotyping. The report goes on to say that the "harms [of these practices] are borne disproportionately by African Americans, and there is evidence that this is due in part to intentional discrimination on the basis of race" (USDOJ, 2015, p. 4). The discrimination faced on a daily basis in Ferguson at the hands of the police has led to severe mistrust between many city residents and the police. The USDOJ investigators found that the claims made by many observers from outside of Ferguson that the riots and discontent over biased policing and the killing of Michael Brown were the result of outside agitators were unsubstantiated. Instead, they claim the police culture that normalized and promoted unjust and aggressive law enforcement by FPD officers primarily aimed at African Americans was to blame.

Sadly, reports of the police killing unarmed African American men for minor offenses occurred in a number of other cities in 2014 and 2015. In July 2014 Eric Garner was choked to death by a New York City police officer when he resisted arrest for selling untaxed cigarettes. A friend of Garner's recorded the arrest, which went viral on social media. In the video Garner could be heard multiple times pleading for breath. Like the hands-up gesture in the Ferguson case, Garner's final words, "I can't breathe," became a call to arms during the widespread protests that followed (Kauzlarich, 2015). Then, in April 2015 a 50-year-old, unarmed Black man, Walter Scott, was shot in the back while running away from police in North Charleston, South Carolina, as he tried to flee on foot after being stopped for a minor traffic violation. Michael Slager, the white officer who killed Scott, was arrested for murder after a video of the incident surfaced that debunked the officer's claims of self-defense and that he rendered aid to Scott following the shooting (Schmidt & Apuzzo, 2015).

Only eight days after the incident in North Charleston, Freddie Gray, a 25-year-old African American man, was arrested by Baltimore police officers for possession of a switchblade. After a brief foot chase, Gray was apprehended and placed into a police transport van to be taken to police headquarters for booking. During the transport the handcuffed Gray was apparently thrown about in the back of the police van because he had not been secured in place with a seatbelt. Some have speculated that the police officers took Gray for a "rough ride," an unsanctioned practice of bouncing handcuffed prisoners off the walls of the van as a form of "street justice" for failing to cooperate (Fernandez, 2015). Gray suffered three broken vertebrae and injury to his voice box. His spine was 80% severed at his neck. When Gray died on April 19, violent protests erupted in Baltimore as they had in Ferguson just months earlier.

The deaths of Eric Garner, Michael Brown, Walter Scott, and Freddie Gray—among others—helped give rise to the Black Lives Matter movement, which began in 2012 following the shooting death of Trayvon Martin (Black Lives Matter official website: http://blacklivesmatter.com). Martin, a black teen, was shot and killed by George Zimmerman, an armed member of the local neighborhood watch in the Florida community where Martin was temporarily living. On the night of the killing, Zimmerman was suspicious of Martin, whom he noticed walking leisurely through the neighborhood in the rain, so he called police. Prior to their arrival—and against the advice of police dispatchers—Zimmerman followed, then confronted, Martin and a struggle ensued. Zimmerman shot and killed the unarmed Martin during the struggle. The police initially failed to charge Zimmerman, calling his actions "self-defense." Only after widespread protest in cities and on college campuses across the country was Zimmerman eventually charged with murder. Following a month-long trial, Zimmerman was found not guilty by a Florida jury.

The verdict spawned protests across the United States over racial profiling and gave life to the Black Lives Matter movement. On its website, the Black Lives Matter organization describes itself as "a chapter-based national organization working for the validity of Black life. . . . working to (re)build the Black liberation movement" (http://blacklivesmatter.com/about). The Black Lives Matter movement currently has 17 chapters in the United States and one in Toronto, Canada. It has played an important role in organizing the protests in Ferguson, Baltimore, and New York, among other places where unarmed African Americans have recently died at the hands of the police. In November 2015 while protesting the killing of an unarmed Black man, five Black Lives Matter protesters were shot by three white men with alleged ties to White supremacist groups (Wagner & Peralta, 2015).

The Black Lives Matter movement has helped galvanize people to action in growing numbers to stand against what appears to some as racist tendencies in policing. But the police say they are being demonized en masse for the mistakes of a few, which many officers believe has put them in greater danger of being targets for hate-motivated violence.

When the Police Are Viewed as Victims of Hate Violence

Ismaaiyl Brinsley suffered much of his life from mental problems. In his 28 years, he had been arrested on numerous occasions, mostly for minor problems such as theft. Brinsley was extremely agitated by the slayings of Michael Brown in Ferguson and Eric Garner in New York. On December 20, 2014, Brinsley, armed with a Taurus 9-millimeter pistol, which he had used hours earlier to shoot his girlfriend in her abdomen, boarded a bus in Baltimore and traveled to New York City to take revenge. While en route, Brinsley put the following post on Instagram: "I'm Putting Wings On Pigs Today. They Take 1 Of Ours...... Let's Take 2 of Theirs #ShootThePolice." When he arrived in New

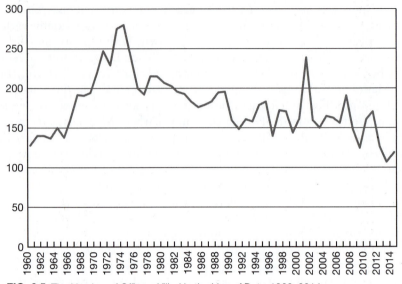

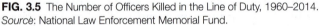

FIG. 3.5 The Number of Officers Killed in the Line of Duty, 1960–2014.
Source: National Law Enforcement Memorial Fund.

York, Brinsley traveled to Brooklyn, where he walked past a patrol car near Myrtle and Tomkins Avenue. He approached the police vehicle from behind and fired four shots into the vehicle, killing officers Wenjian Liu and Rafael Ramos. Brinsley fled from the scene and traveled to a subway station, where he committed suicide by shooting himself (Barker & Baker, 2014). Following the slaying of officers Lui and Ramos, the National Fraternal Order of Police called on Congress to expand federal hate crime laws to include violent attacks against the police. In his appeal to Congress, Chuck Canterbury, president of the national police organization, cited the rising number of attacks on law enforcement officers in the previous year. He used as examples the ambush killing of officers Lui and Ramos and the murder of Corporal Bryon Dickson of the Pennsylvania State Police, who was killed by a sniper as he left his barracks. Canterbury also cited the assassinations of Las Vegas police officers Igor Soldo and Alyn Beck as they ate lunch at a local pizzeria (Fraternal Order of Police, 2015).

The police argue that recent criticisms of their actions are unjustified and have created an atmosphere that puts them at greater danger for hate-motivated violence than in years before.

But this claim is not yet supported by the data. According to the FBI, assaults against the police have dropped by 21% since 2008. And according to the National Law Enforcement Memorial Fund, the killing of police officers in the line of duty is at the second lowest point since 1960 (see Figure 3.5).

Explaining Bias in Policing

There are a number of explanations for what appears to be excessive violence by the police against African American men. From the outside it looks like the violence is based in prejudice, either conscious or unconscious (explicit or implicit) as described in chapter 1. From inside the police system, it looks this way too, but as the result of "a few bad apples" rather than a widespread problem within the ranks of the entire force. Police leaders claim that when elected leaders criticize their efforts and publicly question their methods for providing public safety, they create an atmosphere of discontent that puts officers in increasing danger. Recently, the police have banded in protest against those officials they feel have betrayed them. For example, at the funeral of Officer Liu in New York City, dozens of NYPD officers turned their backs on Mayor de Blasio as he was delivering a eulogy for the fallen officer. The protest was in retaliation for the mayor's earlier criticisms of police (Worland, 2015).

Bourdieu's Theory of Practice: A Sociological Perspective on Police Violence

It would be helpful to place police violence in proper perspective. Sociologist Pierre Bourdieu's (1930–2002) theory of practice was built around three main concepts, which he offered as "thinking tools": field, capital, and habitus (Bourdieu & Wacquant, 1989, p. 50). Bourdieu used the term *field* to envisage all behavior as occurring on something like a football field (i.e., a bounded site where a game is played). According to Bourdieu, the games being played on the many social fields are competitive and rule bound, and there are positions on the fields that yield various types of power and prestige that players seek. These positions are themselves recognition for playing the game well (or not so well) and are referred to by Bourdieu as forms of *capital*. In common usage we generally think of capital as being only economic in form, but for Bourdieu there are other forms of capital that help players advance their power and position on the field. For example, cultural capital involves being recognized for having great skills in the particular game being played on the field. It may also include recognition for having encyclopedic knowledge of the current rules of the game.

In the field of policing, *cultural capital* might include the recognition that a particular officer has highly valued technical skills or language capabilities that most other police officers do not have but are often needed. *Symbolic capital* includes awards, commendations, or official titles that exemplify a player's important contributions on the field. In policing, symbolic capital includes ribbons, commendations, promotions, and transfers to elite units. *Social capital* is the recognition that certain players on the field amass dense networks of people who support them and their goals by providing resources, knowledge, and skills. In policing, this may include recognition for having key informants in the neighborhoods who can help the police identify criminal suspects or who introduce undercover officers into criminal networks. It may also include recognition for having connections to key politicians or government leaders who are available to support particular initiatives related to the police mission.

Finally, Bourdieu describes *habitus* as a "disposition" toward the game being played. The habitus is a person's structured and durable tendency or inclination to think and act a certain way, particularly relative to the game being played on the field. According to Bourdieu, behavior in the game is often not based on a rational thinking process, but on "common sense" notions about how the game should be played based on social conditioning and habitual ways of thinking and acting.

Bourdieu uses the following equation to summarize the relation between these three concepts:

$$[(habitus)(capital)] + field = practice$$

In other words, practice (in any field) is the result of one's structured and socially influenced disposition to the game (habitus) and one's position on the field (capital) given the current conditions of the game (field).

Now, let's try to apply this sociological explanation to the current problems of violence in policing. In recent years, the field of policing has taken a turn toward "toughness" as a standard for practice (Schulhofer, Tyler, & Huq, 2011). The game being played on the field of policing in many American cities is aggressive "law enforcement," aimed at fixing "broken windows," a term popularly used to refer to minor forms of social and physical disorder in neighborhoods. The police profession today is so devoted to the mission of law enforcement that the terms policing and law enforcement are often used interchangeably. Below is an example of a published police mission statement for an urban east coast police department that outlines "law enforcement" as a key component of their overall mission.

> The mission of the . . . Department of Police is to work to . . . raise the level of public safety through law enforcement, and thereby reduce the fear and incidence of crime.

In recent years the idea that *law enforcement* is the raison d'etre of modern policing has been reinforced by the broken windows concept (aka, zero-tolerance policing) and further popularized by practices called "quality of life" enforcement. This term refers to the targeted enforcement of minor crimes in particular neighborhoods or neighborhood "hot spots" in hopes that penalties and inconveniences for these violations will deter potential criminal offenders from behaving badly in these places, thus fixing the broken windows. Minor crimes include such things as vagrancy, public consumption of alcohol, loitering, parking in the wrong direction on streets, and playing a radio too loudly. The broken windows philosophy—and quality-of-life enforcement strategies—have worked in tandem with social policies such as the war on drugs to promote aggressive police action against the poor. Over the years this has resulted in large numbers of arrests of people from poor neighborhoods for relatively minor crimes.

So, the game being played on the field of policing is law enforcement. The place to find large numbers of people congregating in visible places violating minor infractions of the law is in poor neighborhoods where racial minorities often live and where the police do not live and where they often appear only when enforcing the law. The police, therefore, are often viewed as an occupying force rather than as friends and helpers. The neighborhoods targeted for aggressive enforcement are also places where fines, court costs, and other criminal penalties serve to exacerbate problems rather than alleviate them.

In contrast to this contemporary approach to American policing, the earliest police forces drew officers from the community who continued after employment to be part of the neighborhood. They were tasked with helping residents remain safe rather than making arrests. The policing field today draws boundaries between the police and community, separating them and creating an atmosphere of hostility. Aggressive law enforcement strategies widen the divide between the police and community. This is particularly true with drug enforcement, where a key strategy is to develop informants who are deployed into their neighborhoods and asked to betray family and friends in return for attractive plea deals. This strategy has been counterproductive in the long term. The backlash from this includes Stop Snitching campaigns that remind residents not to talk to the police or get involved in public safety efforts (Woldoff & Weiss, 2010).

On the field of contemporary policing, the players (police officers) gain status by making arrests. And it really doesn't matter in many departments whether the person arrested is later convicted or not. It only "counts" that an arrest has been made (Moskos, 2008). Officers are recognized with commendations and ribbons (symbolic capital) for felony arrests and for interrupting in-progress crimes. They are often given transfers to elite assignments (symbolic capital) such as drug units or federal task forces because they have demonstrated their abilities as aggressive law enforcers. Officers with good reputations as law enforcers tend to get promoted in rank (economic and symbolic capital) and they become the mentors (cultural capital) for younger officers learning about how to do law enforcement according to the rules of the game. Examples of this might include officers who are held in high esteem for their abilities in such things as writing search warrants and wiretap orders or conducting protracted drug conspiracy investigations.

Candidates for the position of police officer often come to the profession with expectations that they are entering the field of *law enforcement*. Their aim from the beginning is to catch "criminals." Once they are hired, young officers are then socialized into the profession during the police academy and during the initial field training. They are introduced at this time to ideas and dispositions that promise success in the game of aggressive law enforcement (habitus).

Just as boxers often face off in a ring before a fight with a physical demeanor that is tough, mean, and imposing, police officers are socialized to carry themselves confidently onto the field, ready to face down those who they believe are opponents or potential opponents. From a sociological point of view, this police disposition is not based entirely on individual traits (psychological or biological), but it is brought forth primarily by what is going on in the field. So, as depicted by Bourdieu's equation (see above), police behavior might best be explained as a function of the habitus—a socially produced police disposition (i.e., a tough, no-nonsense law enforcer engaged in battle), and forms of capital (i.e., a variety of rewards and statuses for knowledge, skills, and abilities in law enforcement), which are played on a field (i.e., the setting for the game of law enforcement, as compared to a game with a different focus such as problem solving or relationship building). The contemporary game, which seeks to measure success by amassing large numbers of arrests for minor crimes and traffic violations, is often played out in poor communities that offer the police the best opportunities for success.

Sociologists like Bourdieu provide a perspective that extends beyond "bad apple" blaming, looking instead at the barrel in which the apple lies. Conceiving police behavior as the product of a structured game played on a field is helpful. Most of us know how games are played and how rule bound they can be. It is also helpful in understanding police behavior to recognize that certain behaviors are rewarded and others are not. It is important to recognize that officers receive power and status by being tough crime fighters and not problem solvers or community builders. We think it is also helpful to consider police officers' dispositions toward the game as being coproduced by conditions on the field rather than solely the inherent and immutable personality traits of the officers themselves.

Through this sociological lens one can see more clearly how some current police practices, many of which have lived on beyond the conditions that once made them effective, continue to be reproduced in each new generation of police officers. Most importantly, it is with this sociological understanding that one can see new ways to reduce violence in policing that extend beyond the traditional sensitivity training paradigm where biased police officers are sent to a classroom to learn to appreciate racial, gender, ethnic, and gender diversity, among other forms.

Following along in this line of thinking, one might ask the question: How will changing the structured aspects of the policing field affect crime rates when, from the same sociological paradigm, criminal behavior itself is structured? There are patterns of behaviors in every community that are produced and reproduced by "conditions on the field" and the dispositions of those involved. In the section below we consider this issue using a hypothetical (but realistic) example of law breaking and law enforcing at the intersection of Right and Wrong Streets.

The Traffic Enforcement Analogy: A Sociological Explanation

Under the law enforcement paradigm, the police are often called to enforce traffic laws. One may argue that traffic laws themselves are unbiased, but perhaps we can imagine how the enforcement of traffic laws by the police may lead to biased outcomes and contribute to other problems along the way. Using Figure 3.6 as a guide, let's consider the following description of a concrete situation where biased outcomes are structured by the problem itself and the police response to it rather than just the explicit or implicit biases of individual police officers.

Imagine that you, the reader, are a police officer and that you are now responding to the intersection of Right and Wrong Streets to investigate a traffic accident. Because you are regularly assigned to the police district where this accident occurred, you know that this is a frequent event. There are many traffic accidents at this intersection so you and your colleagues on the force often

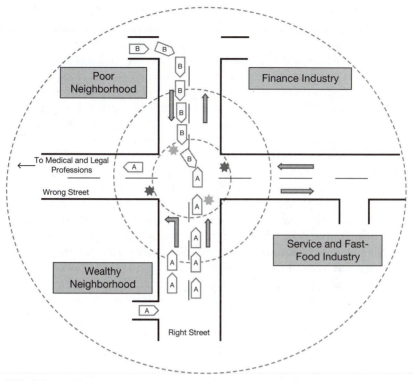

FIG. 3.6 The Intersection of Right and Wrong Streets: A Sociological Explanation of American Policing.

spend time enforcing traffic laws there in hopes of deterring the violations that lead to the accidents.

When you arrive at the scene, you immediately notice the two vehicles that collided in the middle of the intersection. Your focus as a law enforcement officer is on the vehicles in the intersection itself—depicted inside the smallest dotted circle in Figure 3.6. For ease of explanation, we refer to the vehicles in the intersection as A and B. In speaking with both drivers and with other witnesses at the scene, you clearly recognize that the driver of Vehicle B was at fault. By all accounts, both drivers had green lights indicating they could proceed into the intersection. But Vehicle A had the right of way because it was going straight on Right Street through the intersection and Vehicle B was making a left turn from Right Street onto Wrong Street. The traffic laws are clear and unbiased on this issue. Vehicles turning left must yield to vehicles going straight.

Following standard police policy, you issue a traffic summons to the driver of Vehicle B and you run a check on both drivers for warrants. You find that Driver B is wanted on a court-issued warrant for failure to appear on a different traffic violation. According to training and policy you take Driver B into custody, handcuffing him and towing his car, and you transport him to Central Booking where he will be processed on the warrant (fingerprinted and photographed) and taken to court for a bail hearing.

After booking Driver B you return to your sector. Still a bit concerned over the number of traffic accidents occurring at the intersection of Right and Wrong Streets, you decide to do "preventive" activities. As a "law enforcer" you are still focused on the activities in the intersection—inside the smallest dotted circle. In a short time you notice many cars involved in near misses, mostly involving vehicles making a left-hand turn from Right Street to Wrong Street (Vehicle B) cutting in front of vehicles heading straight on Right Street through the intersection (Vehicle A). In about one hour's time you issue five traffic summonses in hopes of deterring drivers from making this bad decision. Your last traffic summons was issued to a driver who was wanted on a warrant for failure to pay a fine, so you arrest him and transport him to Central Booking as you had done earlier. At the end of your shift you report to your supervisor that you have issued six traffic citations and arrested two people on outstanding warrants. Your supervisor tells you that you are doing good work and that your stats (arrests and citations) for the week are among the best on the shift. You are clearly behaving in ways consistent with police policy and training and you are being recognized by your supervisor for being a good officer—one of the best!

Now, imagine that instead of focusing your attention on the traffic violations themselves—again, inside the smallest circle—you expand your view to the level of the second dotted circle. From this view you now see that as they approach the intersection, the drivers of Vehicle B may feel the pressure of the long lines behind them all waiting to make a left onto Wrong Street. Also from this position you can see that there are a number of solutions to the traffic problems that may be more effective than law enforcement. For one, the traffic lights controlling traffic might be reconfigured so that Vehicles A and B do not get the green light at the same time. You also recognize that a turning lane could be created to allow some vehicles to turn right onto Wrong Street, thus reducing the line waiting to make a left turn. Perhaps the construction of a roundabout at the intersection would also be an alternative to the current conditions. In short, with this more expansive view inside the second dotted circle, you can see real solutions to the problems. But these solutions may reside outside the scope of your law enforcement duties. Your job as a police officer is to enforce laws, and besides, this intersection is a source of many traffic citations and arrest warrants, which are beneficial in sustaining your status as a "good officer."

Expanding your view to the outer dotted circle provides an even greater understanding of how the field of policing (i.e., law enforcement) may unwittingly contribute to other problems. Notice that the line of vehicles B is coming from Poor Neighborhood. The police may correctly argue that they are unbiased in the enforcement of traffic laws, but as it turns out almost all of the citations at this intersection are issued to drivers of vehicles B (i.e., from Poor Neighborhood). Because they are poor they are often unable to pay the fines and so ticketed drivers often do not show up for court. When they are arrested for failure to pay their fines, drivers of vehicle B are often sent to jail, which sometimes results in a loss of income. Many of them are fired from their jobs in the service and fast-food industries because of their arrests. On reflection, one might even notice that the large numbers of hit-and-run accidents in the intersection are the result of the fact that the drivers know they are wanted on traffic court warrants and do not want to be arrested.

From this expanded view it is also clear that drivers of vehicles A are mostly from Wealthy Neighborhood and are heading to work in the finance industry, which is straight through the intersection of Right and Wrong Streets. Some drivers of vehicles A also make a left on Wrong Street, heading to work in the medical and legal professions. Many drivers of vehicles A have been involved in traffic collisions with drivers of vehicles B. Drivers B are almost always at fault, and this creates hard feelings and poor perceptions about the driving habits and moral character of these drivers. Because they are poor, a large percentage of drivers B do not have insurance, and this too becomes a hardship for drivers A. Over the years, residents of Wealthy Neighborhood have developed a stereotype about residents of Poor Neighborhood based on their experiences at the intersection. They notice that people in Poor Neighborhood drive cars that are old and beat up. They have come to believe that drivers B are always in a hurry; you cannot trust them to show up for court or have insurance. Most drivers B leave you stranded; after they hit your car they take off because they are wanted. They are criminals!

Over the years, the residents of Poor Neighborhood have had many negative interactions with the police, particularly related to traffic violations at the intersection. They don't like or trust the police and the feeling is mutual. Because they do not trust the police—and because many residents are wanted for failure to pay fines or appear in court on traffic violations—they cannot call the police when they need help settling other types of disputes. Therefore, residents of Poor Neighborhood must rely on the "code of the street" in resolving heated interpersonal conflicts rather than working through a civil or criminal legal system. The availability of guns often makes these disputes deadly. And, since the residents of Poor Neighborhood do not like or trust the police, they do not help them solve crimes when they occur in Poor Neighborhood—which leads to very low clearance rates. Lack of trust in the police and court system, combined with the inability to help clear crimes with an arrest, further diminishes the legitimacy of the police in Poor Neighborhood.

It is important to note that we are not arguing that police officers lack biases, because they do have them. As human beings we all have biases, some of which we are aware of and some we are not. In the above example, we apply a sociological perspective that highlights how the structured institution of policing (i.e., field, capital, and habitus) influences police officer dispositions, attitudes, and behaviors. The law enforcement "game" keeps officers focused on the inner dotted circle in Figure 3.6 (i.e., inside the intersection itself). Inherent in the game is the expectation that police officers will investigate the traffic accident, determine fault, and issue a summons to the driver. An important assumption in this policing game is that enforcing the law is an effective way to prevent traffic accidents. The logic is this: the fines and inconveniences associated with going to court, receiving points on a driver's license, and the possibility of higher insurance rates all serve as a deterrent to the errant driver (a specific deterrent) and to all others who might be deterred from aggressive driving by the threat of these things (i.e., a general deterrent). The assumption that law enforcement actually works this way is never challenged and the game of law enforcement is reproduced again and again in each new police academy and in each generation. Now, perhaps we can use this hypothetical traffic accident scenario to imagine what might happen were the field of policing to change and how that might affect police officer dispositions, attitudes, and behaviors.

Imagine that the field of policing has changed in a way that the game being played now focuses on solving problems rather than enforcing the law. In this revised game, individual officers are recognized, rewarded, and given status for solving problems (like reducing the number of traffic accidents in the intersection) rather than for the numbers of arrests they produce or citations they issue. In this new game a "good" police officer who notices the large number of accidents at the intersection of Right and Wrong Streets would likely look at things from the intermediate level—inside the middle dotted circle of Figure 3.6. From this view—and with organizational rewards and statuses aligned with the goal of fixing problems rather than law enforcement—the officer would likely act to change the structure of the intersection rather than simply issue traffic citations.

Now, try to imagine that the field of policing has changed once again. The game being played now is focused on relationship building, rather than problem solving or law enforcement. The new game of relationship building is based on the assumption that strengthening relationships in communities and between the police and the community creates an environment where people will act informally to help each other as needed. On this new field of play, and with rewards, promotions, and new ways of gaining status in the profession now aligned with this new purpose, a police officer approaching the problems at the intersection of Right and Wrong Streets might look at the situation from the more expanded view (i.e., the outer dotted circle of Figure 3.6). From here the officer would see the growing tensions between residents of Poor Neighborhood and Wealthy Neighborhood. For years the only interactions between residents of these neighborhoods have been related to traffic violations and traffic accidents. There are hard feelings in each neighborhood against the other for a variety of reasons, but most are related to the conditions under which they often meet (i.e., in collisions and near collisions at the intersection). On a field of play where relationship building is the goal, the police officer may decide to use the problems at the intersection as a reason to bring people from the neighborhoods together for a meeting. The officer may also consider inviting members of the business community to the meeting, particularly those affected by the problems at the intersection (i.e., the finance, service, and fast-food industries in this hypothetical scenario).

Police officers will know that the problem itself can be fixed without bringing these groups together, but since the purpose of the game is relationship building—rather than just fixing the problem or enforcing the law—it will be important to host several meetings with residents and members of the business and government sectors. Together they may brainstorm solutions to the problem. An officer skilled in this new game will seek to connect people across groups at these meetings so that the seeds of strong relationships may be planted and take root. The assumption from the relationship-building approach is that strong relationships prevent crimes in many ways. Therefore, by using traffic or crime problems as an excuse to bring people together across groups to both solve the problem and to build relationships may pay crime-prevention dividends far beyond what law enforcement or problem solving alone can provide. And by working together to address these shared problems, participants from the neighborhoods may experience each other in a more favorable light, one that highlights similarities rather than differences.

In this section we explored the current state of affairs in American policing relative to hate violence. It seems that the police are sometimes viewed as perpetrators of hate violence and other times they are viewed as victims. In the above section we provided a sociological perspective on the subject that we hope will contribute to the discussion of these important issues. In the following section we deal more specifically with the issues in policing related to the identification and investigation of hate crimes.

Policing Hate Crimes

In the late 1980s and early 1990s, "hate crime" was a new term and essentially a new type of offense for police to investigate and report. Although some of the larger police departments in the United States, such as New York, Boston, and Baltimore County, Maryland, among others, had already adopted policies and procedures for dealing with hate crimes, most law enforcement agencies had not. The big push for law enforcement to do something about hate crimes came with the 1990 passage of the HCSA. The national hate crime data collection program developed by the FBI required state and local law enforcement officers to identify crimes motivated by bias and report these crimes as part of their participation in the UCR program.

With the development of a national hate crime data collection program came training for police. The FBI training program contained modules for identifying, investigating, and reporting hate crimes. To its credit, the FBI went beyond the basics and developed a training segment on the causes of prejudice and discrimination, which made the training sessions much richer (FBI, 2006). The USDOJ and the Federal Law Enforcement Training Center (FLETC) also developed comprehensive training material for police (USDOJ, 1998).

Federal and state-level efforts to train police officers in the proper ways to respond to hate crime investigations were met with resistance from rank-and-file officers for several reasons. For one thing, hate crimes can be very political, which can complicate investigations, as evidenced by Jeannine Bell (2002), who spent nine months assigned to a bias crime unit in a large police department in an unnamed city (with a population between 500,000 and 900,000). In the following description she demonstrates how the politics of hate crime reporting can sometimes make things difficult.

> A 15-year-old White youth was shot in the buttocks while in a Black neighborhood. The White community demanded that this be treated as a hate crime and given all the special attention it deserved. The residents in the minority neighborhood said that the incident should *not* be treated as a hate

crime because it was just "a drug deal gone bad." The police were faced with making a decision in this politically charged environment that pit White activists against minority residents. What did they do? Later in the investigation the police learned that the White male had put a pistol in his back pocket for protection. During the drug transaction he went to his pocket and the gun accidently went off [injuring him in the buttocks] (Bell, 2002, p. 13).

In addition to the politics involved in hate crime investigations, police departments often have an organizational climate that is less than supportive of officers trying to do the right thing regarding hate crimes. As Bell (2002) learned during her study, being assigned to a special bias crimes unit was not always a welcomed event. At one point she found a sign hanging in one police precinct, supposedly placed there by members of the community, which described their dislike for the bias crime unit known by the initials ABTF. The sign read as follows:

ABTF: These are the initials of the Anti-Bias Task Force of the [name of city] Police Dept. This unit is made up of the dregs of the . . . police department. Most normal cops don't want anything to do with this unit, and we don't blame them. They must have been trained in [area of the city], because all they do is follow young White boys around and then pick them up every chance they get. Their boss used to be called "Ben Dover" [in an area of the city with a large gay and lesbian population] for obvious reasons. Not one member of this unit has any balls, and instead of preying on young White boys in [name of section of city], they should be guarding a harem for some rich sheik, where they couldn't get into any trouble. (Bell, 2002, p. 115)

There are incentives, disincentives, and other forces within the field of law enforcement that affect police participation in hate crime reporting (Nolan & Akiyama, 2002; Shively, Cronin, & McDevitt, 2001). In the following situation, which occurred recently in the state of West Virginia, filing a hate crime report was viewed as a disincentive by law enforcement officials. Although this incident clearly fits the FBI definition of hate crime ("motivated in whole or in part by the offenders' bias"), no hate crime charges were initially brought against the defendants.

In September 2007, Megan Williams, a 20-year-old African American woman, was kidnapped and tortured for six days in a Big Creek, West Virginia, home by seven White defendants. Williams was repeatedly stabbed, mutilated, sexually abused, and forced to drink toilet water and eat animal feces, while her tormentors verbally abused her with racial slurs. Local authorities in the case were reluctant to file hate crime charges against the defendants, stating that they preferred to focus on the crimes that carried the stiffest penalties: kidnapping, which is punishable by life imprisonment, and sexual assault, which is punishable by up to 35 years in prison. In addition, prosecutors in the case were reluctant to pursue hate crime charges because the victim had had a previous "social relationship" with one of the offenders and was therefore not a random target (CBS, 2007).

In this case, the victim was selected *because of* her race; however, the fact that she had had a social relationship with one of the defendants may have made the hate crime charge somewhat murky compared to the other charges, such as kidnapping and rape. Therefore, police were not inclined at first to identify this as a hate crime, even though there was a public outcry from citizens and advocacy groups to do so. Without being able to recognize the benefits of correctly labeling an incident as a hate crime, regardless of the strength of the case or the ability to prove bias beyond a reasonable doubt, the police will likely remain slow to acknowledge that hate crimes occur, serving to reinforce negative stereotypes about the police with regard to their own biases.[12]

On the other hand, there are also *incentives* to adding a hate crime charge in some cases. Consider the following situation from New York: In Queens, New York, in February 2008, Alexandra Gilmore, a 36-year-old White female, was charged with a hate crime for taking advantage of Artee McKoy, a 93-year-old White male Alzheimer's patient. Gilmore claimed to be McKoy's daughter in order to swindle him out of $800,000. Gilmore and her accomplice, 30-year-old Rebecca Tharpe, were charged with second-degree larceny, motivated by hate, and faced up to 25 years if convicted (Livingston, 2008). Gilmore pleaded guilty in 2009 and received a two- to six-year sentence (Barnard, 2010).

This case showed clear evidence of material and economic motivation, but prosecutors found the crimes so despicable that they tacked on hate crime charges as well, since New York's definition requires simply that a crime be motivated *in part* because the victim is perceived to be from a different group. Clearly, there was an incentive to charge this offense as a hate crime, regardless of whether it was truly recognized by citizens and advocacy groups as such.

In addition to these incentives and disincentives, there are other forces that affect police participation in hate crime reporting. Using focus groups and survey research methods, Nolan and Akiyama (2002) identified a list of "social forces" that either encourage police participation or discourage it. They found that high-ranking police administrators are generally supportive of special hate crime policies for reporting and investigation when they believe that recognizing these crimes will improve police–community relations, that victims will really get the assistance they need, that it is the right thing to do politically and morally, that it is consistent with the values of the department, and that citizens appreciate the efforts of police when they recognize hate as a motivation for the crime and charge the offenders accordingly.

On the other side of the issue, police administrators will not want to promote hate crime policies for investigating and reporting when they believe these crimes are not a "real problem," it is not "real" police work, it is wrong to make these crimes "special," police action would support the political agendas of gay and minority groups, it creates too much additional work, and they are not as serious as many other crimes (Bennett, Nolan, & Conti, 2009; Nolan & Akiyama, 2002).

In addition to the above, at a much more practical level, many police officers state simply that hate crimes are very difficult to identify. Although cross

---

[12] One of the offenders in this case was eventually charged and convicted of a hate crime. This probably would not have happened had it not been for the publicity and pressure on police and prosecutors by citizen groups.

burnings and gay bashings in general are easy to recognize as being motivated by hate, many other crimes are difficult because hate may be only part of the motivation. In the section below we present a conceptual framework for recognizing several types of hate crimes for different law enforcement purposes.

Seeing Hate Crimes

Individuals in all professions, including law enforcement, have what is known as "professional vision." This means that through training and the daily routines of a profession, individuals learn to *see* things that the untrained eye might miss (Goodwin, 1994). For example, it doesn't take long for an urban police officer to learn to distinguish between a "lookout" (someone on the corner watching for police and ready to warn their criminal co-conspirators in the event a patrol car approaches), and a regular law-abiding person standing on the corner waiting for a bus or taxi.

Therefore, we emphasize the word *seeing* in the subtitle of this section, because we want to first stress the fact that *seeing* is *not* a transparent psychological process, as if everyone sees certain events in the same way. In contrast, what someone sees often depends on where he or she is situated socially, politically, economically, and professionally. In regard to the concept of "professional vision," Goodwin (1994) wrote the following: "All vision is perspectival and lodged within endogenous communities of practice." To emphasize this point, he compared the professional vision of the farmer with that of the archeologist while both are looking at the same patch of dirt. Where the farmer sees in the dirt the potential for certain crops to grow, the archeologist sees "stains, features, and artifacts that provide evidence of human activity at this spot" (p. 606). In the same way, we want to make the point that it is *learning to see hate crimes* that is the first step in improving the reporting and investigating of these crimes. Seeing requires that people know what they are looking for.

A phenomenon or event of interest is usually captured in a term which has a specific *meaning* within the culture or profession. John Dewey (1910/1997) identified two steps that must occur for a term like "hate crime" to take on meaning. The first step is "intension," meaning to single it out by defining it. The second step is "extension," which involves marking off the things that do and do not fit the definition. Dewey provided an example of this process using the term "river." He wrote: "The river meaning (or character) must serve to designate the Rhone, the Rhine, the Mississippi, the Hudson, the Wabash, in spite of their varieties of place, length, quality of water; and must be such as *not* to suggest ocean, currents, ponds, or brooks" (p. 130). Where *intension* is the definition of the term "river" in principle, the application of the term to distinguish what is and what is not meant by the word "river" is *extension*.

Intension and *Extension* of the Term "Hate Crime"

After passage of the HCSA, the FBI, in collaboration with other law enforcement groups, NGOs, and criminologists, developed the following definition of the term "hate crime":

"a criminal offense committed against a person or property which is motivated, in whole or in part, by the offender's bias against race, religion, disability, ethnic/national group, or sexual orientation group." (FBI, 1997)

The first key element of this definition of hate crime is that the incident must be a violation of an existing "criminal" law, such as assault or robbery, and that the motivation for the crime was the offender's bias against one or more groups from a very circumscribed set of categories. Clearly, the murder of Aaron Wood by Tom Gibison and Craig Peterson described at the beginning of this chapter is an event that fits within this definition. Or is it? The underlying crime was murder and the motivation was a bias against African Americans. But, was this really the primary motivation for the crime? From reports and interviews it seems that Gibison and Peterson did in fact hate Black people. But perhaps the primary motivation for the murder of Aaron Wood was for *status* in the Eastern Hammerskin organization, a group that espouses hatred for African Americans. This is where the second key element of the definition becomes important. The motivation for the crime can be the offender's bias for the specific group either "in whole or in part." Perhaps this language adjusts for the real-life situations that are much more complicated than the "ideal" hate crime that is solely motivated by hate. However, does this aspect of the definition—"in whole or in part"—confuse matters too?

In 2003 researchers at Northeastern University set out to find out why police departments were having trouble identifying and reporting hate crimes. While conducting reviews of records from a sample of large and small police departments in the United States, the researchers discovered incidents like the two described below that created difficulty for officers in deciding whether to classify them as hate crimes. In other words, by *extension* of the definition of hate crime to these two real-life events, do they fit? Are they hate crimes?

Incident 1: While driving on a state highway, a White male cut in front of a car driven by a Hispanic male. In response, the Hispanic male pursued the car driven by the White male and followed it to a local fast-food restaurant. The Hispanic male exited his car and approached the White male driver and his female passenger while yelling, "You shouldn't mess with Mexicans." He then proceeded to assault the White male (McDevitt, Cronin, Balboni, Farrell, Nolan, & Weiss, 2003).

Incident 2: While playing in a local neighborhood, a young White child accidentally knocked over a soda can [belonging] to an African American child, thus spilling its contents. The mother of the White child approached the mother of the African American child to explain the incident and apologize for the mishap. The African American woman yelled at the White woman "Get your white ass out [of here]" and "I will kick your white ass." The White woman said she did not want any trouble and would not fight back. The African American woman then proceeded to assault the White woman. The investigating officers reported that the African American woman had a history of "causing trouble" in the neighborhood (McDevitt, Cronin, Balboni, Farrell, Nolan, & Weiss, 2003).

Both of these incidents involve an underlying criminal behavior, that is, assault. In addition, they both seem to have been motivated, at least in part, by a bias against the victim's group. But are they hate crimes as intended by the definition?

In her ethnographic research of a bias crime unit within a large metropolitan police department, Bell (2002) found that it was somewhat common for there to be some difficulty in applying the criminal definition of hate crimes to real-world events, such as the ones above. Bell found that bias crime detectives had two basic requirements for classifying offenses as hate crimes: (1) the victim and the offender had to be from different groups, that is, racial or ethnic groups, and (2) the context in which the crime occurred must suggest a bias motivation rather than some other reason for the crime. Interestingly, she found that detectives would actually do the *reverse* in order to determine whether an incident was a hate crime; they would try to find some *other* motivation, such as anger or revenge for a neighborhood dispute or a traffic accident. Detectives would then classify these crimes as being "less than 51% bias motivated," and, therefore, not hate crimes. To these bias crime detectives a typical nonhate crime was "a traffic accident between someone Asian and someone white. Racial epithets, slurs are exchanged" (p. 144).

In addition to the problems faced by officers in applying the FBI definition of hate crimes to their actual events, there are also problems created by the fact that hate crimes defined in state criminal statutes often don't match the statistical definition provided by the FBI as a result of the HCSA. For example, the West Virginia hate crime statute reads in pertinent part as follows:

a. All persons within the boundaries of the state of West Virginia have the right to be free from any violence, or intimidation by threat of violence, committed against their persons or property because of their race, color, religion, ancestry, national origin, political affiliation or sex.
b. If any person does by force or threat of force, willfully injure, intimidate or interfere with, or attempt to injure, intimidate or interfere with, or oppress or threaten any other person in the free exercise or enjoyment of any right or privilege secured to him or her by the Constitution or laws of the state of West Virginia or by the Constitution or laws of the United States, because of such other person's race, color, religion, ancestry, national origin, political affiliation or sex, he or she shall be guilty of a felony, and, upon conviction, shall be fined not more than $5,000 or imprisoned not more than 10 years, or both.[13]

The West Virginia criminal statute 61-6-21 prohibits behaviors such as assault, intimidation, or robbery but which are committed "because of such other person's race, color, religion, ancestry, national origin, political affiliation or sex." The statute also includes categories of bias not included in the FBI statistical definition (ancestry, sex, color, political affiliation) and it does not include a sexual-orientation bias category, which is included in the FBI definition. The

---

[13] West Virginia Criminal Code, §61-6-21. Prohibiting violations of an individual's civil rights; penalties.

fact that these definitions are not the same can also interfere with what events actually get classified as a hate crime.

The case of J. R. Warren is indicative of the problems of defining hate crimes in West Virginia. On July 3, 2000, Warren, a 26-year-old gay Black male from rural Grant Town, West Virginia, met with three White teens at a vacant house in this predominately White rural town. The teens had been painting a vacant house that day and, prior to their meeting with Warren, had also been "drinking beer, huffing gasoline, and snorting tranquilizers" according to official sources (Smith, 2001). Shortly after he arrived at the house, Warren became engaged in an altercation with the group. The three teens took $20 from Warren then beat him until he was unconscious—and believed dead. Two of the youths put Warren's body into the trunk of a Camaro and drove to a remote area to dump it. While en route to the dump site, the teens discovered that Warren was still alive. They stopped the car in a secluded spot alongside a remote rural road, dragged his body out of the trunk, and while Warren was still conscious, repeatedly drove their vehicle over his slender body, crushing him to death (Nolan, McDevitt, Cronin, & Farrell, 2004).

The J. R. Warren case was considered a hate crime in the minority communities of West Virginia and by the local media because it had all the right elements: the victim was Black, slightly built, and openly gay while the offenders were young White males from a rural southern town. Immediately following the commission of the crime, the community held peace vigils, while advocacy groups like the Marion County NAACP and the West Virginia Lesbian and Gay coalition called on the police to investigate the incident as a hate crime (Fischer, 2000; Smith, 2000). The police refused to recognize the episode as a hate crime because, as Bell had found in the police department she studied, officials claimed to have uncovered an *alternative explanation* for the crime. Police claimed the murder was the result of a "drug- and alcohol-fueled rage" that was brought on by the belief on the part of one of the defendants that Warren had told others of a "long-standing sexual relationship that the two had shared" (Smith, November 25, 2002).

Thus, J. R. Warren's murder was not considered a hate crime because bias against Warren's race or sexual orientation was not viewed as a primary motivation for the killing. In addition, even if police had decided that the crime was motivated "in part" because Warren was gay, sexual orientation bias is not a category in the West Virginia criminal code.

Classification of Hate Crime Incidents

Throughout this chapter we have described several incidents that have been evaluated by police to see if they fit the definition of hate crimes. These incidents include (1) the Aaron Wood murder (Tom Gibison and Craig Peterson, the offenders), (2) the road rage assault (Hispanic on White), (3) the spilled soda assault (Black on White), and (4) the J. R. Warren murder. As we describe our categories below we will refer back to these cases for clarification purposes.

Our categorization of hate crime incidents begins with the two primary definitions of hate crimes, one from the FBI for statistical purposes and the other defined by the state's criminal code for law enforcement and prosecutorial purposes.

In Figure 3.7 there are two overlapping circles that represent sets of events. The one on the left (set I) represents the set of events that clearly fits the FBI's statistical definition of hate crime. For example, an African American family moves into a White neighborhood and residents burn a cross on their lawn in order to "send a message" that Black people are not welcome. The event clearly fits into set I. Set II (the circle on the right) includes events that fit the criminal definition of hate crimes as indicated in the state criminal statute. The cross burning described in set I would also fit into set II in West Virginia because the state criminal statute includes this behavior as prohibited by law. Therefore, the cross burning would best be defined as an event that fits into Region 3 of Figure 3.7, or at the intersection of sets I and II.

The complication with identifying and recording hate crimes for investigative and other purposes arises when the bias motivation is not the primary motivation, such as in the Wood murder, the road rage and spilled soda assaults, and in the J. R. Warren incident. These crimes can be explained by other motivations, but they can also fit within our classification of hate crimes. McDevitt, Cronin, Balboni, Farrell, Nolan, and Weiss (2003) identified two types of events that provide police with motivations other than bias, which can cause them to overlook offenses that are actually hate crimes. These are "reaction events" and "target selection" events. Reaction events are criminal behaviors that are triggered by something other than bias. However, because of the offender's bias the incident escalates into a violent crime such as an assault. In the road rage and

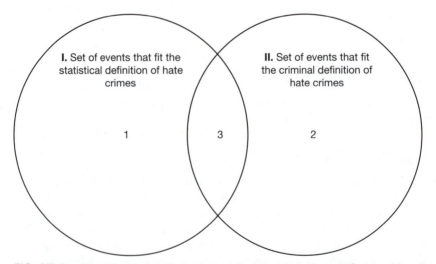

FIG. 3.7 The Set of Events that Fit the Federal Statistical Definition and State and Local Criminal Definitions of Hate Crimes.

spilled soda examples from earlier in this chapter, something other than bias triggered the behavior of the offenders. However, based on what the offender said at the time of the assaults it was clear that bias against the victim's group was at least in part a motivation for the crimes.

The J. R. Warren murder could also be classified as a "reaction event." From what the police investigation revealed, he apparently had been having sexual relations with one of the male offenders. What triggered the behavior of the offenders was the threat that he would tell others of this relationship. Would it have been different if J. R. Warren were a female and having a heterosexual relationship with the eventual offender? This is the type of question that can be answered if police see the incident as a possible hate crime and know to ask it.

Target selection events are situations in which someone chooses to commit a crime for some purpose other than bias but selects a member of a particular group either because of bias against the victim's group or some other reason. For example, Tom Gibison and Chris Peterson were probably motivated to achieve status in their new group, the Eastern Hammerskin skinheads, when they selected a Black man to kill. However, it was the bias against African Americans that directed Gibison and Peterson to Wood rather than to some other victim. There were no triggering events on the part of Wood that created violent behavior from the two offenders. He was simply a member of the right group to kill and he was in the wrong place at the wrong time.

In Figure 3.8 we overlap the four sets of events to create the classification of hate crime incidents. Nine of the 11 regions in the figure fit into three main types of hate crimes: primary motive hate crimes (Regions 1, 2, and 3), reactive hate crimes (Regions 6, 7, and 8), and target selection hate crimes (Regions 9, 10, and 11).

Primary motive hate crimes are crimes in which the principal motivation is the offender's bias against the victim's group. The three regions of Figure 3.8 that compose the primary motive hate crimes are Region 1, statistical reporting only, Region 2, criminal prosecution only, and Region 3 for both criminal prosecution and statistical reporting. If an organized gay-bashing event occurred in the state of West Virginia, this event would fit the primary motive hate crime type and the subtype would be "for statistical reporting only," because, as stated previously, West Virginia does not include sexual orientation as a bias type in its criminal code. If an organized cross-burning event were carried out by White residents of a neighborhood to intimidate or otherwise threaten the new Black neighbors, this would fit in the category of primary motive hate crime and the subgrouping would be "for both criminal prosecution and statistical reporting" (Region 3 of Figure 3.8).

The second main category of hate crime is the *reactive hate crime*. As you may recall from our earlier discussion, reactive hate crimes occur when some triggering incident occurs, such as a fight over a parking space, and the offender threatens, assaults, or in some other criminal way gets even with the victim because he or she is from another group.

If the group is covered in the statistical definition and not the criminal definition, the event would fit into Region 8 of Figure 3.8. We believe the J. R.

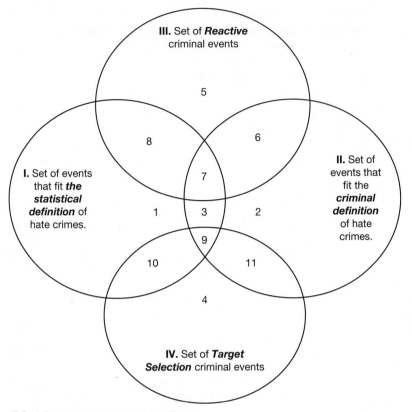

FIG. 3.8 A Typology of Hate Crime Events.

Warren murder is an event that fits into Region 8. If the bias that prompts the offender's violent response is covered in the criminal code and not the statistical definition, such as sex or political party affiliation in West Virginia, the criminal event would fit into Region 6 of Figure 3.8. Reactive hate crimes that occur based on a bias that is included in both the criminal and statistical definitions of hate crimes fit into Region 7 of Figure 3.8. We believe that the road rage and spilled soda assaults that were described earlier in this chapter fit into Region 7. Reactive events that result in criminal behavior, but are not prompted by group differences, fit into Region 5 of Figure 3.8 and are not considered hate crimes.

As suggested earlier, the third main type of hate crimes is the *target selection hate crime*. These crimes occur when the primary motivation for a crime is something other than hate for a particular group or groups, but the victim of the crime is selected because of his or her group membership. Clearly the Aaron Wood murder could be considered a target selection hate crime, and since the bias type was race in this murder it would fit into Region 9 of Figure 3.8.

Rational choice target selection events occur when a victim is selected for reasons other than bias. These types of crimes often look like hate crimes and have the impact of hate crimes on the victim group, but on close examination the selection was based more on rational thinking than bias. For example, Cronin, McDevitt, Farrell, and Nolan (2007) described events that were occurring in a large Midwestern city where patrons of gay bars were being targeted for robbery. When detectives apprehended the suspects they found that the choice of victims was made based on the stereotype of gay men having lots of money and being unlikely to call the police. These types of crimes fit into Region 4 of Figure 3.8.

Why Is This Distinction Important?

We present this classification of hate crime incidents as a conceptual framework for improving the *professional vision* of police officers with regard to the reporting of hate crimes. This is important for several reasons. For one, in order for hate crime laws to have an *instrumental* effect on the occurrence of hate crimes (i.e., actually make a difference), the police must know how to recognize and record them on police reports (Grattet & Jenness, 2008). The accurate recording of hate crimes is a precursor to successful investigations and the arrest of perpetrators, crime analysis and intelligence gathering, crime prevention and community action, and for the achievement of successful criminal prosecutions. By applying a framework like the one we are suggesting here, the police may be able to provide some clarity to crimes that are often very murky.

For example, when police are "looking for" a hate crime, do they think about prosecution only? If so, perhaps they are looking only for incidents that fit into Region 2 in Figure 3.8. This is an extremely narrow view of hate crimes, one that would likely overlook an offense that started because of some other "triggering event" like an argument over a parking space (Region 6 in Figure 3.8). From this view, an officer might also fail to see a hate crime that was motivated by greed, for instance, where the victim was selected because he or she belonged to a certain group (such as men coming out of a gay bar) as well as bias (Region 11).

This framework can also help law enforcement officials *see* hate crimes for purposes other than for prosecution. For example, crime prevention, crime analysis, and criminal intelligence gathering are important aspects of police work. Therefore, enhancing officers' ability to see crimes, police must be able to identify bias-motivated incidents that don't fit the definition of hate crime according to the existing state statute. In the case of J. R. Warren, if West Virginia police officials could have recognized the criminal acts as being motivated *in part* by sexual orientation bias (a category of bias not covered by the state code), perhaps they would have classified this crime as a hate crime and avoided all the negative press and community conflict. As mentioned earlier, the J. R. Warren murder probably fits into Region 8, a category that includes "reactive crimes" that are *in part* motivated by hate, but in a category not covered by the state criminal code.

We suggest that police construct hate crime training modules around this conceptual framework. By taking real-life incidents that occur in their own local jurisdictions and trying to overlay them onto this framework, it is our hope that officers will improve their professional vision in regard to *seeing* hate crimes for criminal prosecutions and for the other important aspects of policing.

Hate Crimes in Europe

Over the past several years, many European nations have been working to institute hate crime laws that deal with a growing anti-immigrant sentiment, among other forms of intergroup hostility. As in the United States many European countries are struggling economically, which seems to have heightened citizens' awareness of the "other." Where racial differences spark many hate crimes in the United States, intergroup violence in Europe is more often ignited by expressions of ultra-nationalism. This means that *any* outsider—visitor, international student, migrant, refugee, or asylum seeker—is a potential victim of hate crimes.

Religious intolerance is also a growing concern in Europe, particularly with regard to Judaism and Islam, according to independent monitoring organizations. In its publication *2008 Hate Crime Survey*, Human Rights First found that anti-Semitic violence in Europe had increased since 2006 and that reported hate crimes were mostly spontaneous acts committed against people who were visibly Jewish, that is, wearing distinctive clothing or jewelry associated with the Jewish faith. This organization also reported that anti-Muslim hate crimes continue to be a problem in Europe and that these offenses seem to be a result of mixed motives, triggered by both religious intolerance and an aggressive anti-immigration sentiment. Below is an excerpt from the organization's 2008 hate crime report:

> Acts of aggression against Muslim individuals and places of worship are being committed in the context of a longstanding strain of political discourse in Europe that has projected immigrants in general and Muslims in particular as a threat not only to security but to the European homogeneity and culture. The situation has worsened in recent years in the context of terrorist attacks and the response of governments to them. (p. 67)

On November 13, 2015, a series of coordinated terrorist attacks in Paris left 130 people dead and 368 injured. The terrorist group known as Daesh claimed responsibility for the attacks. Daesh is popularly referred to in the Western press as the Islamic State or ISIS, leading people to believe their murderous activities are based in Islamic beliefs. At the time we are writing the fourth edition of this book, it is still uncertain how France will respond with regard to Muslim citizens and to what degree the terrorist act itself, its coverage in the media, or the backlash from French citizens related to fear will create an atmosphere that is unwelcoming to European Muslims or other so called "outsiders." In a November 17, 2015, blog entry by the organization Human Rights First, Rebecca Sheff wrote the following:

> On the heels of the horrific attacks in Paris, far-right groups in France are already escalating their xenophobic rhetoric and mobilizing supporters

to turn their anger against refugees and immigrants. Muslim and immigrant communities across the country face a greatly increased risk of hate crimes. Indeed, violent confrontations are already happening. (Sheff, 2015)

The Roma in Europe

When pop singer and cultural icon Madonna took time out during her August 2009 concert in Romania to speak up against discrimination directed at the Roma people, thousands of concertgoers booed and jeered her. The incident was covered by the international media and broadcast throughout the United States. It was likely the first time that many Americans ever even heard about the Roma, also called Gypsies or Sinti by some Europeans. Madonna, herself, seems to have only recently become aware of the situation because of her relationship with the Roma musicians who are part of her show. She said to the crowd of 60,000 people, "It has been brought to my attention . . . that there is a lot of discrimination against Romanies and Gypsies in Eastern Europe. . . . It makes me sad." She was also booed for admonishing the crowd about discrimination against gay people. Unlike the situation of Roma in Europe, hate and discrimination against people because of their sexual orientation and gender identity are well known in the United States (Sidduque, 2009).

As a group, Roma are probably the most despised and disadvantaged minority group in Europe and perhaps throughout the world. The group's origin has been traced back to India, somewhere between the ninth and fourteenth centuries. Since that time populations of Roma have dispersed to many areas throughout Europe, and with a total population estimated at around 10 million, they are the largest minority group in Europe (European Parliament, 2008; Iganski & Levin, 2015).

The plight of the Roma people throughout history is marked by discrimination, endemic poverty, lack of institutional support mechanisms, and social marginalization. Roma lack the very basics for human existence in a modern world. Many have no real home address and lack documentation and citizenship anywhere. These facts alone deprive individuals of the opportunity for attaining health care, schooling, or employment. In addition to these structural barriers to full integration into European society, the social and political atmosphere there works against the Roma in significant ways. Popular references to Roma include such stereotypes as untrustworthy, dishonest, dirty, lazy, violent, criminal, thieves, and kidnappers. Local political leaders often speak openly about their desire to get rid of Roma from their communities. In Italy, for example, the prefect of Rome, Carlo Mosca, declared that he would sign expulsion orders against Roma without hesitation. He told the press that "the hard line is necessary to deal with these beasts" (Human Rights First, 2008, pp. 111, 112).

The problems faced by Roma in Europe run deep and often call for action by international monitoring organizations to step in and help. In February 2007, for example, the UN Committee on the Elimination of Racial Discrimination (CERD) wrote in its report on Ukraine that the "lack of personal and other relevant identification documents effectively deprives many Roma of their right to equal access to the courts, legal aid, employment, housing, health care, social security, and education" (p. 110). CERD recommended that the government of Ukraine take immediate steps to fix this situation.

The social conditions of Roma make them targets for widespread violence, and even the authorities are hesitant to help at times. For example in August 2007, six Roma were returning to their homes when they were attacked by a dozen skinheads. The victims all required hospitalization. When interviewed the victims said they called the police but that the police refused to send assistance (Human Rights First, 2008).

Many people in Europe hold a benign prejudice view of Roma, blaming them for their own deplorable situations and the "well deserved" discrimination that results. These Europeans fail to see that prejudice and discrimination are the *cause* of the Roma situation and not the other way around. Until this view changes, the fate of the Roma people will remain bleak (Iganski & Levin, 2015).

Sexual Orientation and Gender Identity Violence

Reports from nongovernmental agencies suggest that hate crimes based on sexual orientation and gender identity are rising in Europe (Human Rights First, 2008). The victims of this form of violence include people who describe themselves as LGBT. In 2007 the sharp rise in violence against LGBT people caused the European Parliament to pass a resolution on homophobia. Of particular concern was the local banning of gay pride marches and an increase in threatening and inflammatory homophobic speeches made by leading politicians and religious leaders (Organization for Security and Cooperation in Europe [OSCE], Office of Democratic Institutions and Human Rights [ODIHR], 2008).

In its annual report on hate crimes, the OSCE expressed the following view of the social climate in Europe in regard to the acceptance of LGBT people.

> Violent homophobic incidents and crimes continue to occur in a climate that was often hostile or intolerant to LGBT people. Homo- and transphobic bullying among youngsters in schools had particularly drastic effects on LGBT persons and represents an example of the climate of intolerance that LGBT communities across the OSCE region continued to face. Bullying and harassment of young people who are, or are perceived to be LGBT has been known to have serious effects on one's self, of confidence and health. (p. 109)

For example, in Ukraine in March 2007 a 16-year-old boy committed suicide by hanging himself from a tree. The boy had reported to a school psychologist that he thought he was homosexual and was being harassed and mocked by fellow students and his own stepfather. The boy became very depressed as a result of this seemingly hopeless situation and decided that he would be better off dead than alive.

In addition to the effects of a hostile climate on a person's sense of well-being, it can also affect the rate at which victims report these incidents and seek assistance from authorities like the police in the case of hate crimes. LGBT hate crimes are believed to be among the most underreported and underdocumented of all crimes. In Europe, many countries do not even recognize LGBT as a category in their hate crime laws; only 10 of the 56 countries in the OSCE region recognize this category. The attitudes among officials, including the police, are often so hostile toward LGBT issues that many victims would not even think of going to law enforcement for help (Iganski & Levin, 2015).

In March 2009, the second author traveled to the Balkans region of Europe as part of an international training team on the topic of hate crime. The training was developed for senior officials from national police organizations. During the training, when the topic turned to sexual orientation and gender identity hate crimes, the participants (men and women), who up to that point had been quite reserved and very professional, became agitated and vocal about their intolerance toward homosexuals. At one point a member of the group made the remark, "They should be sent to institutions," referring to gay men being sent away for psychiatric treatment. Another member of the group, a police officer assigned to a war crimes investigative unit, said that homosexuality was akin to bestiality. Other officers nodded in support of this statement.

Along with the open hostility among police officials toward LGBT issues, there is also the belief among victims of LGBT hate crimes that nothing will happen to the offenders even if they are caught. In Italy in November 2007, for example, a father killed his gay son by shooting him 12 times. The father admitted to the killing and explained that he had previously sent his son for psychological care due to his homosexuality. The father was released by Italian authorities after only four days of detention (OSCE, ODIHR, 2008).

Conclusion

Although crimes motivated by hate have long been a dark part of our collective history, it is only in recent years that the term "hate crime" has become part of the public lexicon. The passage of the HCSA in 1990 was important in this regard because it set into motion programs and policies within law enforcement that required officers on the streets to know about hate crimes and the impact they have on victims and communities. Police departments throughout the country have had to begin collecting data on hate crimes. Although almost everyone agrees that hate crimes are vastly undercounted, still the information provided by the FBI by way of the NIBRS program gives us a glimpse into the nature of hate crimes in the United States.

Hate crime statutes are controversial, many times because of misinformation about them. Misinformation about hate crime laws often deals with issues of free speech rights and victim hierarchies, such as the argument that hate crime offenders receive more severe penalties because the victim is Black or gay or female. The U.S. Supreme Court has weighed in on these arguments in *Wisconsin v. Mitchell*. It seems that there are no First Amendment problems when using speech as an element of a crime if it provides insight into the motivation for the crime. In addition, the Court finds no particular constitutional problem with penalty-enhancement laws that recognize bias motivation as an aggravating circumstance, therefore providing the opportunity for more severe penalties. Finally, in order to pass constitutional muster hate crime laws must protect anyone who is victimized because of bias—not just Blacks, but Blacks, Whites, Asians, and Latinos; not just Jews, but Jews, Catholics, Protestants, and Muslims; not just gays, but gays and straights.

Some people say that passing hate crime laws is a way to articulate high standards of social conduct and to send a message that it is not okay to strike out against other people because of prejudice. On the other hand, some argue that many of our social institutions are racist, including the criminal justice system, so why should we expect that hate crime statutes will even work? Both of these beliefs contain an element of truth, and perhaps we won't know for a while if hate crime laws actually work or not. What we can say for sure is that the police are much more actively involved today in hate crime investigations than they were in the past, mostly because of the HCSA. Linking the FBI's national hate crime data collection program to UCR was a very good idea. It resulted in thousands of police officers receiving training ostensibly for statistics, but really for identifying, investigating, and reporting these crimes. The HCSA resulted in a heightened level of awareness within law enforcement about the significance of hate crimes both to the individual victims and to whole communities. The idea that hate crimes are different from other similar crimes is now deeply embedded in the consciousness of thousands of police officers throughout this country.

Notwithstanding the increased attention to hate attacks, the relationship between the police and members of minority communities has been strained in recent years by the killing of unarmed African American men in Ferguson, Missouri; Baltimore, Maryland; New York City; North Charleston, South Carolina; and Chicago, Illinois, at the hands of the police. The Black Lives Matter movement, which was fueled by these violent events, has helped organize major protests against the police in a number of major cities throughout the United States. It remains to be seen how this will unfold, but the police know that change must occur. In this chapter we provided a sociological perspective to these contemporary problems in the hope of adding to the discourse about the types of change that are possible.

In terms of work to be done in policing relative to investigating and reporting hate crimes, we believe the police should continue to sharpen their "professional vision." By this we mean that officers must be trained to *see* hate crimes for purposes other than prosecution. There are many instances where hate crimes occur and cause fear and divisiveness in communities, but the police don't recognize them because they don't fit the criminal statute exactly. The impact of these crimes on victims, communities, and on police–community relations is lost. Without a framework for seeing hate crimes for multiple policing purposes, including criminal prosecutions, statistical analyses, community relations, intelligence gathering, and the implementation of hate crime prevention, it is difficult to resolve this problem. We offer such a framework in this chapter and hope that police officials, among others, will be able to use it to see the many types of hate crimes that occur, extending the definition of the term beyond a small circumscribed set of behaviors that fit local criminal hate crime definitions to a diverse number of bias-motivated crimes that will never make it into a court of law.

Finally, the measure of an open society is the extent to which it can effectively alleviate fears about the "others" in peaceful ways that build relationships and create greater understanding. In Europe, particularly following the terrorist attacks on Paris in November 2015, the challenge will be to recognize the widespread fear caused by the attacks without succumbing to extremist rhetoric that exacerbates difference and establishes an atmosphere conducive to increasing hate violence.

CHAPTER 4

A Typology of Hate

Hate crimes are committed against people and places because the offender holds a bias against the victim's group. But many people, in fact most of us, have biases; so why are some people moved to act violently because of them while others are not? This chapter focuses on the motivations and circumstances of the people who commit hate crimes as well as on the people who encourage and support them. The typology presented here not only encompasses but is also much broader than the hardened hatemongers and dabblers in hate who are directly responsible for attacking people who are different (Levin & McDevitt, 1993, 1995b). In addition, the typology includes those who sit on the sidelines, the sympathizers and spectators, without whom crimes of hate would be far less problematic.

Hatemongers

When a sadistic offense is committed because a victim is different, there seems to be much reason to suggest that the motivation contains important elements of hate. Sadism is essentially designed to give a perpetrator a sense of power, control, and dominance, but at the expense of a set of victims. The three White supremacists who were charged with James Byrd's murder in Jasper, Texas—John King, Lawrence Brewer, and Shawn Berry—beat the Black hitchhiker until he was unconscious, chained him to their pickup truck, and then dragged him down the road on his back for almost three miles to his death. For the first two miles, not only was Byrd alive, but he was also conscious. Only when he was decapitated by a boulder at the side of the road was the victim's suffering ended and his life mercifully taken.

The Role of Organized Hate

Investigators discovered a Ku Klux Klan manual among the possessions carried by one of the suspects; and two of the suspects wore White supremacist body tattoos depicting the Confederate Knights of America. King, Brewer, and Berry were definitely ardent admirers of the Klan who used White supremacist propaganda and enjoyed being identified with White supremacist symbols of power.

In addition to the murder of James Byrd, there have been several particularly dangerous and deadly high-profile hate crimes committed by the members of White supremacist organizations (Fox & Levin, 2006). In August 1999, Buford Furrow walked into a Jewish Community Center in the Los Angeles area and opened fire on a group of children as they played. Although he failed in his attempt to kill his young victims, Furrow then shot to death a Filipino letter carrier who just happened to be in the wrong place at the wrong time. A photograph later released to the public showed Furrow a few years earlier dressed in a Nazi uniform at the Hayden, Idaho, compound of the racist organization known as Aryan Nations.

More recently, as a cultural phenomenon, there are literally millions of Americans who, in varying degrees, dislike the members of various minority groups in society. Most of them would, however, never even think of committing an act of violence against someone because they are different. The relationship between hate and violence is far from perfect. Hate can and does occur without violence; violence against outsiders can and does occur in the absence of hate.

Organized hate groups provide the situational facilitators in whose presence hate violence becomes more likely to occur. Not unlike a gang or a cult, the organized hate group comes to represent the family of a newly recruited member. Typically, the members of organized hate groups have lacked a sense of belonging. They aren't getting along with their parents, can't make it at school with their peers, and are forced to take dead-end jobs, at best. Many of them are unemployed or work in dead-end jobs as manual laborers (Borgeson & Valeri, 2007). But in Posse Comitatus, Aryan Nations, National Alliance, Creativity Movement, or the Klan, they gain what has been missing in their lives, a sense of belonging and a vague feeling of their own importance. Hatemongers espouse hate and violence, but their underlying motivation is more complex (Ezekiel, 1995).

In social psychology, it is well known that the group can make the difference between attitude and action, between thinking about violence and actually perpetrating it. Acting in a group rather than alone reduces feelings of personal responsibility. Because blame or responsibility is shared, it is also weakened. Individuals may be willing to take more risks, to engage in dangerous behavior, simply because they don't feel that they can be held accountable for their actions.

Hate from a Distance

No more than 5% of all hate crimes nationally are committed by members of organizations like the Ku Klux Klan, Aryan Nations, or the White Aryan Resistance. Still, groups of White supremacists continue behind the scenes to inspire murder, assault, and vandalism. They encourage and support much larger numbers of violent offenses committed by nonmembers who may be totally unsophisticated with respect to the ideology of hate—racist skinheads, alienated teenagers, hate-filled young men looking to have a good time at someone else's expense (Levin & McDevitt, 1993).

While serving time behind bars for burglary convictions, two of the suspects in Jasper apparently had links with the Aryan Brotherhood, a prison hate group whose members are often recruited by White supremacists after they have been released. Established in many states around the country, the Aryan Brotherhood introduces inmates to the theology of the Identity Church, according to which a race war is inevitable. Prison may be a school for crime, but it is also a crash course in hatred and a training ground for leaders of the most dangerous White supremacist groups in our society.

Hatemongers often retaliate in an organized fashion. They want more than just to stop a particular event from happening or a particular individual from intruding; they believe that the very presence of certain groups of people in *their* town, *their* state, *their* country represents an intolerable threat to their personal well-being and to the survival of their group's way of life. Hatemongers provide propaganda to individuals looking to justify their own hateful behavior; they train youngsters in the art of bashing minorities; they recruit on college campuses and in prisons and workplaces; and they operate cable-access television programs featuring interviews with one another. These are the Americans who join Posse Comitatus, the Identity Church, the White Aryan Resistance, the Ku Klux Klan, the National Socialist Movement, and the like. There aren't many who qualify as hatemongers, but the few who do are responsible for some of the most vicious acts of violence perpetrated against citizens (Levin & McDevitt, 1993).

Biblical Bigotry

The underlying religious inspiration for many organized hate groups is provided by the Christian Identity Church, a worldwide movement whose ministers preach that those who call themselves Jews are actually the children of the devil and that Blacks, Latinos, and Asians are "mud people" whose spiritual development remains at the level of animals rather than human beings. According to the Identity Church, the true Israelites in the Bible are the ancestors of those Americans who came from northern European countries.

White Aryan hatemongers are not the only ones who preach biblical bigotry. The beliefs of the Black Hebrew Israelites bear a remarkable resemblance to the theology of Christian Identity practiced by many White supremacists. Members of the Black movement depict themselves as divinely blessed by God with moral superiority; they are God's authentic chosen people of the Old Testament. They see Whites as blue-eyed devils and conventional Jews as imposters.

Black Hebrew Israelites who have migrated from the United States to Israel are usually peaceful. In America, however, they are known by the police for their violence and criminal activities, due in large part to the Miami-based Nation of Yahweh that was headed by Yahweh Ben Yahweh. In the 1980s, members of the Nation of Yahweh, under the direction of the man they thought of as the Messiah, committed several homicides (Levin & Fox, 1991).

As do the Christian Identity group and certain civilian militia groups, Black Hebrew Israelites draw on the Khazarian legend to explain why those who refer to themselves as Jews are actually imposters. The Kingdom of Khazaria, one of the most diverse countries of medieval Europe, existed in an area of what is known now as southern Russia. In the eighth century, Bulan, who was the king of Khazaria, adopted Judaism. In one version of the story, he was forced to become Jewish after his kingdom was invaded by Jewish tribes from the Crimean Peninsula. In another version, Bulan voluntarily converted to Judaism only after carefully considering the relative merits of Islam, Christianity, and Judaism. Soon afterwards, Khazarian aristocrats also converted and Judaism became the official religion of the kingdom of Khazaria, although other religions were also tolerated. Most Khazarians became Jews, but some converted to Islam or Christianity. The appeal of Judaism may have been enhanced by the fact that Khazaria had, at the same time, become a destination for substantial numbers of persecuted Jews from Europe and Asia who sought a safe haven (Brook, 1999).

After 250 years, the medieval kingdom of Khazaria was overrun by Russian soldiers. Those Jews who remained in Khazaria were forcibly baptized. The remainder fled to Hungary, Ukraine, Lithuania, Belarus, Slovakia, Romania, Poland, and parts of Russia (Brook, 1999).

The existence of the kingdom of Khazaria is an indisputable historical fact. Yet most of the details surrounding the association of Eastern European Jews with Khazaria and the dissolution of the kingdom constitute unsubstantiated legend wholeheartedly adopted by organizations and individuals—members of the Black Hebrew Israelites, Christian Identity, and some militia groups—eager to discredit Judaism and to substantiate their conspiratorial views concerning the Jewish people. They argue that the origins of most of European or Ashkenazi Jewry can be traced back to the kingdom of Khazaria and not to Jerusalem. Thus, from this viewpoint, European Jews were converted and therefore cannot make claims to the land of Israel (Patriot Fax Network, 1996).

One part of the legend supports the notion that Jews seek to control the world's peoples. Their claim is that for more than 1,000 years, ever since the dissolution of the Khazarian kingdom and the dispersion of European Jews throughout the world, Khazarians have passed along to their offspring a secret plot to amass great wealth and political power and ultimately to take over all of the countries around the world (Patriot Fax Network, 1996).

For anti-Semites both Black and White, the term "Khazarian" serves more than one purpose. First, the Khazarian legend traces in detail the historical basis for the centuries-old charge that Jews represent an international conspiracy to gain control over the world's economic resources. Second, the term "Khazarian" (as a replacement for "Jew") has become a code word for those who do not wish to be accused of anti-Semitism. They are not anti-Jewish, only anti-Khazarian. Third, the term "Khazarian" has greater scope than Ashkenazi Jew, including within it not only all Jews of European descent but also certain Christians and Muslims who are considered the enemies of freedom and whose ancestry can be traced back to Eastern Europe (remember that some Khazarians converted to Christianity and Islam). Thus, some opponents of the concept of a "one-world order" identify the Rockefeller family and former president George

Bush as non-Jewish Khazarians. Finally, focusing on Khazarians also lends credibility to the accusation that Jews, especially Ashkenazi Jews, represent a racial group rather than just a religion. Treating Jews as a race becomes important to those who argue that they are a breed apart from the rest of humanity and must be eliminated rather than converted to Christianity.

The Militia Movement and White Supremacy

Several years ago, the first author spent the day in a small town north of Boston at a "Patriot Potluck" attended by 75 members of the so-called Patriot movement—militia members, survivalists, and other political discontents who listened attentively to the words of a long list of speakers. The first and featured speaker was a leader of the militia movement in New Hampshire, Ed Brown, who spoke among other things about the evils of the Khazarians. As he warned the audience to be on guard, a voice in the audience could clearly be heard to agree with Brown's cautionary words. "Right, Ed," said the man in the crowd. "It's the Ashkenazi." Brown immediately admonished him about using the word "Ashkenazi," which is a reference to Jews of European ancestry. "Stick to the term Khazarians," he advised. "They are the true source of evil."

Militias have been linked, at least in the public mind, with everything from the Oklahoma City massacre in which 168 people lost their lives to Atlanta's Olympics pipebomb murder. According to the stereotyped version, militia members are nothing more than a collection of gun-loving hatemongers and thugs who preach First and Second Amendment rights as an excuse for waging war against the federal government. And the first author is certain that there are some militia members who fit the image. But that is also why he was so surprised when the 75 men, women, and children at the Patriot potluck he attended seemed so hospitable and friendly, even innocuous.

The first thing that struck him about this gathering was its diversity in terms of age, social class, and geography. They were men, women, and children from several states who hardly resembled the image he had expected to see. From a distance, in fact, they could easily have been mistaken for a group of bridge players or a convention of social workers.

The author was also surprised by the utter boredom of their speeches. Through a five-hour procession, he heard almost nothing about guns and bombs and a great deal about financial hardship and economic disaster. Speaker after speaker after speaker talked about money and how to keep it or make more of it—about how to defeat the Internal Revenue Service (IRS) through common-law courts, about how to withdraw from the Social Security system, about the effect of free trade on the unemployment rate, and about how to avoid going into debt. The author got the strong impression that these were Americans who had suffered through hard times and were looking for some way to survive. Their response was to blame the federal government, the United Nations, the so-called one-world order, the communists, and international bankers. Some, but by no means all of them, also blamed Jews, Blacks, Asians, and Latinos (Levin, 1997a).

It is interesting to note that Ed Brown, the New Hampshire militia leader who spoke at the Patriot Potluck, was subsequently convicted, along with his dentist wife Elaine, for the crime of tax evasion—the couple had concealed almost $2,000,000 in income from the IRS. In January 2007, refusing to turn themselves in to the FBI, the Browns barricaded themselves in their Plainfield, New Hampshire, home. Finally, in October, after being holed up for almost nine months surrounded by armed federal agents, the Browns were arrested under-cover and taken to serve their lengthy prison sentences (Associated Press, 2007).

If there is a bit of overlap between militia groups and White supremacists, it is because both believe that the federal government has let them down and is now illegitimate. Both have committed themselves to the defense of their ver-sion of America. The militia movement gained dramatically in both membership and publicity during the deep recession of the early 1980s, at a time when much of the attention of the nation was on big city problems. Some militia members came from the ranks of automobile workers who lost their jobs in Detroit's massive layoffs, but many more had been miners, farmers, ranchers, and people in the timber business who had been put out of business, who simply could no longer make ends meet, and who were looking for help from government officials—help that never came or came too late to make a difference. In addi-tion, some militia groups were convinced that communists had taken over all branches of the federal government and that the United Nations and one-world order types were conspiring to rob the United States of its sovereignty.

So concerned are militia members about the erosion of their constitutional rights that they stand ready and willing to defend our country against itself. They often cite what they regard as a federally instigated conflagration at Waco, Texas, and before that the killing by federal agents of the wife and son of a White supremacist at Ruby Ridge, Idaho, as proof that the government is out to get its citizens. They refuse to give up their firearms, believing that they might very well need all the weapons they can get to resist the coming onslaught by foreign and communist forces. Some hate Jews and Blacks, but there are also Jewish and Black militia members.

For a period of time in the late 1990s, civilian militia groups lost much of their appeal. More recently, however, as terrorism, immigration, gun con-trol, and unemployment have become major issues, the militia movement again experienced growing membership rolls and popular appeal. According to the Southern Poverty Law Center, there were 512 militia groups in the United States in 2009, up from 149 a year earlier. In response to the election of President Obama and a bad economic situation, the number of such groups reached an all-time high in 2012, totaling some 1,360 militias before falling somewhat to 874 in 2014. At this point, anti-government activism began to modify its tac-tics, relying to an increasing extent on the Internet as well as lone wolf attacks (Potok, 2015).

Not unlike militia groups, the members of organized hate groups like the Klan, Posse Comitatus, Aryan Nations, World Church of the Creator, and White Aryan Resistance also despise the federal government, but for different if overlapping reasons. They refer to the federal government as ZOG and they emphasize their belief that Jews and Blacks have conspired with other enemies of the republic to benefit themselves at the expense of White Christian Americans.

According to Ezekiel (1995), the leaders of White supremacist organizations are motivated less by sheer hate than by a burning desire to assume a position of power and to be important in the eyes of others. Their followers are recruited from the ranks of marginalized and alienated Americans, many poorly educated and financially troubled, who are searching for a sense of belonging that they never had at home, but they find readily available in organized hate (Langer, 1990).

Expanding the Influence of Organized Hate

At the same time, marginality and alienation do not always depend on impoverishment. Although most White supremacists are from working-class backgrounds, there are also some who seem to be well educated and wealthy. One of the most tragic examples of the appeal of racism and anti-Semitism to an economically advantaged White supremacist can be found in the July 1999 three-day rampage of 21-year-old Benjamin Smith, in which the Indiana University student murdered a Korean graduate student on his campus and a Black basketball coach at Northwestern University. He also fired bullets at a group of Orthodox Jews, injuring six of them before taking his own life.

Smith, whose father was a physician, grew up in an affluent suburb northwest of Chicago. His mentor was, however, not his father, but 27-year-old Matthew Hale, the son of a police officer and law-school graduate from East Peoria who, based on his racist beliefs and practices, was denied the privilege of practicing law by the state of Illinois. In his role as head of the White supremacist group World Church of the Creator (now known as the Creativity Movement), Hale was able to express his racist views to a group of followers who were eager to hear them. Before serving a lengthy prison sentence for conspiring to murder a judge, Hale had been in contact with Smith for several days prior to the young man's murderous rampage through Illinois and Indiana and considered Smith a martyr and a friend. Some questioned whether Hale had inspired Smith's killing spree.

Hale also preached Ra-Ho-Wa—the inevitability of a racial holy war from which Whites would ultimately emerge the winners. He despised Jews, Blacks, Latinos, and Asians, considering them to be subhumans at the same level as animals. He also argued that Christianity was merely a tool of deception used by power-hungry Jews to nurture a mind-set that would enable them to take over the world. Smith was reportedly furious when he learned that the state of Illinois had denied Hale's bid to practice law. This may have been the catalyst that initiated his killing spree.

Peer pressure may also have been a factor. Smith's girlfriend, 20-year-old Christine Weiss, was also a member of Hale's World Church of the Creator. Like her boyfriend, Weiss had grown up in a wealthy Chicago suburb. She had played soccer and classical music for 11 years and had attended the same high school as Smith, one of the best in the country. Then, Weiss learned on the Internet about World Church of the Creator and Matthew Hale. After graduating from high school, she disavowed her Episcopalian roots and joined up. She started talking about preparing for the racial holy war espoused by Hale and about caring only for "her own kind"—the White people of the world (CNN, 2000).

The Internet and its thousands of hate websites give to hatemongers a degree of influence well beyond their small numbers (Daniels, 2009). Thanks to the Internet, Matthew Hale's message of hate has reached thousands of young people around the country who may have racist and anti-Semitic feelings and are thrilled to learn that they are not alone in these beliefs.

According to former racist Tom Leyden, the Internet is probably the best thing ever to happen to the White supremacist movement. Any child with a computer can access hundreds of hate websites, including that of Matthew Hale's organization. In fact, six-year-olds can even visit the website called World Church of the Creator for Kids, where they can find a crossword puzzle to solve and a White power coloring book to download.

Leyden should know about hate. He has preached tolerance for the Simon Wiesenthal Center in Los Angeles, but he's not Jewish. For 15 years, he was a neo-Nazi skinhead whose body was covered with racist and anti-Semitic tattoos. In his younger days, when he wasn't in jail, Leyden was in the streets, fighting, attacking, and beating up people he considered to be his enemies (Leyden, 2008).

Leyden later married another White supremacist. But when he had children, he felt it was time to make a profound change in his life. There was no way, he reasoned, that he was going to raise his sons in the image of the Nazi movement. There was no way that he was going to contribute to the making of the next generation of hatemongers. Now, he works for the other side, seeking to make up for the time he lost in his early years that was filled with hate and prejudice.

Leyden's reference to the Internet should not be taken lightly. As he suggested in a CNN (2000) interview with correspondent Art Harris, there are youngsters in small towns and big cities around the country who feel alone in their racism. They don't have friends; they have trouble getting along with their peers. But when they boot up their computers and log onto the Internet, they've got good friends literally around the world who love them and who agree with their racist views.

Because of the Internet, hate websites originating in the United States have also had a powerful impact on youngsters in other countries where the restrictions on hate are more rigorously applied (Daniels, 2009). According to German law, for example, the dissemination of Nazi propaganda is strictly forbidden. Yet, German laws banning hate on the Internet have been easily circumvented by the spread of websites in the United States operated by neo-Nazi extremists and accessible in the German language to German youths. Protected by the First Amendment to the Constitution, U.S. sites offer propaganda, insignias, music, and computer games that have been officially outlawed from German society but are nevertheless within easy reach of German youths.

There are many computer hate games available from American sources, including Concentration Camp Manager, an extremely popular game among German teenagers in which players choose who lives and who dies in the gas chambers. Other computer games have been modified by American Nazis who add an element of hate to what would otherwise be an innocuous form of high-tech entertainment. In the game Grouse Hunt, for example, the virtual pheasants to be shot were replaced by yarmulkes (Jewish prayer caps) and Stars of David. According to a German Interior Ministry estimate, the number of Nazi sites outside Germany that are directed at German citizens has recently soared (Finn, 2000).

Mass Murder in the Name of Hate

During the civil rights movement of the 1960s that swept American society, it would have been less than surprising to learn about a mass murder involving Whites killing Blacks (or their sympathizers). In 1963, for example, four Black girls were killed, when four members of the Ku Klux Klan planted dynamite beneath the front steps of the 16th Street Baptist Church in Birmingham, Alabama. In June 1964, three civil rights workers—two White and one Black— were abducted and shot to death in Neshoba County, Mississippi, by members of the White Knights of the Ku Klux Klan. The three victims had been working to register African Americans to vote.

On the surface, it appears that the complexion of hate-motivated mass murder has not changed much over the decades. In June 2015, the murder of nine African Americans at a historic church in Charleston was committed by a White supremacist who might have perpetrated the same sort of violent crime against the same sort of victims decades earlier if he had been around during the civil rights era (Levin & Fox, 2015).

Actually, in contrast to the past, race has become vastly more complex in twenty-first-century America. The struggle for equality has grown far beyond the relationship between Blacks and Whites to encompass a broad range of ethnic groups whose members compete for their share of power, prestige, and wealth. A wide variety of race and ethnic groups reside in cities of America where they share schools, neighborhoods, and public services, not always in an agreeable manner. On occasion, the battles between various minorities can be every bit as brutal and violent as any between Blacks and Whites.

Moreover, hatemongers rarely specialize. They might despise Blacks and Latinos, but they also hate gays, Jews, Muslims, Asians, and immigrants of virtually all nationalities. The complexity of intergroup relations can, of course, be seen most vividly in tragic episodes of mass slaughter. Not unlike hate-motivated violence generally, multiple homicide is no longer only a case of Whites attacking Blacks based on their racial identity.

Blacks have mass-murdered Whites. In March 2000 in Wilkensburg, Pennsylvania, 39-year-old Ronald Taylor, an African American who hated Whites, became enraged about a broken door in his apartment that hadn't been repaired. In retaliation, he shot to death the White maintenance man and White customers at two fast-food restaurants.

Whites have mass-murdered individuals representing a range of racial and religious backgrounds. In April 2000 outside of Pittsburgh, Pennsylvania, immigration lawyer Richard Baumhammers proclaimed his hatred for immigrants, Jews, and people of color. Driving from place to place, he killed five people including his 63-year-old Jewish next-door neighbor, a 22-year-old African American man leaving a karate school, a 34-year-old Chinese restaurant manager, a 27-year-old Vietnamese American cook, and a 31-year-old Indian immigrant who was picking up groceries on his lunch hour.

Whites have mass-murdered both Blacks and Whites. In July 2003, in Meridian, Mississippi, Doug Williams, a known racist, killed four co-workers including one White and three Black employees.

Whites have mass-murdered Americans of Asian background. In August, 2012, in Oak Creek, Wisconsin, 40-year-old Wade Michael Page, a member of a White supremacist group and White power band, fatally shot six people at a Sikh temple.

Whites have sought to mass-murder Jews. In April, 2014, in Overland Park, Kansas, Frazier Glen Miller, a 72-year-old former leader of the Carolina Knights of the Ku Klux Klan, shot to death three people whom he believed to be Jewish at the Overland Park Jewish Community Center. Actually, all three of his victims were Christians who happened to be in the wrong place at the wrong time.

Dabblers

For hardened hatemongers, bigotry becomes the basis for a full-time preoccupation, if not a career. They join an organization that espouses racism or other forms of prejudice. They completely limit their friendships to those who hold their bigoted beliefs. And they practice what they preach by waging a continuing campaign of intimidation against the "outsiders" they despise. Most hate-motivated multiple homicides are committed by dedicated hatemongers who believe they are on a mission to rid the world of evil.

Getting a Thrill

Yet in everyday life, not all hate incidents are so clearly hate-filled. Certain individuals *dabble* in bigotry (Iganski & Levin, 2015; Iganski, 2008; Levin & McDevitt, 1993). They convert their prejudices into behavior, but only on a part-time basis as a hobby, for example, by going out on a Saturday night with their buddies to assault someone, to burn a cross, or to spray-paint graffiti. Dabblers are typically young people, usually groups of teenage boys or young adults who aren't getting along at home, in school, or on the job. They may hate themselves as much as they hate their victims. But in committing a hate crime, they gain what seems to be missing from their lives. They feel superior to the extent that they make their victim feel inferior. They feel important by their actions in reducing their enemies to the status of garbage. Moreover, many hate attacks directed against Blacks, gays, Latinos, Asians, and Jews are committed by dabblers who gain "bragging rights" with their friends at the same time that they fill their idle hours with excitement. Their attack constitutes a bonding experience, much as a difficult pledge or initiation period reinforces the loyalty of fraternity brothers or the members of gangs.

At the extreme, a thrill hate crime can result in brutal murder. Thirty-year-old Jennifer Daugherty was an intellectually challenged woman from Greensburg, Pennsylvania, who trusted just about everyone and regarded friendly people as her close friends. In February 2010, she was abducted and then murdered by six men and women ages 17 to 36 who posed as her good friends. For 36 hours, they tortured Daugherty in unspeakable ways, first tying her up and then forcing her to eat feces, urine, and detergent, beating her, shaving her head, painting her face with nail polish, and forcing her to write a fake suicide note before they stabbed her to death. After taking her life, the six perpetrators wrapped her in Christmas decorations, placed her body inside a garbage can, and dumped her in the parking lot of a local school. Two of the offenders got the death penalty while the other four received lengthy prison sentences (Levin, 2011).

Not all of those who band together to bash vulnerable victims are responsible for instigating an attack. Indeed, in any group of dabblers, there is usually a leader who has sadistic tendencies that he is eager to satisfy by making life miserable for the enemy. In addition, there are usually at least a few "fellow travelers" who go along with their friends so as to avoid being rejected (Watts, 1997). In questioning college students in Boston, for example, we identified some who had not verbalized an objection when their friend threatened to do harm to a member of another group. One young Asian woman remarked:

> A friend of mine threatened someone else who was of a rival gang. My friend was Asian and was racially biased against other races, but would only threaten to hurt those who were in gangs. I was shocked that he would say that and quietly hoped he wouldn't follow through on the threat.

The phenomenon of the fellow traveler may have applied very neatly to a hate crime involving a group of eight Southern California teenagers who brutally attacked five elderly Latino nursery workers, apparently just for the fun of it. Bored and unable to think of any legal forms of entertainment to amuse themselves, the youngsters drove slowly through the darkened streets of the city, searching for a little excitement. Finally, they came upon the Latino nursery workers. At first, the teenagers only shouted ethnic slurs at the Latinos from their passing car. Then, five of the boys got out of the car and began shooting the workers with pellet guns and beating them with rocks. All the while, three of the teenagers participated minimally in the attack, seated uncomfortably in the car where they talked together in hushed tones about being scared and about how things were getting out of control. One of them reluctantly retrieved ammunition to re-arm one of the teenager's pellet guns, but apparently he never directly participated in the attack (Roth, 2001).

Struggling with a high unemployment rate and widespread resentment toward Jews and foreigners, the former East Germany has had more than its share of thrill hate attacks—some of them deadly. In 1989–1990, just prior to unification of East and West, there were fewer than 200 acts of hate aimed at foreigners, Jews, and political opponents; most of these were perpetrated by German adults who were linked to neo-Nazi hate groups.

Throughout the 1990s and into the twenty-first century, however, as the unemployment rate grew and immigration increased, the number of violent attacks almost quadrupled. In 2004 alone, there were 776 cases of racial or ethnic assaults—mostly beatings, attempted murders, and arson attacks—in German cities and towns. From the fall of the Berlin Wall to the years of the early twenty-first century, neo-Nazis have murdered more than 100 foreigners, according to reports in the German press (Nickerson, 2006).

Even the personal characteristics of activist bigots changed after unification. During the 1980s, most of the racist demonstrators were older and connected with organized neo-Nazi groups. By contrast, after unification, the vast majority of attackers were under the age of 20—teenagers who were driven more by personal misery than by political ideology. Fewer had ties to organized hate groups or were in touch with Nazi beliefs. Like their counterparts in the United States, the German bigots tended to be alienated and marginalized young people who saw little hope for the future and blamed refugees, Jews, and guest workers for all of their woes (Watts, 1997).

Some episodes of hate violence turned particularly brutal. In June 2000, three young racist teenagers in the city of Dessau missed the last train back to their hometown of Bitterfeld and, being bored, decided to go out and get drunk. Two were high school dropouts; one was out of work. All of them enjoyed listening to the lyrics of anti-Semitic violent music such as "Auschwitz, Dachau, Buchenwald, we're going to bump off the Jews again" and "Our faces are full of hatred. We love violence" (Leparmentier, 2000).

Shortly after midnight, having been thrown out of the train station where they had been drinking heavily, the trio staggered through the streets of Dessau and into a local park, where they encountered Alberto Adriano, a 39-year-old Black man of Mozambican descent. He had come to the town of Dessau 12 years earlier and was married to a German woman. Shouting "filthy nigger, get out of our country," the three bigoted teenagers knocked down their victim and repeatedly hit and kicked him in the head, even as he lay helplessly on the ground and appeared to be dead. Then, to humiliate Adriano, the three young men tore off his clothes so that he was left lying in the park with nothing on except his socks and shoes. Their sadism suggests strongly that the three young racists in hate were motivated more by a profound psychological need than any political end.

In August 2000, a judge handed down sentences to the trio for the brutal murder of Alberto Adriano. The two 16-year-olds received nine years in prison; their 24-year-old companion received a life sentence. When asked by the judge what he had against foreigners, one of the 16-year-old defendants replied simply, "I hate niggers."

Not unlike the killers of Alberto Adriano in Germany, many dabblers in countries around the world suffer from marginality based on economic and/or educational disadvantage. Some may come from wealthy families, but nevertheless they feel a profound sense of social marginality in relation to their families or peers. In the United States, anxious advocates of nativism envision huddled masses of impoverished, uneducated, disease-ridden criminals who sneak across our porous borders to steal jobs and murder our citizens.

Typically, dabblers do not limit their attacks to any specific group. The interesting thing theoretically is that a dabbler who hates someone because he or she is Black is also likely to hate someone who is Latino or gay or Asian or Jewish or Muslim (Sniderman & Piazza, 1993). This lack of specialization in the selection of a victim probably reflects the dabbler's psychological need to feel good about himself at somebody else's expense. Our culture supplies the dabbler with a range of enemies who would be appropriate to vandalize, bash, threaten, intimidate, or assault. He makes his selection from this range of cultural villains based on what is convenient at the time.

Not unlike those individuals who are different with respect to race, religion, or sexual orientation, street people are frequently stereotyped as little more than trash to be hauled away and eliminated. During a 10-year-period (1999–2008), 244 homeless individuals were murdered, typically by groups of young men and teenagers looking for a thrill. Some of the perpetrators videotaped their attacks, laughing audibly as they beat their victim to death with a baseball bat or a nail-studded board. In response, Maryland was the first state to add homeless individuals to its hate crime statute. Similar efforts to add homeless men and women as a protected category in hate crime legislation have been successful in Alaska; California; Puerto Rico; and Washington, DC. Moreover, the state of Maine passed a separate law in 2006 whereby judges are allowed to take into consideration a victim's homelessness when considering an appropriate sentence for the perpetrators (National Coalition for the Homeless, 2013).

Thrill hate attacks seem to increase and decrease as young adults and teenagers become more or less involved in violence generally as a way of filling their idle hours. As shown in Figure 4.1 the trend in the prevalence of hate (in this case, anti-Semitic incidents) tends to follow closely the trend in serious violent crimes perpetrated by young people. As the rate of murder committed by individuals aged 18–24 soared between the mid-1980s and the mid-1990s, so did the rate of anti-Semitic incidents. When the homicide rate decreased after 1993, the prevalence of anti-Semitism also declined.

Being Defensive

Not all dabblers are looking for just a thrill. According to Levin and McDevitt (1995a), a second type of dabbler is motivated to commit hate crimes that are believed to be *defensive*. Such attacks are typically precipitated by a threatening episode, for example, a gay

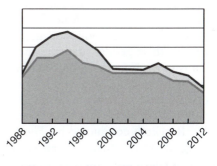

□ Homicide Rate ■ Anti-Semitism

FIG. 4.1 Homicide Rate (Ages 18–24) and Anti-Semitic Incidents, 1988–2012.
Source: Federal Bureau of Investigation, Homicide Data, and Anti-Defamation League, Anti-Semitism Audit, 1988–2012.

rights parade, Blacks moving into a previously all-White neighborhood, a terrorist attack by Muslim extremists, or the first Latino or Asian student on a campus. Failing to elicit the desired response (e.g., the immediate withdrawal of a Latino family from a previously all-White neighborhood), there may be an escalation of violence. A verbal attack by phone may become a personal visit with a firearm; a hate crime that begins as vandalism may turn more deadly.

September 11, 2001, was a threatening episode for those Americans who wanted to "defend the homeland." One of the benefits of having a national hate crime data collection system like the one described in chapter 3 is that it enables us to see how this significant event affected hate crimes perpetrated against certain groups. Comparing the hate crimes reported to the FBI via NIBRS for four years before September 11, 2001, and four years after, researchers found that the hate crimes following 9/11 were 123% more likely to be violent crimes, 18% more likely to involve offenders over the age of 40, 89% more likely to involve a bias against Arabs or Islam, and 55% more likely to target religious institutions. This event didn't just affect Arabs and Muslims. Post 9/11 anti-Jewish hate crimes were 40% more likely to result in serious injury (broken bones, internal bleeding) to the victim and nearly 40% more likely to involve multiple offenders in a single incident (Nolan, Bennett, & Rodrigues, 2008). Into the twenty-first century, hate crimes were more likely to be committed by older perpetrators rather than teenagers and individuals in their twenties (Levin & Reichelmann, 2015).

Even prior to the 9/11 terrorist attack, many Americans felt threatened by the presence of groups considered to be outsiders. Those who argue that hate crimes increased through the 1980s and 1990s note also that intergroup competition rose as well during this period (Olzak, Shanahan, & McEneaney, 1996). Whether or not economically based, growing threats to the advantaged majority group may have inspired a rising tide of hate incidents directed against members of challenging groups. Over the past 25 years or so, there have been dramatic increases in interfaith and interrace dating and marriage; migration especially from Latin America, the Middle East, and Asia; newly integrated neighborhoods, schools, college dormitories, and workplaces; individuals who change their gender identity, and gay men and lesbians coming out (and, in many cases, organizing on behalf of their shared interests). As first suggested in chapter 2, Green, Strolovitch, and Wong (1997) have shown that hate crimes occur most frequently in "defended" White neighborhoods, that is, in predominantly White areas that have experienced an in-migration of minorities.

Research conducted by *The Chicago Reporter* (Gordon & Pardo, 1997) suggests that Chicago-area suburbs with growing minority populations have experienced increasing numbers of hate offenses against Blacks and Latinos. In many previously all-White suburban communities, minorities have reached a critical mass, causing White residents to feel threatened by the influx of newcomers. This seems to be the point at which hate crimes escalate. Broadening Green's concept a bit, we suggest that dabblers in hate may defend any aspect of their lives they feel especially entitled to hold—not only their neighborhood, but their campus, their dormitory, their office, or their social relationships.

The concept of defended neighborhood is illustrated by a hate crime that occurred in Salt Lake City on the Saturday evening before Labor Day in September 1998. A 25-year-old man, Michael Magleby, and his 15-year-old accomplice snuck onto the lawn of a modest single-family house. Asleep in their home were Ron Henry, who is Black, his wife, who is White, and their 12-year-old son. Awakened by a sudden noise outside, the three ran to a window and watched as a cross burned brightly on their lawn.

As a consultant for the prosecution, the first author was able to interview Ron Henry in the course of Magleby's trial. It was clear to him that Ron understood the symbolism of the burning cross all too well. It was intended to intimidate him, to threaten him with violence, and to scare him into leaving the neighborhood. For two weeks afterwards, Ron was frightened enough to install a security system in his home. He began carrying a baseball bat whenever he and his son took walks around the neighborhood. He considered leaving the area.

Trial evidence confirmed that Henry's fear was not misplaced. Michael Magleby was known to visit hate websites, collect racist propaganda, read White supremacist novels such as *The Turner Diaries*, and listen to White power CDs including the racist lyrics of Skrewdriver. Just before he was convicted in federal court, the prosecuting attorney identified Magleby's motive. He argued that only a racist would even think of burning a cross on the lawn of a Black family. It was clear, he said, that the defendant wanted Henry out of the area, and the burning cross was meant to convey a message to that effect (Rayburn, 1999).

The prevalence of defensive hate crimes has historically risen and fallen, depending on the particular economic circumstances of the times. During periods of economic downturn in the 1980s and 1990s, for example, Asian Americans often became the targets of hate. Just as Jews had been blamed for Germany's economic woes during the Nazi era, Asians were held responsible for America's declining position in the global economy. In 1982, during the deepest recession since World War II, a Chinese American man, celebrating just prior to his wedding day, was killed by two recently out-of-work automobile employees in Detroit who blamed the Japanese for their financial problems and failed to distinguish Chinese from Japanese or Asian Americans from Asians (McDevitt, Levin, & Bennett, 2002).

Ten years later, just as an epidemic of corporate downsizing hit the American economy, the Los Angeles office of the Japanese American Citizens League received a bomb threat in which the caller warned, "I'll show you a year of remembrance, you dirty Japs. What we remember is Pearl Harbor." During the same period, an Asian American from Sacramento was stabbed to death by someone who sought to "defend our country" from the onslaught of Asian newcomers (Ancheta, 1998, p. 74).

In a 1992 study of hate crimes reported to the Boston police, it was found that Asians and Latinos were the two groups at greatest risk for victimization.

At the time, these were the "new kids on the block," the newcomers who were seen as threatening the economic well-being of groups of Americans who had been here longer and who felt they must protect their stake in the country (Levin & McDevitt, 1993, 1995a; McDevitt, Levin, & Bennett, 2002).

According to the most recent data released by the U.S. Census Bureau, such "defensive" hate attacks might be expected to increase over the next several years. In the 2000 census, the number of Latinos soared to the point where they surpassed Black Americans to become the largest minority group in the nation. More specifically, Latinos represented 6.4% of the total population in 1980; by the year 2000, they were 12.5% (Rodriguez, 2001), and by 2014, they represented more than 17% of the population. Similarly, the Asian population grew by leaps and bounds, especially in and around large cities. In New Jersey, for example, there was a 94% increase. In Pennsylvania, the Asian population grew by 83% (Armas, 2001). By the year 2014, Asian Americans were almost 6% of the national population (Quick Facts, 2014).

Some hate crimes include elements of both thrill-seeking and defense. During the early morning hours of July 12, 2008, a group of drunken teen-aged boys—all high school football players and residents of rural Shenandoah, Pennsylvania—were walking home from a block party when they encountered 25-year-old Mexican immigrant Luis Ramirez. The Mexican man, who worked in a local factory, was walking with his 15-year-old Anglo girlfriend. One of the boys punched Ramirez, causing him to fall to the ground and hit his head on the concrete road. Eyewitnesses also saw one of the White boys kick the immigrant in the head when he was down, causing it to snap sharply to the right. Ramirez died two days later in a nearby hospital.

Prosecution and defense attorneys disagreed as to whether Ramirez or the football players had thrown the first punch. They also disagreed as to whether or not the White boys had shouted racial slurs at the victim. In either case, the Shenandoah area had experienced an upsurge in anti-immigrant sentiment as larger numbers of newcomers from Latin American countries recently relocated into the local community. The fact that the group of high school students had been drinking at a party before encountering the victim suggests that a thrill hate crime was committed. As a secondary motivation, however, the boys may also have decided to protect Ramirez's White girlfriend from her romantic relationship with the Mexican immigrant. The desire to defend "our women" from men who come from some other racial or ethnic group is a motivation for violence found almost universally around the world. An all-White jury found one of the boys not guilty of murder; they convicted two of the boys of simple assault, but acquitted both of them of ethnic intimidation charges (CNN, 2008).

Getting Even

The growing concern about terrorism coming from radical elements of Islam has created a new wrinkle in the complexion of intergroup relations among America's Muslims, Christians, and Jews. In the aftermath of 9/11, there was an escalation in defensive hate crimes committed against Arabs and Muslims in the United States. Operating on the basis of diffuse anger and a profound sense of frustration, some Americans decided to carry out vigilante actions against individuals whom they regarded as the disloyal supporters of anti-American terror. Thus, Middle Easterners and Muslims (as well as individuals who only looked like Middle Easterners or Muslims) were vulnerable to attack, regardless of their personal loyalties and beliefs. The perpetrators never stopped to determine the unique characteristics of those singled out for abuse and punishment. A foreign accent, dark skin, a veil, or a turban made all the difference.

Recently visiting the campus of the University of Michigan in Dearborn, the first author met a young single mom from the Middle East who had recently relocated to the United States in order to enjoy the liberty and freedom that this country provides its citizens. As long as she remains in Dearborn—a city that has a large Arab population—the young woman feels secure. But when she and her three-year-old daughter venture out of the community to a nearby fast-food restaurant, she is harassed by angry Americans who, seeing her dark skin and hearing her accent, regard her as a terrorist and hold her responsible for the terrorist attack on September 11, 2001. While holding her daughter in her arms, she was slapped across the face. On another visit, she was knocked to the floor.

On occasion, hate crimes perpetrated by the members of one group trigger a *retaliatory* strike by members of the victims' group. In such a case, the victims of hate offenses become the perpetrators; they seek revenge for the injustices they have suffered. Their targets are typically selected on a random basis, so that each and every member of a group is a potential victim. A retaliatory hate crime may have occurred on March 4, 2006, when Mohammed Reza Taheri-azar, a 22-year-old native of Iran who had spent most of his life in the United States, allegedly drove his rented sport utility vehicle through a crowded gathering place on the campus of the University of North Carolina, where he had recently graduated. Six students, including a visiting scholar on campus, were slightly injured. According to FBI sources, Taheri-azar indicated that his motive was to avenge the shoddy treatment of Muslims around the world (Dalesio, 2006).

On March 10, Taheri-azar sent the following letter from Central Prison in Raleigh to a reporter at the local ABC-TV affiliate:

> Allah gives permission in the Koran for the followers of Allah to attack those who have raged war against them, with the expectation of eternal paradise in case of martyrdom and/or living one's life in obedience of all of Allah's commandments found throughout the Koran's 114 chapters. . . .
>
> The U.S. government is responsible for the deaths of and the torture of countless followers of Allah, my brothers and sisters. My attack on Americans at UNC-CH on March 3rd was in retaliation for similar attacks orchestrated by the U.S. government on my fellow followers of Allah in Iraq, Afghanistan, Palestine, Saudi Arabia, and other Islamic territories. ("Taheri-Azar Writes to Eyewitness News," 2006)

Most defensive and retaliatory hate crimes in the United States and England take the form of vandalism, intimidation, and simple assault (Iganski, Kielinger,

& Paterson, 2005: Levin & McDevitt, 2002). On occasion, however, the defensive aim of an attacker is transformed into a *mission*. The hatemonger is no longer satisfied just to remove one Black family from the neighborhood. Now he dedicates himself to eliminating as many Black Americans as possible. In some cases, the hatemonger takes his defensive stance to a new and more deadly level. He commits a pre-emptive strike against the enemy.

Shortly after midnight on February 2, 2006, 18-year-old Jacob Robida walked into Puzzles Lounge, a popular gay gathering place in the city of New Bedford, Massachusetts, 50 miles south of Boston, and ordered a drink at the bar. Then, after having one more shot of whiskey, he walked to the back of the room near a pool table and took a hatchet from his black trenchcoat. Two men were able to grab the hatchet from the assailant's hands, but not before Robida had slashed both of them in the face. He then pulled out a 9 mm pistol and shot a third man in the stomach. Next, he put the gun to his own head and pulled the trigger. When it failed to fire, Robida ran out of the front door of Puzzles Lounge and into the night.

Robida's rampage had just begun. After escaping from the gay bar where he left three men seriously wounded, he drove to Charleston, West Virginia, and picked up 33-year-old Jennifer Bailey, a woman with whom he had previously lived. The couple drove to Gassville, Arkansas, where Robida confronted police officer James Sell, who had asked him to pull over to the side of the road in a routine traffic stop. Robida first gunned down Sell, then shot to death his female companion. He finally turned the gun on himself, taking his own life as the police closed in on him (Southern Poverty Law Center, 2006).

It was no coincidence that Robida had initiated his rampage by targeting gays. The first thing he had asked the bartender before slashing and shooting patrons was, "Is this a gay bar?" According to those who knew him well, he hated gays and lesbians, but he also despised Blacks and Jews. His MySpace page contained a photograph of himself wielding a firearm with a swastika in the background. His bedroom walls were covered with anti-Semitic writings and swastikas. Robida had an extensive collection of Nazi memorabilia, including books about the Third Reich, Nazi flags, and a sword. Among his books was a copy of *The Turner Diaries*, a neo-Nazi novel that many believe had inspired Timothy McVeigh's 1995 massacre in Oklahoma City (CBS4Boston, 2006).

Young people may be disproportionately involved, but they have had no monopoly on the commission of vicious hate attacks. In June 2009, an 89-year-old White supremacist, James W. von Brunn, entered the lobby of the Holocaust Museum in Washington, DC, and shot to death a security guard who had opened the door for him. Apparently hoping to kill as many victims inside as possible, von Brunn never got the chance. Instead, he was critically wounded by other security guards who managed to stop him before he could get through the metal detectors and open fire on tourists.

Von Brunn was a long-time White supremacist and Holocaust denier who was on a mission to eliminate Blacks and Jews. Years earlier, he had served an 11-year prison sentence for his failed attempt to storm the Federal Reserve building with a shotgun and kidnap its occupants. He bragged about having spent a year behind bars for fighting a deputy sheriff in Maryland. Just days before attacking the Holocaust Museum, he walked into the Naval Academy in Annapolis, Maryland, to complain that minority enrollments were too high and to demand a meeting with officials.

Von Brunn had published an anti-Semitic treatise online entitled *Kill the Best Gentiles*. He also maintained a website, where he was free to articulate his conspiratorial and anti-Semitic ravings and rantings. After being released from prison for his kidnapping attempt, von Brunn became well known in White supremacist circles. In 2004, he lived for a period of time in Hayden, Idaho, at that time the headquarters of the neo-Nazi organization known as Aryan Nations (Emery & Robbins, 2009).

Sympathizers

Millions of Americans may not be active hatemongers or even dabblers, but they agree in principle with those who are. Such "timid bigots" can be regarded as *sympathizers*—their prejudiced attitudes are generally at a verbal level only (Merton, 1957). They may repeat a joke to their like-minded associates and that is as far as they are willing to go, but their voices give encouragement and comfort to those who express their hatred in discrimination or violence. Moreover, because of their refusal to cooperate with those who seek to bring bigots to justice, sympathizers also share responsibility for the acts that their sympathetic stance makes possible.

The sympathy for bigotry is not always clear-cut or consistent. This was indicated by a college student in the Boston area whom we recently questioned about her prejudices. She was a White woman who confessed having been told a joke that referred to another race in a derogatory way. When asked how she responded to the bigoted joke, she answered,

> It was humorous. However, this doesn't necessarily mean I agree with using the terms, because I don't (not in a serious manner). I thought the joke was funny and remembered it for my repertoire of good jokes that I tell other people who share my ideas about members of that group.

Behind Closed Doors

Though hardly represented among violent bigots, sympathizers play an especially important role in perpetuating institutionalized forms of discrimination against underrepresented groups in society. In the atmosphere of an executive boardroom, a real-estate agency, or a university admissions office, verbal bigotry may be just what it takes to stifle the ambitions of individuals who seek jobs, homes, or a place in the classroom. The individual hatred of powerful decision-makers can easily be transformed into company policy.

This was seen when it was disclosed that certain Texaco directors, while meeting together to formulate company policy concerning racial discrimination, had been caught on tape voicing racist feelings about their Black employees. Using a metaphor to discuss with sarcasm the failure of Black workers to be promoted, one director asked, "Isn't it funny how the black jelly beans seem to get stuck to the bottom of the bag?" Another complained, "I'm still having trouble with Hanukkah. Now we have Kwanzaa."

Some observers connected directors' attitudes with the fact that tiny numbers of Black workers had attained executive positions in the Texaco hierarchy. Indeed, Texaco had no Black heads of departments or vice-presidents. No Blacks sat on its board of directors (White, 1996).

An Eliminationist Anti-Semitism

Given the appropriate conditions, some sympathizers can be moved to dabble in bigotry or even to become hatemongers. According to Goldhagen (1996), tens of thousands of German citizens during the Nazi era of the 1930s, reacting to Hitler's interpretation of a terrible economic situation, translated their sympathy for anti-Semitism into mass murder.

At the Nuremberg War Crimes Trials, defendants sought unsuccessfully to elude responsibility for their participation in the Nazi slaughter by arguing they had been mesmerized into obeying the orders of a charismatic Adolf Hitler. Rather than admit that they approved of what he represented, they spoke instead of Hitler's domineering presence, his irresistible magnetism, his ability to cast a hypnotic spell. Their defense was meant to let them off the hook: "No Hitler, no Holocaust" (Weiss, 1996).

According to Weiss (1996), even the most powerful orators cannot possibly convert those who have not already bought into their ideas. Radical demagogues have the capacity to confirm but not to convince. It was not Hitler's style so much as the substance of his rhetoric that persuaded hundreds of thousands of German citizens to participate in, or at the very least not to oppose, the massacre of Jews.

Of course, there may be some limited circumstances, for example, among prisoners of war, where the control over an individual is absolute or complete. Under such conditions, it may actually be appropriate to speak in terms of "brainwashing," "mind control," or "thought reform" (Lifton, 1961). But in most of the circumstances of everyday life, individuals possess an element of free will that can only be manipulated so much. The most authoritarian and charismatic leader cannot completely undermine individual autonomy and voluntarism. In fact, it is pure myth to suggest that the members of a society collectively lack any power to resist while under the spell of a madman. Even extremely vulnerable individuals possess an "active self" that severely limits the power of the most persuasive leader to mold or shape the behavior and beliefs of his followers (Tabor & Gallagher, 1995).

Cultural Hate

It would be comforting if we were able to characterize hate and prejudice as deviant, irrational, and pathological behavior—as an aspect of the domain of a few "crazies" on the fringe of society whose psychosis is in urgent need of treatment by psychotherapy, psychotropic medications, or both. Unfortunately, hate hardly depends for its existence on individual pathology or abnormal psychology. Nor is it a form of deviance from the point of view of mainstream society. Even if the admission of being prejudiced is unacceptable, hate itself is instead normal, rational, and conventional. It is part of the culture—the way of life—of the society in which it exists, appealing typically to the most conventional and traditional of its members (Barnett, 1999; Feagin & Vera, 1995; Levin & Rabrenovic, 2009; Westie, 1964).

Even in such an extreme set of circumstances as the atrocities committed under Nazism, genocide was carried out and encouraged not by ideological fanatics and schizophrenics but by ordinary citizens. Even the perpetrators were normal by conventional mental health standards. The power of Nazism was indeed strong, but it hardly prevented most ordinary citizens from making ethical decisions and functioning in a normal way (Barnett, 1999; Browning, 1992). For example, Polish authorities suggested for decades that the Nazis had been responsible for a 1941 massacre of the Jewish residents of the town of Jedwabne. New evidence argued that it was not Nazi soldiers but ordinary Polish farmers who herded 1,600 of their Jewish neighbors into a barn and set it on fire (Stylinski, 2001).

Where it is cultural, sympathy for a particular hatred may become a widely shared and enduring element in the normal state of affairs of a group of people. Even more important, the prejudice may become systematically organized to reward individuals who are bigoted and cruel and to punish those individuals who are caring and respectful of differences (Katz, 1993). In such circumstances, tolerance for group differences may actually be regarded as rebellious behavior and those who openly express tolerance may be viewed as rebels.

Sympathizers draw their hate from the culture, developing it from an early age. As a cultural phenomenon, racism is as American as apple pie. It has been around for centuries and is learned by every generation in the same way that our most cherished cultural values have been acquired: around the dinner table; through books and television programs; from teachers, friends, and relatives (Levin & Levin, 1982; Levin & Rabrenovic, 2004b, 2009).

In the American experience, White racism has a long and deep cultural history, being traceable back centuries to the impetus in the New World for enslaving large numbers of Africans rather than White Europeans. Racism can therefore be seen not as a conscious conspiracy of powerful people or the delusional thinking of a few radical bigots. Rather, it is an important, if largely unconscious, aspect of America's historical experience and of our shared cultural order, arising from the taken-for-granted assumptions that Americans learn to make about themselves and others (Kovel, 1971; Lawrence, 1987; Smith, 1995).

Stereotyping also seems to have a cultural basis that is dependent on the cognitive development of an individual. As a result, the particular cultural images of a group of people may not be accepted, or even understood, by a child until long after she has already developed an intense hatred toward its members.

Later on, education seems to be effective in reducing stereotyped thinking. In addition, legislation can, within limits, reduce discriminatory behavior. Yet, the emotional component of hate may persevere over the course of a lifetime, regardless of attempts to modify it. Beginning so early in life, hate may become a passion for the individual who acquires it, being much harder to modify than stereotypes or the tendency to discriminate (Levin & Levin, 1982; Levin & Rabrenovic, 2009).

The cultural element of hate can be seen in its amazing ability to sweep across broad areas of a nation. Individuals separated by region, age, social class, and ethnic background all tend to share roughly the same stereotyped images of various groups. In the United States, for example, some degree of anti-Black, anti-Asian, and anti-Latino racism can be found among substantial segments of Americans—males and females, young and old, rich and poor—from New York to California, from North Dakota to Texas.

Similarly, in Nazi Germany, Hitler's condemnation of the Jews reflected not only his personal opinion, but also the beliefs of hundreds of thousands of German and Austrian citizens. While the police looked on approvingly, university students joined together to beat and batter their Jewish classmates. Faculty members and students voiced demands to rid the universities of Jews and cosponsored lectures on "the Jewish problem." Because of their genuine conviction, thousands of German soldiers and police helped to murder Jews. Civil service bureaucrats aided in doing the paperwork to expedite carrying out Hitler's extermination program. Many important business, banking, and industrial firms cooperated in the task of enslaving and murdering Jewish citizens. Thousands of German physicians cooperated in sterilizing or eliminating the "undesirables." Finally, whereas the church in other European countries denounced racist anti-Semitism, Germany's religious leaders (both Catholic and Protestant) failed to protest the final solution (Weiss, 1996).

At the cultural level, the emotional character of racial or religious hatred is reflected collectively in laws and norms that prohibit intimate contact between different groups of people. In the Deep South, Jim Crow laws created separate public facilities: "colored" and "White" restrooms, waiting rooms, water fountains, and sections on public buses. In the South African version of apartheid, Blacks were similarly restricted to living in segregated communities and could work among Whites only under the strictest supervision.

In Nazi Germany, the same sort of enduring sympathy for hate might be found among citizens concerning anti-Semitism. In explaining the particular stronghold of Hitler's "final solution," Goldhagen (1996) has argued that an "eliminationist anti-Semitism" was a long-standing feature of German culture that dated back centuries. The majority of ordinary German citizens believed that the Jews, ostensibly being responsible for all of their country's economic woes, had to be eliminated at any cost. Thus, rather than some dark and repulsive secret, gruesome stories about the Nazi's brutal anti-Jewish policies—the death camps, gas chambers, hideous experiments, and mass murders—were told and retold proudly across the land to ordinary German citizens who were eager to hear them.

Nazi anti-Semitism was located at the end of a continuum of cultural bigotry that seems to have helped determine the fate of Jews not only in Germany but in other European countries as well. Nations such as Poland and Hungary, which had a long-standing tradition of anti-Semitic attitudes and behavior, were also nations in which a large proportion of Jews was murdered; countries such as Denmark, Belgium, and Bulgaria where a tradition of tolerance and respect for religious diversity was strong were also countries where a relatively sizable proportion of Jews survived (Fein, 1979).

Culture Transcends Generations

At precisely the same time in the 1800s when it was on the decline in other western European countries, anti-Semitism increased rapidly among the populations of Germany and Austria. By the 1890s, anti-Jewish feelings had gained widespread acceptance throughout the same generation that would later bring Hitler to power. Nazism was initially only one of the political movements to espouse anti-Semitic policies. In 1919, political parties across the ideological spectrum merged to fight a more effective battle against the "rule of the Jews." Huge amounts of anti-Jewish political propaganda were disseminated to the masses (Weiss, 1996).

Moreover, even long after Hitler's death and the defeat of the Nazi movement during World War II, anti-Semitism continued to thrive and prosper. An analysis of anti-Jewish attitudes in eastern and western Germany found that strong anti-Semitism remained in western Germany even after "four decades of re-education . . . and a nearly total taboo on public expressions of anti-Semitism" (Watts, 1997, p. 219). A survey of German youngsters recently found that more than a third believe that Hitler's regime had "a good side" and nearly 40% said that Nazism had its good points. In the former East Germany, where the economy continues to be shaky, 15% of all 14- to 16-year-old respondents thought that Nazism was a good idea (Helm, 2001).

On the other side of the racial ledger, it is also no coincidence that the country of Bulgaria, whose people actively defied Hitler to a greater extent than any other Nazi-allied country, has remained at peace with itself, despite an unemployment rate varying between 13 and 15% and an ethnic mix that resembles that of its next-door neighbor, the former Yugoslavia. Just like its opposite, respect for differences often also has a cultural component.

Spectators

As we have seen, Daniel Goldhagen (1996) proposed that the specifically German form of anti-Semitism that he labels "eliminationist" in its objective was responsible for the mass extermination of Jews under Hitler. Taking a cultural viewpoint, Goldhagen argued that German anti-Semitism during the 1930s was deeply rooted in German history, finding its origins in a long-standing desire among German citizens for the liquidation of their Jewish neighbors, dating back to the nineteenth century, if not earlier. Thus, the mass murder of German

Jews under the Nazi regime involved more than a million "willing executioners." These were average German citizens who actively participated in the slaughter or who, at the very least, regarded the mass extermination of Jews as necessary for the survival of German society. Those who did the killing hardly tried to conceal their deadly jobs from family and friends; instead, they bragged and joked about their role in death camps to an eager audience of ordinary citizens.

The Failure to Act

But Goldhagen has been widely criticized for relying so heavily on German national character and culture as an explanation for the Nazi holocaust (see Shandley, 1998). Most other scholars agree with Goldhagen that anti-Semitism was a predisposing factor, but not the only one nor perhaps even the most important. Other European countries, not just Germany, had virulent forms of anti-Semitism. And many Germans, although perhaps indifferent to the plight of Jews, were hardly enthusiastic in their support of the Nazi program.

Looking at the rise of anti-Jewish policies and practices across nations, Brustein and King (2004) have suggested that cultural bigotry cannot by itself adequately explain the escalation of anti-Semitic practices in Western societies just prior to the Nazi Holocaust or variations in anti-Semitic practices across countries and time. The rise in anti-Semitism between 1879 and 1939 varied significantly depending on the extent to which Jews were perceived as a threat to non-Jews. In five countries—Germany, Romania, Great Britain, Italy, and France—anti-Semitism grew when the nation's level of prosperity deteriorated and the level of immigration of eastern European Jews increased.

This was certainly the case in Nazi Germany. There were important situational and economic factors in the German experience. For example, the breadth and depth of inflation in its economy, the charismatic leadership of the Third Reich, and the vulnerable status of Germany after World War I may have contributed significantly to the appeal of eliminationist thinking. Moreover, although the massacre of Jews was at a genocidal level, many other groups (Gypsies, elders, eastern Europeans, gays, and people with disabilities) also suffered tremendous losses.

When questioned about their cooperation with the Nazi movement, many German citizens characterized themselves as "little people" who were powerless to influence the course of Hitler's final solution. What they failed to acknowledge, however, was that millions of ordinary people throughout Germany gave their support, whether active or inactive, to Nazism. Of their own free will, many joined the Nazi party, worked to enact its policies, or encouraged their own husbands and sons to fight for the Fatherland (Katz, 1993).

In fact, many Germans were motivated to acquiesce less by cultural anti-Semitism than by self-interest. Some could not muster the courage; others took a practical path that they felt would be more beneficial. The Nazis never gained more than 37% of the vote in a free election. For a relatively few German citizens during the 1930s, eliminating Jews was a top priority; for the largest part of the German population, however, it was not (Browning, 1992).

Indeed, there seemed to be less active support and more passive acceptance of Nazi policies born of indifference, discomfort at the thought of the fate of German Jews, and fear of the Nazi leaders (Barnett, 1999).

As suggested by Elie Wiesel (1977), apathy is actually a version of complicity that facilitates the spread of hatred and bigotry. Although not acting out of an eliminationist anti-Semitism, most German citizens nevertheless accepted legal, economic, and political measures that would eventually drive Jews from Germany and into death camps. They supported measures carried out in an orderly and a legal manner such as those removing Jews from public positions in 1933, socially isolating Jews in 1935, and confiscating their property in 1938. The same German citizens who supported the legal persecution of Jews were opposed to violent anti-Semitism, for example, the boycott of 1933, the collective vandalism of 1935, and the Kristallnacht bloodletting of 1938 (Browning, 1992). When it came to the fate of the Jews, however, German citizens seemed to be increasingly apathetic. The indifference of "ordinary Germans" gave the Nazi regime exactly what it needed, the freedom to proceed toward a "final solution" (Browning, 1992).

During the 1930s, spectatorship was alive and well in German life. Very few Germans were willing to stand and be counted in opposition to the removal and massacre of Jews. Aside from cultural considerations, there were severe economic exigencies to which Hitler had promised an effective response. There were new laws allowing the persecution of Jews that would have to be violated. And there was always the threat of being discovered, turned in, and treated as a traitor (Staub, 1989).

During the Nazi era, moreover, many otherwise decent German citizens benefited in a material sense from the confiscation of Jewish property (Browning, 1992). Personal belongings and furniture were auctioned to the highest bidder, and tens of thousands of Jewish apartments were taken over. In addition, the expulsion of Jews from prestigious or lucrative occupations seriously reduced the competition for well-paying and high-status jobs. On the other side, citizens of Germany and Nazi-occupied European countries who aided Jews by concealing them from German soldiers exposed themselves to the possibility of paying the ultimate price. In one Ukranian village, for example, an entire family—including husband, wife, and three children—were shot to death for sheltering a Jewish woman (Hilberg, 1992).

The concept of the spectator can be expanded well beyond individual citizens to characterize companies, religious groups, banks, and entire countries whose decision-makers respond to bigotry with a form of passive acceptance that is tantamount to complicity. Hitler's regime was aided and abetted in moving toward its final solution by countries around the world that refused to admit Jews who were otherwise on their way to death camps, by church leaders who refused to condemn Nazism, by political leaders outside Germany who allied themselves with the Third Reich, and by western companies that supplied Hitler's subordinates with machines needed to increase the efficiency of the process for identifying, transporting, and exterminating Jews and other victims of the Nazis.

Middleman Minorities

The visibility of Jews in the social structure of Germany during the 1930s also gave them special vulnerability. During the Nazi period, German Jews represented only one-half of 1% of the country's population. But they were disproportionately located in middle- and upper-middle-class occupations—the butcher down the block, the doctor on the next street, the teacher at the local school, the reporter at the town's newspaper. Jewish wealth, therefore, tended to be of the "in your face" variety, a constant reminder to impoverished Germans that many of their Jewish neighbors were economically better off than they were. In this sense, German Jews can be regarded as a "middleman minority."

According to Beller (1997), German anti-Semitism was in part a consequence of the middleman role of Jewish citizens in German and Austrian society. He focuses particularly on the city of Vienna, where early on anti-Jewish policies and practices took hold. In the aftermath of the crash of 1873, many Austrians lost confidence in liberal political and social policies to produce prosperity for the masses. Because of restrictions on their educational and occupational opportunities, Vienna's Jews remained a distinct and separate socioeconomic community that was disproportionately represented in finance and commerce and the professions considered to be "liberal." Their friendships, alliances, and marriage partners were primarily confined to other Jews. And even though there may have been some "spatial mingling" in apartment blocks and schools, Jews kept pretty much to Jews and Christians kept pretty much to Christians.

Viennese Jews took pride in the fact that as a group they were better educated, were less involved in violent crimes, and had fewer children out of wedlock than the rest of Viennese society. Moreover, their general orientation was much more bourgeois than the overall population of Vienna, a fact that was deeply resented by Christians who were not. And, finally, Jewish writers and artists were very critical of many aspects of Viennese life. Overall, Jews were far from "humble," refusing to quietly fit into Viennese society. Even though their ancestors had been in Austria longer than those of many of their neighbors, Jews were considered outsiders, intruders, or foreigners who didn't quite belong.

In light of their poor public image and the gains that accrued to Viennese Christians, wholesale discrimination against Viennese Jews was indeed "sensible." Excluding Jews from professorships, bureaucratic positions, and student organizations meant more jobs and customers for non-Jews. Similarly, economic boycotts of Jewish companies meant more jobs and customers for non-Jews. Jews comprised almost half of Vienna's physicians and more than half of its lawyers. Excluding Jews from these professions, in a very tight and competitive job market, resulted in a major occupational advantage for Vienna's Christian population.

The vulnerability of German and Austrian Jews as a middleman minority, although arguably implicated in the development of genocidal policies on the part of the Nazi regime, is otherwise hardly unique. Hatred of middleman minorities underscores the competitive basis for much of prejudice. Throughout history, there have been certain groups of outsiders who have occupied an intermediate position between the economic elite and the masses of a particular society, often incurring the wrath of both groups. These middleman minorities often come from mother countries where they were well educated and middle class. In their host society, they typically come to play the role of small business-people and professionals. During periods of economic or political turmoil, middleman minorities have often been looted, vandalized, injured, murdered, and expelled. They have included Jews in Europe, Indians in East Africa, Chinese in the Philippines and Thailand, Cubans in Puerto Rico, and Koreans in the United States.

Middleman Minorities in the United States

Because of their position in the social structure, middleman minorities are frequently victimized not only by members of the dominant group but also by those underrepresented groups against whom they are forced to compete for small amounts of power, prestige, and wealth. Violent reaction to the middleman role of Korean Americans occurred in 1992 in the aftermath of the Rodney King beating and the subsequent trial and acquittal of the police officers involved in the attack. At the time of the Rodney King incident, many of the merchants in Black and Latino Los Angeles neighborhoods were of Korean descent. During the 1960s, many shopkeepers in Black neighborhoods were Jewish. Thus, Blacks saw Jews and then Koreans as outsiders who were taking advantage of them, didn't appreciate their business, were rude and arrogant, and had climbed the ladder of success over Black bodies to own shops and stores in the local neighborhood.

Of course, at least some part of the conflict, but not all of it, between Blacks and other groups may have been a result of cultural differences that could not be resolved. In fact, it is even reasonable to have predicted that Blacks might get along better with Jews or Koreans than with other Americans because these merchants down the block took a chance by opening marginally profitable businesses in places that were largely ignored by large corporations that opt for the vastly more profitable White suburbs or downtown shopping centers. As a result, stores in Black areas tend to be small, family-owned and -run businesses whose proprietors are required to work long hours to survive.

It is certainly not difficult to understand that in 1990s Los Angeles, at a time when they were feeling very much squeezed not only by Whites but by an increasing number of newcomers, Blacks would feel in competition with neighborhood merchants of Asian descent. Where groups differ in socially significant ways, for example, by race, religion, sexual orientation, disability status, or gender, there exists the potential for intergroup conflict. The potential is realized when the characteristics, attributes, or possessions of one group threaten (or are perceived to threaten) the well-being of another group. But the presence of a threatening difference doesn't necessarily lead to violence and discrimination, not unless there is also a sufficient degree of prejudice and hate to justify a collective effort to enslave, exile, or eliminate members of the threatening group. Thus, hate in the culture and personality provides the basis for doing harm to others by justifying an attack. When groups are in competition for scarce resources, their members are unlikely to get along. When hate and prejudice are available to characterize the opposing groups, animosity can easily turn into violence.

The American Version of Spectatorship

The forces of spectatorship at work so dramatically when Hitler's regime was in power have existed in countries around the world, including the United States. In the agrarian south, for example, slavery was widely viewed as a necessary aspect of the southern economic order generally and the plantation system of agricultural production in particular. But the one in four White southerners who owned slaves were not the only southerners who benefited from the enslavement of Black Americans. Many more were spectators who never made money directly from slavery, but they did gain indirectly from the fact that Blacks were not allowed to compete with them for jobs and they enjoyed being members of what was considered a superior caste.

Moreover, the willingness of so many Americans during World War II to play the role of spectator made possible the rounding up of thousands of Japanese Americans, forcibly removing them from their homes, confiscating their property, and relocating them to internment camps (army-style barracks ringed with barbed wire and military guards) located thousands of miles away from their homes, where many of them remained throughout the war. Even before they were relocated in 1942, Japanese Americans had already been forced to give up their jobs and were subjected to a 6:00 a.m. to 6:00 p.m. curfew as well as a five-mile limit as to where they could travel from their homes (Kochiyama, 2001).

German and Italian Americans also suffered, but not so extensively, from the same policies to reduce domestic sources of sabotage. In fact, within 72 hours of the attack on Pearl Harbor, the FBI had almost 4,000 Japanese, German, and Italian immigrants in custody. The government labeled hundreds of thousands of Italian immigrants as enemy aliens, forbidding them to leave their homes after dark, seizing their personal property, and forcing them to carry identification cards. Thousands of Italian immigrants were arrested and hundreds more were interned in military camps. Similarly, thousands of German immigrants were arrested and interned for the duration of the war. Unlike such policies regarding German Americans and Italian Americans, however, the government's treatment of Japanese Americans failed to distinguish native-born citizens from foreign-born newcomers. More than two-thirds of all Japanese Americans forced into internment camps were not immigrants. They were American citizens who were regarded as a security risk based only on their Japanese ancestry (Holian, 1998; Hummel, 1987). Using Executive Order 9066 as a legal basis, the federal government gave as its rationale that the United States was at war with Japan and simply could not afford to permit disloyal Americans of Japanese descent to sabotage the war effort. Not immigrant status, but racial identity (defined by identifying one Japanese great-grandparent) was the sole basis for being treated as the enemy and removed from American society.

Yet active cultural bigotry was only part of the story of sending Japanese Americans to internment camps. Knowing that they would be gone for some period of time, many of them sold their houses and personal property in a few days for next to nothing. Moreover, real-estate agents eagerly bought up the land left by farmers of Japanese descent. Whites could have offered to rent the residences of their Japanese American neighbors and associates, but very few made the effort. Even though many White Americans recognized the unfairness of forcibly relocating an entire group of Americans, it was hard to discover anyone who had the courage—at the risk of being regarded as disloyal to the United States—to speak out against government policy (Kochiyama, 2001).

Even today in the arena of prejudice and hate, the largest number of Americans can probably be characterized as spectators. They appear to be indifferent or apathetic rather than hateful because they do little if anything to put an end to bigotry. Whatever their mind-set, their advocacy of values embodying the "American Creed"—democracy, equality of opportunity, and respect for diversity—is limited to verbalized agreement. As a matter of abstract principle, spectators may espouse support for the equal treatment of Blacks, Latinos, Asians, and White ethnics in the major public areas of everyday life—in schools, neighborhoods, workplaces, and public accommodations. In the context of everyday decision-making, however, they stand idly by, hoping not to get themselves involved, to look different, to stand apart from others, or perhaps they are even betting on being rewarded for their indifference.

In a recent questionnaire study, we discovered many college students who were spectators in the expression of hate and prejudice. In response to a racial slur or joke, they might feel offended, but they remain absolutely silent. One such student said:

> A co-worker was talking about the American Music Awards and how disgusting many of the "colored" people dressed and acted. I was so shocked that I didn't say anything—I just ignored it.

Another student reacted as follows to hearing the word "gay" repeatedly uttered by her friends to characterize others in a negative light:

> The word gets thrown around so often among a group of friends. It is used to insult each other. I guess I am fairly used to them saying it to each other, so that I don't even respond anymore. Yet, I would never say it.

Even if they believe in principles of democracy and equality of opportunity, spectators enjoy the advantages of bigotry. Rather than participate actively, they just go along to get along. They are bystanders to a situation that they may feel powerless to change. Of course, their very inactivity, their failure to act on their convictions, tends to give license to those who are raving bigots. At the same time, spectators benefit from whatever advantages their group receives from the perpetuation of prejudice. As a result, they laugh along with their friends at the most bigoted jokes, they walk right by teenagers painting hateful graffiti, and they make no effort to stop schemes aimed at harassing their Black neighbors.[1]

Conclusion

Relatively few hate crimes are reported to the police every year, and most of those that are reported are committed not by members of organized hate groups but by dabblers in hate. In the typical hate offense, a group of bored and idle teenagers or young adults goes out on a Saturday night looking for someone to intimidate or assault. What often gets overlooked is that those who commit hate offenses are encouraged and supported by two categories of citizens: first, by sympathizers with bigotry who would perhaps never commit a hate offense themselves but are only too thrilled that others do. Those in sympathy with hate draw their thinking from the mainstream culture in which hate is widely learned and shared by members of a society. The second set of individuals, the spectators, probably represents the majority of citizens. Although they have not internalized the cultural stereotypes and emotions, they nevertheless remain passive bystanders in the face of destructive bigotry. These are the citizens who benefit from the status quo.

As we have seen, cultural standards alone cannot always explain the tremendous appeal of hate. Wherever prejudice becomes part of the culture of a society, where it is learned from an early age and widely shared, we can expect strong pressures for it to persist from generation to generation and to influence the behavior of society's members. At the same time, bigoted behavior persists not only because it becomes incorporated into cultural norms and roles and—at the individual level—is incorporated into the personality of hatemongers, dabblers, and sympathizers, but also because some of society's members believe they have a personal stake in their acceptance of hate and prejudice. We have seen, for example, how the leaders of various White supremacist groups are able to satisfy their craving to be important, while their followers gain a sense of belonging that was previously missing from their young lives (Ezekiel, 1995).

Sympathizers and spectators together create the conditions for hate crimes and ethnic violence to persist. To the extent that the culture of a society contains biased images of a particular group, then hate and prejudice will persist. For hate to be translated into hate crimes and intergroup violence, citizens must also believe that they are likely to benefit from bigotry and to suffer from tolerance. Those who are sympathetic to bigotry but who see no profit in supporting it will tend to express their hate verbally.

Indeed, even those individuals totally lacking in personal hatred may be supportive of bigoted behavior as a rational choice because they are convinced that a particular decision, even if distasteful in some of its aspects, will help to bring them the wealth, prestige, or power they believe that they so much deserve to possess or might keep them out of harm's way. It typically takes more

---

[1] In some states, gender is also included among those characteristics protected by hate crime statutes, but it is not counted among hate offenses reported nationally.

than a sympathetic attitude toward hate to create the conditions conducive for hate crimes and discrimination to thrive and prosper; it also takes convincing a sufficient number of society's members that they will benefit from their decision in support of bigotry. In many cases, this means that they support the status quo, that they simply go along with the masses, and that they become not activists but passive spectators. Moreover, when hate is being considered as a viable political option, they might take an active stance in favor of a particular law, leader, political party, or public policy that supports or encourages hate. Under different circumstances, they might be respectful of differences; but when hate and prejudice are rewarded, they are seen to be what Merton (1957) referred to as "fair-weather" liberals.

Of course, such choices may not always perfectly reflect actual self-interest, only a perception that self-interest will benefit. The appeal of rational choice is complex, involving short- versus long-term interests; personal versus social identity; an array of objectives in the economic, psychological, and social spheres; and differences in access to information about a law, leader, political party, or policy (Brustein, 1996). The consequences of spectatorship may often be ambiguous, but the intentions are clear enough.

CHAPTER 5

The Benefits of Bigotry

The concept of "interdependence" is important to our understanding of physical, social, and spiritual life. In general, the term means that the parts of a whole relate to each other in a way that assures the identity and functioning of the collective. In the physical sciences, interdependent parts are observed in molecules, in water, in food, and in all types of machines. In the social sciences, the interdependent functioning of a collection of people might be called a working group, an athletic team, a religious organization, or a society. In addition to the physical and social realms, interdependence is observed in the sacred teachings of our most prominent religious traditions, that is, the Covenant in Judaism, the Five Pillars in Islam, and the Holy Trinity in Christianity. These religions also teach us to see microcosm in macrocosm and vice versa, which is a way of experiencing interdependence at different levels of aggregation.

The related term "interdependent co-arising" means that every phenomenon that appears in the world is the result of everything else, or stated more succinctly, "This is, because that is," where "that" refers to a whole range of variables (Hanh, 2006). This is a simple but profound truth. For instance, if we look at a tree and try to explain why it exists, we have to mention the sun; the clouds; the rain; the Earth, and the position of the Earth relative to the other planets in the solar system; along with the presence of human beings, as a start. If you can finish the list you realize that you then must go on to explain the existence of all the things you just mentioned, because without any one of them the tree would not be there. If you follow this line of thinking fully, you will soon realize that everything in the universe is necessary for the tree to exist (Hanh, 2006). Western science, including social science, typically searches for cause and effect within a narrow range of variables, sacrificing knowing the entire story, given the impossible task of understanding "everything," but settling for knowing something about a few important variables.

This concept of interdependent co-arising is further explored in the story of Indra's net. In Eastern mythology there is a story about the supreme god Indra who possesses a large and wonderful net that stretches infinitely in all directions. Connected to each link in the net is a beautiful jewel. If you look inside each jewel, you will see the reflection of every other jewel in the entire net. The one jewel contains all the jewels, and at the same time it is also a part of all the jewels. This concept can be stated another way: "The one contains the all, and the all contains the one." As the story goes, if any of the jewels is touched, all of the other jewels are affected. The image of Indra's net is used to convey the eternal truth that no single phenomenon exists separate from everything else (Hanh, 2006).

We use the image of Indra's net in this chapter as a way to make an important point: that the causes of and solutions to hate violence can be touched most directly and most effectively by the average person in the local situation. The local situation might be a neighborhood, an organization inside a neighborhood, a university or a department within a university, a business office, or similar places where local people meet and interact. The local situation is often a reflection of the larger society and at the same time it is an interdependent part of the larger society. The local situation contains all the reasons why hate violence occurs. If you look deeply you will see them all right where you are. And by working to dismantle hate violence in the local situation, the whole of society reaps the benefits. Perhaps this will become clearer in the following discussion.

Figure 5.1 is our version of Indra's net as it relates to explaining the existence of hatred and discrimination in our world. For our purposes we used only eight jewels, representing eight different perspectives on the subject.[1] Each of the eight jewels has eight sides. The large letter(s) on one of the sides of each

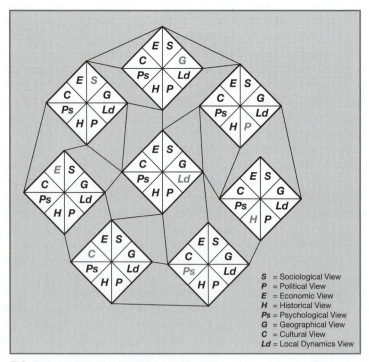

FIG. 5.1 Indra's Net of Hate Violence Theory.

S = Sociological View
P = Political View
E = Economic View
H = Historical View
Ps = Psychological View
G = Geographical View
C = Cultural View
Ld = Local Dynamics View

---

[1] We know there are many more perspectives on hate violence, but in order to make our point that all perspectives are found in every perspective we use only eight.

jewel indicates the dominant perspective of that jewel. You will notice that each jewel represents a single discipline or "way of explaining" the presence of hate violence in our society, but it also contains all the other perspectives as well. In order to explain this concept a little more clearly, let's go back to the murder of the three civil rights workers (Schwerner, Chaney, and Goodman) in Mississippi, described in chapter 3, to examine what we mean.

If we start from the historical perspective (jewel H), we might first look at the structure of racial hatred in the United States from its origins in slavery, then through the American Civil War and the Reconstruction Era, Jim Crow, and, finally, through the civil rights movement of the 1950s and 1960s. However, from the historical perspective we could not help but see the impact of geography and sociology (G and S) on our topic. Rural poverty, social isolation, limited access to resources, and dogmatic and literal views of religion were characteristic of the southern region of the United States at the time of the murders and served to maintain the ideology of White separatism and superiority. In addition, it would be difficult to proceed further in our historical view (jewel H) without also mentioning the psychology (Ps) of the people who promoted and participated in hate violence at the time, along with those who joined and supported organizations like the Ku Klux Klan. For a fuller historical understanding (jewel H) of the hate that existed at the time of the murders, one must make note of the way many citizens (particularly those who wanted to maintain the status quo) were terrorized by the civil rights movement, in part because it promised an end to political domination for Whites. These issues would also be the focus of a sociological (S) and political (P) investigation. In addition, a historical account (jewel H) is not complete without an understanding of some of the tools of oppression, including the use of the mass media, which would come from a cultural (C) and sociological view (S). Negative images of African Americans were perpetuated by the media, which over the course of history served to maintain a pool of marginalized, low-skilled employees who worked long hours for low wages in the service of White business owners. It wasn't until the 1980s that popular television programs like *The Cosby Show* portrayed African Americans in the role of professionals, such as doctors and lawyers.

The importance of this example of the historical perspective on the hatred that existed in Mississippi at the time of the Schwerner, Chaney, and Goodman murders is to show that no matter which perspective one uses to explain hate violence—that is, at which jewel you look—all of the other perspectives are also there. This idea that "all are contained in the one" holds true even if one were to look for explanations of hate and violence in the dynamics of the local situation, which we intend to do next.

In the center of Figure 5.1 is a jewel marked Ld for local dynamics. By local dynamics we are referring to the social forces that affect attitudes and behaviors in the most immediate situation or context. In addition to containing all of the historical, geographic, psychological, sociological, political, economic, and cultural forces of the larger society, local situations are places where roles, norms, and interpersonal dynamics are experienced firsthand. Local situations are also places where collective emotions such as group conflict, organizational trust, and dependence on authorities are found. What makes these group-level attributes come alive in the local situation is the fact that the members of the collective share a common goal or a common fate (Lewin, 1951). What happens in these places, good or bad, affects the overall well-being of all the members. A common goal and common fate create *a priori* interdependence among the people in these local places, which then launches interpersonal dynamics that combine with the other social forces to make things better or worse.

Both the authors know of a sociology professor at a state university who makes this point in a large section of his sociology course on the topic of juvenile delinquency. In this class there are well over 100 students, sometimes over 200. The professor asks students to gather into groups of four or five to discuss a case that he intends to give them. Once they have moved into groups and have introduced themselves to one another, the professor presents the following real-life case study:

Lionel Tate, a 12-year-old African American boy, was left alone playing with Tiffany Eunick, a 6-year-old African American girl, while Tate's mother, an off-duty Florida Highway Patrol trooper, was asleep in another room. By all accounts, Lionel Tate was large and overweight for his age, and he loved to watch professional wrestling on television. His defense attorney claimed that Lionel was emulating his professional wrestling heroes when he lifted 48-pound Tiffany into the air and slammed her onto a living room table. He then kicked and body slammed Tiffany, rendering her unconscious. Tiffany's injuries included a lacerated liver, broken ribs, and a fractured skull; she later died from these injuries. At age 12 Lionel Tate was arrested for murder (Canedy, 2001).

After presenting this short scenario, the professor asks his students the following questions: (1) What *should* happen to Lionel Tate as a consequence of his behavior in this case, and why? (2) To what extent do group members agree that this is the correct response?

The small groups discuss this case for about 30 minutes, and then each group reports its decision and reasons for its decision to the other groups. Inevitably the range of responses is very broad. Many groups argue that Lionel should receive some jail time and a period of parole where he could be supervised by "professional" authorities. They argue that he must be punished for what he did, but he also needs psychological help. On the other hand, some groups think that Lionel would benefit from in-patient care at a mental health facility rather than prison because punishment is not necessary. In every class, some groups argue that Lionel Tate should serve life in prison or be executed for this crime of murder. They say, "He should be tried as an adult and treated like an adult because he committed an adult crime." At the other end of the spectrum, groups argue that Lionel should go free with very structured outpatient mental health treatment.

The broad range of responses to this incident is very interesting, but what is really amazing is the fact that in most groups the consensus for the penalty is described as "100%," or "nearly 100%." In other words almost every student in almost every group agrees to what the group decided and why group members decided it. The professor points out this interesting fact to students: Although the intergroup variability in terms of the prescribed response to Lionel Tate's actions is broad and diverse, the intragroup variability is very small.

In explaining their actions, students usually draw from many social science theories of violence. Those who explain violence as a consequence of the social structure or social learning tend to want to forgive Lionel for his behavior and offer counseling and support. Those who think that Lionel has innate characteristics, such as low intelligence combined with ADHD or some other psychological disorder that makes him prone to violence and perhaps future killings, want to "protect society" by keeping him incarcerated for life or by executing him. So, students use theory to help themselves understand what it is they are seeing in terms of Lionel Tate's behavior. But, as the exercise points out, what they see as a group is so different from what other groups see that it is hard to imagine that each viewpoint can be correct.

The fact that there is so much group consensus in a class where viewpoints are so diverse is hard to imagine. The professor asks his students to explain how it is that groups were composed of such like-minded people. He asks, what is the probability that in a large sociology class with such diversity in thinking, as exemplified in the variety of responses to the Lionel Tate case study, students who think exactly alike would just happen to find each other in time for the group exercise? This appears to be virtually impossible and, therefore, must have another explanation.

The professor then discusses how the simple act of placing people together in a group for a common purpose (or with a common fate) can introduce forces that affect how they think and feel. The effect of the group formation and the local dynamics that occur once it is formed are virtually unnoticeable to group members. When the professor confronts students individually about their decisions, they typically hold fast to their arguments. They say that they came into the group with beliefs and ideas about the causes of violence and would have responded similarly even if they had been assigned to another group. For the most part, they honestly do not even recognize the impact on their thinking that the group has had. Once students have had a chance to publicly take a stand on Lionel Tate's fate, they tend to hold firm or "dig in" to their positions when challenged by other groups, which is another consequence of the local dynamics.

This exercise brings to the surface a point we want to make in this book, that is, that every viewpoint is *not* equally correct. At times in our recent history, university students would probably have explained Lionel Tate's behavior as a consequence of his race, meaning that he was biologically predisposed toward violence because he was Black. Even today, many sympathizers would hold this belief, but they probably would not be willing to talk openly about it except among close friends or family. The mere fact that some people hold negative and *incorrect* views about certain groups based on race, religion, ethnicity, sexual orientation, or gender is not as alarming as the fact that these views are likely to be accepted and unchallenged at the local level, such as in a group, a community, neighborhood, workplace, club or fraternity, or the like. The local dynamics then tend to reinforce these negative beliefs, serving to hold them in place.

The small group exercise conducted by the professor creates the condition of social interdependence. The group members jointly must decide what to do in this simple, but difficult, case example; they rely on one another to come to a group decision in order to satisfy the instructor's requirements. Although the actions of Lionel Tate and the information surrounding the incident are very brief and circumscribed, the incident contains much more. If you look deeply at the situation you see that it contains race and the dark history of racial discrimination in America. It also contains the impact of changing social norms, such as the increasing number of single parent families in America, and the negative effects of a modern society on our overall health and well-being, such as the pervasiveness of unhealthy fast-food restaurants and diets. In addition, the case example touches on the quiet segregation that continues to exist in many elementary and secondary schools across America, as African American children get left behind because they don't conform tightly to White middle-class norms and values. In this situation you will also see conflicting ideologies in our institutions of law and criminal justice. Finally, you will see a lucrative media market that perpetuates a culture of violence through television, radio, and the Internet.

In addition to these broader social forces that affect attitudes and behaviors in local situations, local situations, themselves, produce their own dynamics. This is easy to recognize just by thinking about yourself in high school, where many young people conform to clothing and hair styles, music interests, political and social ideas, and methods of interacting and communicating. The high school experience across cultures and geographic locations has many similarities, but there can be noticeable differences as well. When high school students change schools, for example, they are likely to notice that the rules are a bit different in the new environment and that their successful behavior in the old environment might not work as well in the new. The impact of the local situation on attitudes and behaviors is even further demonstrated if one thinks about the different ways he or she thought or behaved in college, in a church group, in the family household, or in a new career role.

The roles and norms in the local situation are not the only forces that affect how people think, feel, and behave. There are also the group dynamics that occur when two or more people come together for a common purpose or when they share a common fate. For example, groups that value conformity and cohesion may be overly inclined to agree with each other, even when the ideas are bad, a condition known as *groupthink*, or, when acting collectively individuals will sometimes give up their own moral compass and behave in ways they would not have behaved if alone, a condition known as *deindividuation*. In addition to these dynamics there are still others. For example, when conditions are right in local situations, people are more likely to obey authority figures even when they are told to do evil things, such as what happened in Nazi Germany in the 1930s and 1940s. Local group situations can even change people's perspectives, many times without them even being aware—as demonstrated in the classroom exercise.

In the pages that follow, we will explore in some detail the larger sociological explanations for hate violence (jewel S of Figure 5.1). As you read please notice how interconnected this explanation is with psychological (Ps), economic (E), political (P), and cultural (C) perspectives. Then in chapter 6 we will consider ways to overcome some of the forces that perpetuate hate violence that appear in local situations. As Indra's net demonstrates, by touching the forces of hate in local situations, we affect them everywhere. The local situation mirrors the dynamics of the larger social system and at the same time is a part of it. The local situation is where the average person experiences intergroup hate violence and where he or she can most readily take steps to dismantle it from our world.

Protest by Proxy

To some extent, hate thrives on ignorance, and those who are poorly educated tend to present themselves as most prejudiced (Chickering & Reisser, 1993; Selznick & Steinberg, 1969). Clearly, at least some people with higher levels of education simply know better how to respond with politically correct answers regarding racial and ethnic issues, thus masking their true feelings. At the same time, however, education may have a real impact on prejudice by reducing the tendency to rely on stereotyped judgments of other people. Prejudice depends for its existence on rigid thinking. And poorly educated individuals are more likely to be intolerant of ambiguity and uncertainty. As education increases, so does the ability to understand and be comfortable with complex ideas and situations (Farley, 2004).

Yet, information or moral suasion alone does not always reduce bigotry. What may be more important, if less understood, is the fact that numerous Americans, rich and poor, from all walks of life, actually *benefit* from being intolerant and hate-filled, or at least they *believe* they benefit. Their gains may be short term or long term, imagined or real, economic, social, or psychological, but such individuals depend to a considerable extent on hate to give them a sense of well-being and adequacy, to reduce uncomfortable ambiguities in their everyday lives, and to sustain their socioeconomic advantages (Levin & Levin, 1982).

Culture certainly helps to assure that hate sticks around, that it is difficult to stop, and that it thrives and prospers across generations. Cultural prejudices help to identify the groups in society whose members are to be victimized and whose members are to be spared. At the same time, prejudice would never get started in the first place—wouldn't last 20 seconds—if it weren't for the fact that certain individuals and groups are benefitting from it.

The word "hate" in the term "hate crimes" can be misleading. As we have seen, those who commit thrill and mission hate crimes are frequently motivated by a desire to be accepted, to belong, to achieve a sense of importance and power, to gain attention, and to be in charge. Those who commit defensive hate offenses often possess an economic motivation; they seek to keep their jobs or to improve their property values. The cultural stereotypes specify which groups are appropriate to attack, but they do not, by themselves, provide the motivation. This can be seen in the lack of specialization among many hatemongers. If they can't find someone Black to assault, they will go after someone gay. If they can't find someone who is gay, they will victimize an individual who is Latino, or Jewish, or disabled, or Catholic (Levin & McDevitt, 2002).

Certain questions are very telling. Would, for example, there have been a Holocaust in Nazi Germany if Jews had not existed? Given the power of what Daniel Goldhagen (1996) calls an "eliminationist anti-Semitism" in German culture and history, you might conclude, "Probably not." At the same time, considering the horrible economic conditions in Germany during the 1930s and the humiliating post–World War I international policies that brought Germany to its knees, you might conclude that some groups would still have been targeted, even if not at a genocidal level of destruction. And we know that Hitler victimized not only Jews but also gays, the elderly, the disabled, Gypsies, Poles, and the mentally ill.

Would there have been slavery in the United States in the absence of Africans to play the role of slaves? Probably yes. Hate helped to justify enslaving Blacks, but the impulse to find a source of cheap labor was totally independent of prejudice or racism. For a period of time, American Indians were enslaved. For a period of time, Whites of European descent became indentured servants who were treated as slaves for a finite period after which time they earned their freedom. If it hadn't been Africans who were enslaved, it might have been the members of some other "devalued" group.

During the 1960s, when hundreds of civil disturbances spread across the country, Black Americans in large urban centers like Los Angeles looted and destroyed most of the shops and stores in their neighborhoods, many of which were owned and operated by White Jews. Would these stores have been ransacked and burned if their proprietors had not been Jewish? The answer is probably yes. The evidence can be seen in the early 1990s when the Black and Latino residents of Los Angeles' inner-city neighborhoods destroyed thousands of stores and shops owned by Korean Americans.

Given their vulnerability, racial and religious minorities are frequently targets of displaced aggression for members of society who are profoundly frustrated in their efforts to be successful and, for one reason or another, cannot express their hostility toward the true source of their problems. Instead, they engage in *protest by proxy*. That is, they scapegoat on a collective level by constructing an evil force, an enemy, that becomes the perceived source of their predicament and the object of their animosity and therefore deserving of punishment.

The deep recession of the early 1980s convinced some destitute and out-of-work automobile workers, farmers, ranchers, miners, and workers in the timber industry that Jews, Asians, and Blacks were responsible for all of their economic woes. Up to the late 1980s, during the so-called "cold war" era, many Americans traced their personal problems to the conspiratorial activities of the "evil empire" located in the vast and powerful republics under the control of the Soviet Union.

With the demise of eastern European communism, however, it became more difficult to externalize responsibility for America's miseries. The enemy had to be reconstructed. Instead of locating evil in Moscow, more and more Americans found it in Washington, DC; New York; and Hollywood. Since the 1970s, the credibility of all leadership positions in the United States (government, science, medicine, education, business, and even religion) has seriously eroded. Fewer and fewer Americans now believe that people in positions of power represent the interests of the average citizen. In fact, some are convinced that communists have taken over the White House, the Supreme Court, and Congress (Halpern & Levin, 1996; Karl, 1995). In a recent Gallup poll, less than 20% of all Americans rated the honesty and ethics of the following occupational groups as "high" or "very high": lawyers, labor union leaders, real-estate agents, stockbrokers, congressmen, car salesmen, telemarketers, business executives, and advertising practitioners (Saad, 2008).

Protest by proxy gives a sense of satisfaction not possible if one attacks vague and abstract economic and social forces. Thus, instead of blaming global competition, corporate downsizing, and automation for putting them out of work, some Americans prefer to put a human (or subhuman) face on the enemy: communists in the White House, the Satanic Jewish lobby, Blacks and Latinos who unjustly receive special treatment and privileges, or the menace of immigration.

Protest by proxy is connected with a long history of violence being perpetrated, during periods of economic turmoil and bad times, against vulnerable and marginalized groups. Between 1800 and 1930, whenever the cotton crops failed in southern states, Blacks were lynched. At low points in the business cycle, Ku Klux Klan (KKK) membership rose. During the Great Depression of the 1930s, there were 114 organizations whose purpose was to spread anti-Semitism, and there were numerous nativist organizations whose purpose was to reduce the flow of immigrants to zero. It is hard to bash an abstraction; for someone whose life has been torn apart by failure, it may be much more psychologically satisfying to burn a house of worship, to blow up a building, or to bludgeon someone to death with a baseball bat.

As introduced in chapter 2, protest by proxy has been expressed in what some observers have labeled the "new anti-Semitism" (Chesler, 2003; Iganski & Kosmin, 2003). Thoroughly outraged by American policies that support an Israeli presence in the Middle East and anti-immigrant policies in European countries, some Muslims and Arabs as well as Europeans have adopted a posture of hostility and conflict. But rather than aim their attack directly at the West, at capitalism, at the United States, or even at Israelis, certain extremists have instead attacked a more vulnerable group—Jews around the world.

In September 2005, a series of cartoons depicting the Islamic prophet Mohammed unfavorably (e.g., as a suicide bomber) were published in the Danish newspaper *Jyllands-Posten*. By February 1, 2006, the same satirical cartoons had appeared in newspapers across the world from Switzerland to Australia, from Germany to Japan. In response, outraged Muslims hurled gasoline bombs and stones at Danish embassies. In the Middle East, Asia, and Africa, tens of thousands of angry Muslims demonstrated in the streets. Police opened fire on Afghan rioters as they attacked a base of Norwegian NATO troops with grenades and guns. After threats against their lives were issued, the cartoonists whose drawings had inspired a firestorm of protest in the Muslim world reportedly went into hiding under police protection.

Then in January 2015, heavily armed members of the Islamic terrorist group al-Qaeda stormed the offices of the French satirical magazine *Charlie Hebdo* in Paris. The terrorists interrupted a staff meeting, killing 12 people and injuring 11 more. Witnesses say the journalists were shot in the head "execution style." *Charlie Hebdo* was targeted for its controversial portrayals of the prophet Mohammed. Stephane Charbonnier, the magazine's editor in chief, was killed in the attack. Charbonnier had been on a publicized al-Qaeda "hit list" for two years prior to the terrorist assault (CBS/AP, 2015).

The extremity of the Muslim response to the satirical treatment of their religious beliefs may, in part, be a function of differences in theology. For Muslims, depicting the prophet Mohammed in satirical form was nothing short of blasphemous. Westerners were viewed by millions of observant Muslims as initiating a vicious attack on Islamic religious beliefs. From the Muslim point of view, publishing cartoons degrading Mohammed was only the latest in a long series of insensitive acts committed against Islam by Westerners. When asked in a Gallup survey what Western countries could do to improve relations with the Muslim–Arab world, the most common reply from citizens of predominantly Islamic nations (from Morocco to Indonesia) was that they should demonstrate greater respect and tolerance for Islam (Esposito, 2006).

In addition, even prior to the September 11, 2001, attack on America, many White Europeans were already voicing, in angry and intolerant tones, their concern that an influx of guest workers and refugees was changing the basic character of their countries—and not for the better. Increasing numbers of Europeans began to support right-wing political movements aimed at reducing the flow of immigration. For example, a March 2000 Harris survey determined that 60% of French adults believed that too many people of "foreign origin" were in France; 63% told pollsters there were too many Arabs (Australia Immigration Visa Services, 2000).

After September 11, 2001, the conflict only worsened. Muslims were very much aware of the heightened wave of anti-Muslim sentiment sweeping through European nations, part of which was but one aspect of an increasing intolerance for any group regarded as "foreign." A 2005 Harris poll of adults in Great Britain found 73% agreeing that "the current government has been too lax with regard to its immigration policy" (Harris Interactive, 2005). Another survey of violent hate crimes concluded that since the 9/11 attack on America, a message of xenophobia has infiltrated political movements throughout Europe (McClintock, 2005).

In 2015, as Syria's internal conflict exploded and civil war erupted in full force, more than a million migrants and refugees crossed into European countries, seeking to escape the extreme violence in their homeland. Most were Syrian, but others came from the war-torn countries of Afghanistan and Iraq as well as impoverished Kosovo. Struggling to cope with the crisis imposed by an influx of newcomers, member states of the European Union were divided on how to deal with resettling the migrants, most of whom were of the Islamic faith. In most cases, the newcomers were relocated into cultural ghettos, where they hardly interacted with the native population and its mainstream institutions.

Long before the influx of Syrians headed to Germany, Hungary, Austria, and other European countries, right-wing extremists voiced their opposition to Islamic newcomers. In Denmark, where the cartoons satirizing Mohammed were originally published, an anti-immigrant party won 12% of the vote in a parliamentary election in November 2001. Opinion surveys reported that a growing number of Danish citizens were resentful of foreigners, seeing them as welfare recipients, terrorists, and criminals. Campaign posters portraying a young blonde girl said: "When she retires, Denmark will have a Muslim majority" (Finn, 2002, p. A1).

It would seem all but inconceivable for Islamic leaders rationally to blame Jews for producing blasphemous images of Mohammad, but that didn't stop them from going on an anti-Jewish tirade. Rather than attack Christianity, for example, one of Iran's most popular newspapers announced sponsorship of a contest to locate the best Holocaust cartoon (Birsel, 2006). This response was seen as particularly vengeful, in light of the statements attributed to Iran's president Mahmoud Ahmadinejad that the Holocaust carried out by the Nazis was a myth (Australian Broadcasting Corporation, 2005). More recently, Iran's supreme religious leader Ayatollah Ali Khamenei called the offensive cartoons a "Zionist conspiracy" (Associated Press, 2005). Ironically, Arab Americans and Muslim Americans have also become victims of protest by proxy. Americans eager to place the responsibility for the September 11 terrorist attack found it less than psychologically satisfying to blame some shadowy figure named Osama bin Laden, located thousands of miles away, whom they had seen a few times over the years on low-quality videotapes or in fuzzy newspaper photographs. In sharp contrast, their Muslim American and Arab American neighbors and coworkers were easier to identify and close at hand. Some wore headscarves and veils; many stopped to pray several times daily. They had foreign-sounding accents and dark skin. They weren't the terrorists aboard the doomed airplanes that hit the Pentagon and World Trade Center; they weren't involved in the more recent terrorist attacks in Paris and Brussels; but they shared enough characteristics with these Middle Eastern terrorists to provide a convenient scapegoat (Levin & Rabrenovic, 2004b).

Psychological Advantages

In the short run, hate generates some important psychological advantages. It gives a temporary boost to self-esteem and makes sense of a world that might otherwise seem chaotic and unpredictable. Rather than do the hard work of dealing directly with their problems, bigots continue to cover them up, sidestep them, and deny that they exist. In the long run, hate has the capacity to destroy those who hate or, at the very least, make their lives miserable. But in the meantime, they receive a much-needed boost to their egos and the basis for living in an apparently predictable world.

Enhancing and Protecting Self-Esteem

Hate directed against a specific group of people is learned. It is not inborn. Individuals learn to be bigots; they are taught which groups to despise, which groups to avoid, and which groups to oppose. At the same time, there may be predispositions, developed through evolution and programmed at birth into the human being, that tend universally to foster a preference for an individual's own group members and that might contribute to hate if not effectively controlled (Fishbein, 1996).

Individuals tend to identify with groups. Their self-esteem may be some function of how they feel about themselves and how they feel about their group memberships. Thus, they may experience higher self-esteem if they think their group is superior; they may feel worse about themselves if they consider their group inferior to others. Social identity affects personal identity (Brown, 1986; Fishbein, 1996).

According to research by Tajfel, Billig, Bundy, and Flament (1971), it is merely the act of being assigned to a group (any minimal group) that creates the full in-group preference. In other words, just being assigned by the flip of a coin to a group named A rather than to a group called B is enough to make an individual prefer group A over group B. Therefore, just because of their membership in the group, many people tend to attribute positive characteristics and good deeds to individuals in the group to which they belong and negative characteristics and bad deeds to everybody else (Billig & Tajfel, 1973; Locksley, Ortiz, & Hepburn, 1980). Strangers may be devalued simply because they are outsiders who don't belong (Beck, 1999). Moreover, there is a tendency for individuals to better remember the good behavior of the in-group and to better remember the bad behavior of the out-group (Rothbard, Evans, & Fulero, 1979).

The phenomenon of "minimal group favoritism" seems to exist, but it hardly explains the levels of violence, hate, and destruction (genocide, slavery, mass murder) that have been aimed throughout history at the members of various out-groups. Nor does the minimal group effect explain wide variations in the groups selected for victimization—Muslims in one circumstance, Jews in another, Latinos in still another, and so on.

Social psychologists have long argued for the existence of a personality type that encourages the scapegoating of vulnerable victims. Prejudice is part of our culture, but it also serves an important psychological need for self-esteem and respectability. The target of prejudice is selected because he has been widely stereotyped as inferior, as dirty or lazy or stupid or immoral or alcoholic or sly or treacherous or whatever. Through a process of social comparison, the perpetrator is able to gain a sense of her own superiority, for example, as beautiful, smart, or moral, only to the extent that she places the victim in an inferior position.

This zero-sum definition of respectability can be found in early versions of a work called *The Authoritarian Personality* (Adorno, Frankel-Brunswick, Levinson, & Sanford, 1950; Stone, 1993). It describes a psychoanalytic theory generated by a group of refugees from Nazi Germany who sought to locate in early childhood the genesis of anti-Semitism and other forms of bigotry. According to the original conception, the authoritarian personality was a syndrome of symptoms in which prejudice was the basic pathology. First, from this point of view, authoritarians are *ethnocentric*, that is, they express a generalized hostility toward a range of groups considered by cultural norms to be weak or inferior. If they hate Blacks, ethnocentrics are likely to despise Jews, Latinos, and Asians as well. Characteristics of the victim are more or less irrelevant and take a backseat psychologically to the authoritarian aggressor's need for power, dominance, and control. To overcome their feelings of inferiority and powerlessness, authoritarians come to identify with powerful figures (e.g., with Hitler) and to despise any and all groups stereotyped as weak or inferior. Second, authoritarians tend to have extreme right-wing political views. They are antidemocratic; they are fascists and ardent anticommunists who resemble Hitler and his henchmen in terms of political ideology. Third, according to this theory, prejudice has its roots in harsh and threatening child-rearing practices. Imitation of a youngster's parents' bigoted attitudes is not regarded as an important source of hate; instead, it is the way in which the child is raised that determines whether he eventually develops a psychological need for prejudice and takes an authoritarian perspective. Thus, the young child in an authoritarian family is rigidly relegated to the role of the dependent and submissive underling. The child is subjected to severe, even brutal, discipline. Because of being maltreated at an early age, the bigoted youngster grows up feeling a profound sense of powerlessness. As an adult, to compensate, he identifies with powerful elements of society and seeks to distance himself from groups stereotyped as inferior, weak, and powerless. This is the basis for his hate (Adorno, Frankel-Brunswick, Levinson, & Sanford, 1950).

In literally thousands of studies since the 1950s, many of the ideas contained in the theory of the authoritarian personality have been confirmed and others have been rejected or qualified. In the original view, for example, prejudice was associated exclusively with an extreme right-wing political orientation. In light of the systematic anti-Semitism of Hitler's fascist regime from which they had escaped, it seemed to the creators of the theory that fascism and bigotry were integrally connected. They could not imagine what subsequent research would reveal, namely, that prejudice can be located at any point along the political spectrum. Thus, there are bigots on the left, bigots on the right, and bigots in the middle. Indeed, there are even some bigots who are entirely without any political position at all (Rokeach, 1952).

More recently, social psychologists have turned their attention to what they call a "social dominance orientation," a term that identifies individuals who want their own group to predominate and be superior to other groups (Sidanius, Pratto, & Bobo, 1994). Those who have a social dominance orientation agree with the following statements: "Some people are just more worthy than others." "It is sometimes necessary to step on others to get ahead in life." "Some groups are simply not the equal of others." Individuals oriented to social dominance believe that superior groups (including their own, of course) are deserving of greater wealth and power and that inferior groups are deserving of far less. In an effort to justify such beliefs, those with a social dominance perspective often accept the negative stereotypes and prejudices in their culture that characterize minority groups in a negative light (Pratto, Sidanius, Stallworth, & Malle, 1994). Such subhuman images make it possible to behave with moral impunity in accordance with social dominance beliefs.

It is interesting to note the important role of bigotry in various efforts and movements apparently designed to enhance the sense of power and dominance of individuals who have so little of either. The two young members of the "Trenchcoat Mafia" who in April 1999 went on a shooting spree at their Littleton, Colorado, high school timed their attack to occur on Hitler's birthday. Just as they had planned, the two young shooters, Harris and Klebold, even in death gained the attention of the nation. This is apparently precisely what they craved. They wanted to be important by having a major, if deadly, impact on those who had rejected them: classmates, teachers, and society at large. Similarly, Dion Terres, a young man who killed two people randomly in a Kenosha, Wisconsin, McDonald's and then took his own life, was hardly a dedicated Nazi; yet he had hung a large Nazi flag in his living room as a symbol of power and dominance. Terres felt that he had lost all control over his life and blamed his family and friends for all of his misfortunes. Just before going on a rampage, he expressed his admiration for Hitler's quest for world domination, an effort that came very close to succeeding.

The first author hates to admit it, but he has appeared several times on the *Jerry Springer Show*. The author in his own defense hastens to add that he was on *Springer* when the show was actually an intellectual and moral notch above most of the other talk shows. Shortly after his last appearance, *Springer*'s ratings plummeted (could my appearance have helped?) and so apparently did the show's ethical standards.

On his final visit, he was on *Springer* along with three racist skinheads[2] who appeared dressed in Nazi uniforms complete with armbands. One also had a Charles Manson–like swastika tattoo etched in the middle of his forehead. It became very clear over the course of the program that these three young men were totally unsophisticated with respect to Nazi or White supremacist ideology or history. It occurred to the author then that the three skinheads could just as easily have joined a gang or a cult. They were marginalized youngsters who weren't getting along at home, weren't making it at school with their peers, and had little hope of ever having anything more than dead-end jobs. But they were looking desperately to feel important. The Nazi uniforms and tattoo had only one purpose for them: to give them a sense of power. At home and at school, they were treated like outcasts. But among their Nazi skinhead friends, they felt special, in charge of things, like big shots.[3]

---

[2] It should be noted that not all skinheads are racists. In fact, there are groups of antiracist skinheads, gay skinheads, and people of color who are in skinhead groups. The common denominator among all such skinhead groups seems to be a willingness to use violence as a means for resolving differences.

[3] Because this may not seem very important, we are placing it in a footnote. When the first author appeared on *Springer*, during a commercial break, the producer instructed him to be seated next to one of the three skinheads on the program. Not realizing that his mike was open and that he could be overheard in the control room, the skinhead pointed in the first author's direction and whispered to one of his buddies, "I feel like killing this guy." At this point, the producer rushed onto the set and informed the author of the conversation between the skinhead guests. Of course, he did the prudent thing and asked the producer

Many hatemongers who join racist skinhead groups gain a great deal on the psychological level (Ezekiel, 1995; Hamm, 1994). Growing up, many of them were never entirely accepted by their peers. Instead, other students considered them geeks, nerds, weirdos, or bullies. Many were like Harris and Klebold, the mass murderers at Columbine High School who took the lives of 12 students and a teacher. And not unlike Harris and Klebold, many hatemongers rely heavily on fellow outcasts for their sense of identity, belonging, and importance. Or, like Seung-Hui Cho, the Virginia Tech student who, in April 2007, shot to death 32 students and faculty members, before turning the gun on himself, they become totally isolated from any sources of social influence.

Since the April 2007 massacre at Virginia Tech, the issue of bullying has become newsworthy. Cho had been humiliated, teased, bullied, or ignored long before becoming an undergraduate in Blacksburg, Virginia. He had relocated with his family to the United States from Seoul, South Korea, at the age of eight. And from that time on, through his elementary, middle, and high school years, Cho was an object of scorn and ridicule from his schoolmates who, on a daily basis, chastised him for his shyness, poor English, foreign accent, and flat affect. At Virginia Tech, Cho was pretty much on his own, lacking any meaningful friendships with other students on campus. He wanted desperately to be powerful and dominant. In the midst of his killing spree, after killing his first two victims, Cho took a break and walked to the local post office, where he mailed to NBC News a number of photographs, showing himself as a powerful and dangerous person—with guns and knives at the ready—who could no longer be ignored. After placing the photos in the mail, Cho went back on campus and murdered 30 more innocent human beings.

Unfortunately, the recent attention given to bullying in public schools arose out of a collective desire to identify students, like Cho, who might get angry enough to murder their classmates. Although understandable, this motivation fails to recognize two important things about bullying: First, it is a pervasive problem, having profoundly impacted the lives of countless students around the country who, because of some difference from the norm, simply do not measure up to the expectations of their peers; second, that bullying is a long-standing problem, having afflicted students not just during the past few years but for many decades.

Very few bullied students get even with their tormentors, but they continue to harbor resentment and hate not only for their classmates but also for any group considered weak by conventional standards. Many more internalize the stigma and grow up believing that they are inferior. Others become social isolates who come to have a general distrust of other people. Some who experience an intimidating school environment claim that their lives are destroyed; most are at least uncomfortable during their years of attending middle and high

---

to move him to a position on the stage where it would be harder to get him. One more thing is worth reporting. After the show, while being driven to the airport, the three skinheads asked the driver to stop the car and let them out in downtown Chicago. Still wearing their Nazi uniforms, they immediately walked into a Burger King and only came out when the police arrived and carted them off to jail. We understand they were charged with assault.

school (Bonds & Stoker, 2000). Still others become the authoritarian personalities addressed in the theory of authoritarianism and eventually identify with the aggressor. They become the biggest bullies on the block and victimize any student who shows weakness or frailty.

Being from a different race, religion, nationality, or sexual orientation is frequently a basis for victimization by bullies. In March 2001, a 14-year-old girl in Wiliamsport, Pennsylvania, allegedly shot her classmate in the shoulder with her father's .22 caliber handgun. Reportedly, the suspect was protecting an Asian student who had been bullied and harassed by the shooting victim (Reuters, 2001).

Gay students, or those students who appear to be gay, seem to be victimized with special enthusiasm. They get used to finding the word "fag" spelled out in pink lipstick on their lockers or having to confront the taunting words "faggot" or "dyke" just inches from the face of their tormentor (Berrill, 1992). The bullying occasionally takes an especially ugly turn. In one suburban Omaha high school, for example, a senior found a note in his mailbox written in boldface in purple letters: "All fags must die. You first" (Laue, 2000).

In a case of harassment involving a physical disability, a student in Stanwood, Washington, recounted her many years of enduring the intimidating and taunting behavior of her schoolmates. The 19-year-old woman, Taya Haugstad, who was born with cerebral palsy in Calcutta, India, was, from the fifth grade on, the target of intimidation by other students who mocked her body movements, taunted her with obscenities and name-calling, and blocked her wheelchair. In middle school, another student forced Haugstad's hand from the joystick that controlled her wheelchair, causing Haugstad to swerve into a wall and strike her head (DeMillo, 2000; Stevick, 2000).

In response to the constant bullying, Haugstad often put her head in her hands and cried. She begged her tormentors to stop. At night, she cried in her sleep and experienced nightmares in which she relived the harassing behavior she had received during the school day. By the time she reached high school, the young woman had completely withdrawn.

Reducing Uncertainty

In addition to enhancing or protecting self-esteem, hate also provides individuals with the schema or cognitive blueprint they seek in order to organize, recall, and make sense out of the ambiguities of everyday experiences. Stereotyping gives hatemongers an important edge by making their world seem predictable. *Blacks are lazy; Whites can't be trusted; Latinos are dirty; Asians are rude; Women are emotional; Irish are pugnacious; Jews are mercenary; Muslims are terrorists*; and so on. Such information comes not from the difficult process of getting to know someone; it is simply assumed to be true based on preconceived images (Farley, 2005; Wyer & Srull, 1994).

Prejudiced individuals tend to be intolerant of ambiguities. They desire absolute and unequivocal feelings about themselves and others and emphasize and exaggerate strengths in themselves and the accomplishments of their own group. They focus only on the weaknesses of out-group members (Steiner & Johnson, 1963; Triandis & Triandis, 1972).

Locating the enemy takes on particular importance for a hatemonger. In an early study, Rokeach (1952) found that extremely prejudiced subjects were afraid to admit defeat when confronted with the challenging task of correctly matching names with the faces of strangers. Whereas prejudiced subjects made numerous erroneous guesses, subjects with less prejudice more often admitted being confused and were less willing to take wild guesses.

In 1972, Quanty, Keats, and Harkins found that anti-Semites were more willing to label a face Jewish on the basis of limited information than were tolerant individuals. When asked to identify a number of photographs as Jewish or non-Jewish, the anti-Semites thought that they saw more Jews but were also more inaccurate than their unprejudiced counterparts. "They seem more concerned with correctly identifying Jews than they are with falsely labeling a person Jewish" (Quanty, Keats, & Harkins, 1972, p. 454).

The results obtained in a more recent study suggest that very prejudiced people give an inordinate amount of attention to information about the group of people they hate. When asked to determine the racial identity of a racially ambiguous stranger, they take significantly more time to make a decision (Blascovich, Wyer, Swart, & Kibler, 1997). Moreover, prejudiced individuals remember with greater accuracy the information that supports their stereotypical beliefs than the information that contradicts them (Fiske & Neuberg, 1990).

Economic and Status Advantages

As we have seen, some historians have suggested that the appeal of Nazism took advantage of widespread sympathy for a unique theme of hate in mainstream German culture. In this view, Hitler came to power because of his eliminationist anti-Semitism in which Jews were portrayed as the vermin responsible for all of Germany's economic woes. According to Brustein (1996), however, rational choice rather than bigotry may have been responsible for much of the success of the Nazi party in its early efforts to garner popular support and increase its membership rolls. Those who voted for and actively supported the Nazi movement were German citizens who believed they had the most to gain from its success.

Self-interest, or at least the perception of self-interest, may be at the basis of much intergroup hostility. In the expression of hate, perpetrators, sympathizers, and spectators all stand to benefit in a very material sense. Bigotry provides the members of society and its rulers with a number of important economic and status advantages.

Getting the Dirty Work Done

In every society, certain jobs and responsibilities are seen as sinful, undignified, menial, or physically dirty. They may also be regarded as absolutely essential for the well-being of the population or its rulers. Throughout history, much of a society's dirtiest work has been reserved for those individuals relegated to a position outside the mainstream, frequently those who are already stigmatized and vulnerable.

The history of the Jews is replete with such examples. During the Middle Ages, whenever they were regarded by those in power as capable of playing a valuable role, Jews were tolerated and frequently treated respectfully. Beginning in the sixth century, Jews were invited to settle in France, Germany, and Italy so that they could help develop city life, spread trade and commerce, and serve in the monarch's court as advisors and diplomats. The feudal system of the day consisted of nobles, priests, and serfs; it did not include a merchant class. Thus, Jews were left with an important role to play. They soon became Europe's middle class—its merchants, bankers, artisans, judges, and jewelers.

In their position outside both the feudal system and Catholicism, Jews were uniquely qualified to perform the essential service of lending money at interest, an activity absolutely forbidden on religious grounds to the Christian majority. The medieval church considered the lending of money sinful regardless of the amount of interest charged or the purpose for which money was borrowed. Thus, a Christian who today receives 3% interest on a savings account would, during the Middle Ages, have committed a mortal sin. Yet, money lending was, at the same time, considered necessary by both the church and the nobility as a source of outside financing for building, farming, waging war, and engaging in political affairs. In the eyes of the medieval church, Jews were already headed for damnation; their participation in money-lending could add little to the eternal punishment that awaited them in the hereafter. Thus, Christians used Jews to perform important banking functions they could not perform themselves in the same way that Jews often used their Christian neighbors to conduct affairs on the Sabbath that they themselves were prohibited by religious tradition from conducting (Dimont, 1962).

Similarly, the presence of dirty yet essential tasks motivated the development of slavery in the New World. The enslavement of Blacks may have derived its initial impetus from an acute labor shortage existing in colonial America that could not be resolved satisfactorily by means of European manpower. At least half of the White European immigrants to colonial America paid their passage to the New World by obligating themselves as servants for periods ranging from two to seven years (Horton & Horton, 2006; Kolchin, 2003; Schneider, 2006; Stampp, 1956). When sources of White labor threatened to dry up, America shifted its attention to Africa.

Southerners could have turned entirely to White labor, but they would have sacrificed the several advantages that only slavery could have provided. First, an average White laborer was paid more than the cost of investing in and maintaining his enslaved counterpart. Second, the slave owner was far better able to exploit Black women and children. Third, a master could require his slaves to work longer hours under more difficult conditions without having to negotiate with his workers or with their labor unions. Finally, slave ownership was a symbol of status that identified the master with a privileged social class in the South (Horton & Horton, 2006; Kolchin, 2003; Schneider, 2006; Stampp,

1956). As we have seen, the absolute distinction between free and slave labor that developed on the basis of race alone assured that all Whites could feel they were members of a superior racial group. Moreover, slavery was a method for limiting competition from Blacks (Wilhelm, 1970).

Less obviously, the many White northerners who benefited from slavery in the South contributed to its development and maintenance. Many of the ships that carried slaves to plantations in the South were owned by northern merchants and built in northern shipyards. The slave trade in the northern colonies spawned numerous ancillary businesses such as cotton mills, rum distilleries, and iron foundries. Northern insurance companies benefited by insuring slaves, and northern newspapers ran advertisements in which they urged citizens to return runaway slaves in return for large cash rewards. Northern blacksmiths made the chains to keep slaves from escaping and manufactured the barrels for rum whiskey (Robertson & Kerber, 2000).

For a period of time, American Indians also were enslaved by the White colonials, but several factors mitigated against making American Indians into slaves as a general policy. First, their adaptation to plantation life was impeded by cultural factors. Second, American Indians could often escape to the protection of their own tribes that lived near the plantation. Third, early White settlers feared neighboring tribes and sought their friendship more than their labor. As a result, a predominantly African ancestry became the requirement for enslavement (Stampp, 1956).

In the southern colonies, a few powerful Americans, predominantly planters, shared a need for numerous slaves who could be trained and controlled for profitable exploitation (Noel, 1968). As a result, the vast majority of southern slaves filled the roles of field hands and domestic servants, and a smaller number of slaves were employed as needed in saltworks, mines, railroad construction, textile mills, and in other occupations that required specialized skills (Horton & Horton, 2006; Kolchin, 2003; Logan, 1954; Schneider, 2006). Also as a result of the need for exploitable labor, slavery soon came to be regarded as a kind of "White man's burden," as a moral and religious obligation on the part of White southerners that was divinely ordained and ultimately beneficial to the "uncivilized" and "inferior" Black slave (Comer, 1972; Genovese, 1969; Levin & Levin, 1982).

The changing character of California's farmworkers over many decades illustrates the influence of sheer availability on the fate of those selected to do low-paying and physically challenging jobs. American Indians were California's first farmworkers, at a time when agricultural production was restricted to cattle and wheat. But a subsequent influx of Chinese immigrants soon changed the nature of farmwork in California. By 1870, as work on the transcontinental railroad was coming to an end, Chinese laborers turned for work to California's farmland. Partly because of the availability of a large supply of Chinese workers, the state's agricultural patterns shifted from livestock and wheat to fruits and vegetables, crops requiring much larger amounts of hand labor.

The supply of abundant Chinese labor continued until 1882, when Congress suspended Chinese immigration. At about the same time, however, the Japanese government lifted its ban on emigration, permitting sizable numbers of workers from the rice paddies of Japan to travel to the West Coast of the United States. Until the early decades of the twentieth century, when anti-Japanese sentiment arose in full force, Japanese immigrants were a major source of farm labor in California. After 1910, however, the upheaval of revolution south of the border persuaded tens of thousands of rural Mexicans to flee to the safety of the United States. From that time to the present day, Mexicans have continued to represent the most important source of California's farm labor (Daniels, 2002). Some now argue that we are in need of large numbers of immigrants—illegal or not—to do the dirty work that native-born Americans shun. Such jobs include unskilled labor (especially if it requires getting their hands dirty), landscaping, harvesting fruits and vegetables, entry-level construction, and cleaning hotel rooms, as well as busing and cooking in restaurants.

Eliminating Opponents

Getting the dirty work done is hardly the only economic benefit derived from hate and prejudice. Depending on prevailing economic circumstances, the members of a society may become more active in seeking new avenues for assuring their own economic and status survival. When they are threatened, some may attempt to eliminate their competitors for scarce resources. Because of their vulnerability as stigmatized "outsiders," minority group members make especially effective targets of hate and hostility.

Until the eleventh century, the medieval church was, in large part, tolerant of its Jewish citizens, including those who refused to convert to Christianity. In the early centuries of the Middle Ages, Catholics continued to cling to the hope that Jews would someday see the light and abandon their mistaken religious beliefs in favor of the superior Christian alternative. In most quarters, violence was simply not regarded as a necessary proselytizing tactic. Instead, Jews were excluded from the feudal system so that their heretical beliefs and rituals could not contaminate the Christian majority. Still, the Jewish role was considered an important one.

But large-scale persecution of European Jewry began in earnest during the eleventh century as the opening campaigns of the Crusades swept the land, and not only Jews but Muslims as well as recalcitrant non-Christians became potential victims of brutality. Those who refused to convert were seen as a threat to the veracity of the Christian version of a universal deity. Jews were banished from several European countries or fled to escape being massacred.

Motivations for the Crusades were mixed. Countless numbers of Crusaders were devout Christians who sincerely sought to spread the word of God to the infidel. Others had an ulterior and more-worldly motive, however: For their participation, sinners were absolved, criminals were pardoned, and serfs were granted their freedom. Still others joined the Crusades to plunder the wealthy or simply to delight in killing with impunity.

Charges of diabolical Jewish religious rituals suddenly were heard repeated by those who were eager to justify their murderous onslaught. Many argued that Jews murdered Christian children to spray their blood over the Passover matzoh (unleavened bread) as part of an ancient holiday ritual. Or that Jews re-enacted the crucifixion by stealing the communion wafer (representing the body of Christ) and stabbing it with a sharp knife until it bled. Rumors spread that Jews possessed an odor of evil that miraculously disappeared upon their conversion to Christianity. According to other rumors, Jews were held responsible for poisoning the wells of Europe, thereby causing the epidemic of Black Death that swept through many European cities with devastating impact, frequently killing Christians and Jews alike (Weiss, 1996).

Such anti-Jewish stereotypes spread just as the policies of church and state began to shift profoundly in the direction of intolerance and discrimination. The dehumanization of European Jewry effectively supported not only religious persecution but economic disengagement as well. By the year 1200, recognizing the advantages of the money-lending role, Christians began to supplant Jewish bankers. As the feudal system disintegrated around them, Jews were forced out of their positions in the business community, generally to make room for Christians who sought to eliminate their Jewish competitors. By law, Jews were now forced to wear yellow badges on their clothing and were moved into ghettos. When economic conditions worsened and the masses threatened to revolt, Jews rather than ineffective fiscal policies were held responsible. Beginning with England, they found themselves banished from country after country.

The Black experience in the United States has been similarly affected by the extent to which political circumstances have set the stage for Blacks and Whites to compete. There were many slaveowners who argued that Whites had an obligation to maintain their system of enslaving Blacks to assure that they would survive. In the antebellum South, slaves who at least overtly went along with the system and were willing to "stay in their place" tended to be stereotyped as "little Black Sambo" types, as children who lacked the intelligence and initiative to make it as free people.

After the Civil War, however, the presence of Whites in direct competition with ex-slaves for jobs assured the perpetuation of the myth that Blacks were somehow innately ill-equipped for precisely the same skilled work they had competently performed before being emancipated (Bonacich, 1972; Harris, 1964). This was the case, even though an absolute level of segregation and humiliation of Blacks did not set in until the turn of the century, long after decades of racial conflict and competition led by a "relaxation of the opposition" to racism had established a firm hold on the character of American society (Woodward, 1955).

During the period following the end of the Civil War known as Reconstruction, at a time when they had a genuine possibility of gaining economic and political clout, Blacks found themselves stereotyped more as dangerous animals than as naive children. The new image justified not keeping Blacks dependent and submissive, as they had been expected to be during slavery, but treating Blacks as subhumans who, in self-defense, needed to be segregated, repressed, and even killed (Levin & Levin, 1982).

During Reconstruction, the enslavement of Blacks was replaced by increasing episodes of hate violence. From the standpoint of White southerners, the enemy between 1865 and 1877 consisted of reform-minded northerners who sought to "reconstruct" the vanquished South and Black leaders who hoped to divide large plantations into a number of small farms to give to former slaves. The Republican Party sought to enlarge its influence by enlisting the allegiance of newly freed slaves, liberal southerners, and abolitionist northerners who had traveled to the southern states in an effort to achieve reform (Lane, 1997). Constituting what Roger Lane refers to as a guerrilla war of national liberation, new and more deadly tactics were needed to restore the power enjoyed by the dominant White majority before secession.

With the help of the Union army, the federal government remained in charge of many everyday affairs. It was, however, much too segmented, inconsistent, and uncommitted to see to it that White southerners would accept an increased role for Blacks in the power structure of the South. Instead, the southern majority turned to tactics of intimidation, assault, and murder to keep ex-slaves in only the dirtiest, lowest-paying jobs—those unacceptable to Whites—and to keep them from voting. By the year 1877, when the federal troops withdrew and relations between Blacks and Whites were returned to local White southerners, there had been countless incidents of lynchings, riots, and murders committed by individual southerners as well as secret societies including the Ku Klux Klan.

Fear of economic warfare from newly freed slaves became intense among working-class Whites who until the abolition of slavery had enjoyed state support in keeping Black Americans from competing for their jobs. One White worker, writing at the turn of the century, represented the thinking of many White southerners about the "race question":

> Take a young Negro of little more than ordinary intelligence, even, get hold of him in time, train him thoroughly as to books, and finish him up with a good industrial education, send him out into the South with ever so good intentions both on the part of his benefactor and himself, send him to take my work away from me and I will kill him. (Franklin & Starr, 1967, p. 25)

In the reinstatement of local White rule came a permanent system of institutionalized segregation and an onslaught of hate crimes directed against ex-slaves who were audacious enough to continue seeking a share of the power and wealth of White southerners. In Texas, Kentucky, and South Carolina, the murder rate was approximately 18 times that for the New England states. Throughout the South, White on Black murder rates skyrocketed to the point that they represented some 80% of all such homicides nationally. By the 1890s, lynchings of Blacks in southern states had peaked to about 100 yearly. Murder in the South had become social policy.

Although morally reprehensible, there is little doubt that murder was an extremely effective policy for reinstating the rule of Whites and the subjugation of Blacks. During Reconstruction, millions of Blacks for the first time voted and millions more competed for the first time in the job market against White opponents. By the early years of the twentieth century, however, opportunities for former slaves to accumulate power and wealth had completely evaporated.

Racial segregation was mandated in 1896 with the *Plessy v. Ferguson* decision of the U.S. Supreme Court, which institutionalized "Jim Crow" laws. This decision ensured that the "separate but equal" doctrine would remain national policy for almost 60 years and that Black Americans would be kept "in their place."

In the antebellum South, relations between Whites and Blacks had been dictated by laws and customs governing the acceptable conditions of slavery. From the 1600s, separating the children of slaves from their parents was permitted, but legal marriages between slaves were prohibited. Moreover, slaves were not allowed to own books, inherit money, learn to read or write, or vote. Even northern Blacks were subjected to a discriminatory set of norms. They could not vote; enter hotels or restaurants (except in the role of servants); and were segregated from Whites in formal education, trains, steamboats, church seating, and theaters (Burkey, 1971).

Jim Crow reinstated White supremacy in all aspects of everyday life. Blacks were no longer enslaved, but they were nevertheless subjected to a complex set of rules that defined them as inferior. Blacks rode in the back of public buses, drank from "colored" water fountains, waited in "colored" waiting rooms, used only "colored" public restrooms, ate in "colored" restaurants, and slept in "colored" motels. They were segregated from Whites in schools, churches, membership in unions, public accommodations, and housing.

Moreover, southern Blacks were victimized by a set of petty indignities, including prohibitions against interrace dating and marriage, against sexual relations between Black men and White women, and even against Blacks interrupting conversations between Whites. Discriminatory norms observed throughout the South required that physicians serve their White patients before their Black patients, that Blacks remove their hats when in the presence of Whites, that Black domestics enter the homes of Whites by the back door, and that Black automobile drivers yield the right-of-way to their White counterparts (Burkey, 1971).

Jobs are often but not always the primary nexus of competition between groups. In the history of American society, intergroup conflict has often taken the form of organized efforts to secure land and extend political boundaries. Hate and prejudice have developed to justify the ruthless, illegal tactics that were so frequently employed.

The experience of Mexican Americans provides a case in point. After being stereotyped by Anglos as "treacherous, childlike, primitive, lazy, and irresponsible," Mexican Americans found themselves manipulated by politicians, lawyers, and land-grabbers alike. Despite the 1848 Treaty of Guadalupe-Hidalgo, which guaranteed Mexicans the right of full citizenship, land-owning Mexican families found their titles in jeopardy and their land and cattle stolen or taken from them by fraud. Unlike their Anglo counterparts, Mexican Americans could not count on the courts for protection (Jacobs, Landau, & Pell, 1971).

American Indians were severely mistreated at the hands of land-hungry White Americans who eagerly accepted the view that Indians were "treacherous and cruel savages who could never be trusted." The negative stereotype served a purpose: As long as the Indians were needed for their agricultural expertise, their military assistance, or their skill as trappers, White Americans tended to see them in a favorable light and to permit their culture to maintain itself, but when large-scale campaigns became directed toward securing the lands occupied and settled by American Indians, the negative image emerged in full force. If the central business of the "Indian savage" was to torture and slay, then the central business of the "White man" must be gradually to eliminate the "Indian savage" (Jacobs, Landau, & Pell, 1971).

In some cases, the process of elimination was anything but gradual. By 1825, some 13,000 Cherokees maintained their homes in the southeastern region of the United States. They occupied 7 million acres of land, owned prosperous farms, and were at peace. This situation was radically altered by the discovery of gold in the hills of Georgia. To gain possession of the rich Cherokee-owned lands, Georgia legislature, President Andrew Jackson, the U.S. Congress, the Supreme Court, and the military found it "necessary" to drive the Cherokees beyond the Mississippi. In the Cherokee removal of 1838, this group of American Indians was rounded up and taken away, their homes were burned, their property was seized, many were herded into stockades, and thousands died. Such thinking on the part of White Americans also led to the passage of the Dawes General Allotment Act of 1887, which took two-thirds (90 million acres) of the tribal lands previously granted to American Indians by treaty (Berry, 1965).

It isn't only the dominant group in a society that comes into conflict with the members of minorities. Throughout the history of the United States, impoverished groups have frequently competed with one another for neighborhoods, jobs, businesses, and status. As shown dramatically in the aftermath of the Rodney King episode in 1991, the recent influx of newcomers from Latin America and Asia has vastly changed the complexion of intergroup conflict in America. King, a 25-year-old Black American, was stopped while speeding down a highway in the San Fernando Valley. A local resident recorded King being repeatedly kicked and beaten by police officers and the video was telecast on news programs around the country. Millions of Americans thought the police response constituted "excessive force."

In April 1992, when the four White police officers involved were acquitted by a predominantly White jury, many Americans were shocked and angered. Blacks were particularly outraged, considering the "police brutality" they had observed as an act of racism that was whitewashed by a racially biased jury (Levin & Thomas, 1997). Violent demonstrations broke out around the country. In Los Angeles, three days of rioting resulted in 58 deaths, 2,400 injuries, $717 million in damages, and 11,700 arrests (Abelmann & Lie, 1995).

Many people likened the Los Angeles riots to the 1965 civil disturbances in Watts, which involved mostly Black Americans and resulted in numerous deaths and injuries and almost 4,000 arrests. Yet, the 1992 Los Angeles riots were, in important respects, very different from Watts. The 1965 riots had been essentially Black against White. The Los Angeles riots were, by contrast, truly multi-ethnic, involving not only Blacks and Whites but also Latinos and Asians.

One of the accused police officers was partially of Latino heritage; more than half of those arrested by the police were Latinos. Moreover, the majority of the more than 3,000 Korean American companies in Los Angeles were damaged, the amount totaling some $350 million (Abelmann & Lie, 1995; Kim, 1999).

In the 1965 riots, many of the businesses destroyed by rioters were owned by Jews. By 1992, merchants of Asian descent monopolized the local area; they were Korean Americans who had bought deteriorating businesses in Black and Latino neighborhoods. For the most part, their small shops and stores were family-owned and -run. The image of Korean merchants, like the image of Jewish merchants before them, was that of outsiders who were prospering at the expense of the Black and Latino communities. Although Asian Americans had absolutely no part in creating impoverished neighborhoods, they became scapegoats for expressing the frustrations of Black Americans against White Americans (Abelmann & Lie, 1995).

The Rodney King episode was a precursor to the public outcry over police shootings in 2014 and 2015 as described in chapter 3. By examining the riots of 1992 and 2014–2015, we can learn a good deal about the changing conditions under which hate and prejudice are expressed in the United States. For one thing, we see that definitions of racism that neatly fit only the situation of Black and White relations during the 1960s and 1970s have lost much of their relevance to our understanding of race relations in the United States today. For decades, power was treated as a commodity that Whites possessed and Blacks only wanted. Whites had it all and Blacks had none of it. In this absolutist way of thinking, racism equaled prejudice plus power. Thus, only Whites possessed both of the characteristics necessary to be racists, while Blacks were merely prejudiced (Tatum, 1997).

The foregoing conception may have fit the circumstances of Black–White relations traditionally, but it seems more realistic in contemporary America to consider group variations in power as being a matter of degree rather than in kind (Levin & Levin, 1982; Willie, 1996). Clearly, some groups (e.g., White men) have immensely more economic power than do other groups (e.g., people of color and women). Yet, no one group has absolute power in every respect. Individuals within even a relatively powerless group in economic terms can make their presence felt in a negative way as individuals. In 1992 Los Angeles, for example, Latinos and Black Americans as a group certainly had far less economic clout than their White neighbors, but they were still able to impose their will physically against those of their Korean American neighbors who were put out of business during the melee.

Focusing almost exclusively on Black versus White, the traditional model of intergroup conflict rightly emphasized prejudice against Black Americans as a central problem in our society. Even then, of course, the degree of economic power varied, but by ethnic group (there has long been intense and pervasive competition for scarce resources among White ethnic groups—Italian, Irish, Jewish, Polish, and so on) who left their homelands in Europe to make a go of it in the United States. But the new mix has become even more complex, based, as it is, on differences not in ethnic but racial characteristics. Although Europeans differed in learned cultural characteristics such as language, dress, and religious rituals, they were, for the most part, White and so didn't cross racial boundaries. The new mix introduces the added complexity of racial divisions, always a thorny issue for Americans to resolve (Daniels, 2002; Parillo, 2005).

The incredible complexity of racial issues facing the United States in the early twenty-first century is represented in the recent history of affirmative action policies in higher education. Between 1970 and the mid-1980s, the number of Asian Americans attending colleges and universities dramatically increased, while enrollments of other minorities, especially of Blacks and American Indians, flattened out and then declined (Takagi, 1992). Over the same period of time, the backlash against affirmative action also began to grow. Not coincidentally, hate incidents (both criminal acts and verbal insults) targeting Black college students were on the rise on campuses around the country (Levin & McDevitt, 1993; Takagi, 1992).

Early in the rising skepticism concerning affirmative action in higher education, it was generally argued that White students were victimized by a system that unfairly gave preferential treatment to Blacks, Latinos, American Indians, and Asians. By 1986, as the notion that Asian students were *better qualified* than Whites took hold, the argument shifted, at least temporarily, so as to identify Asians and not Whites as the primary victims of affirmative action policies intended to increase the enrollment of Blacks. In other words, Black students were regarded as being in competition with Asian students for scarce seats in institutions of higher education (Takagi, 1992).

On the other side of the issue, Asian students argued that they were victims not of policies designed to attract more Black students but of blatant anti-Asian discrimination. Some university administrators countered by suggesting that Asian students were actually overrepresented relative to their proportion in the population of the United States and that the disproportionate numbers of Asian students in the classroom threatened the enrollment of truly underrepresented groups, especially Blacks and Latinos and also Whites. From this viewpoint, Asian students were depicted as qualified but usually less than outstanding. They were regarded as narrowly excellent only in science and math, as opposed to other students who had a much broader range of curricular and extracurricular interests and talents. In the face of increasing racial incidents, declining enrollments of Black Americans, greater pressure from Asian Americans to gain acceptance, and general concerns about academic standards, Asians were less often seen as deserving members of a "model minority" and more often as good but hardly outstanding students (Takagi, 1992).

Racial tensions on campuses around the country reflect a much more general trend toward intergroup conflict. Tensions between Blacks and Whites remain to be resolved, but they have been joined by escalating levels of conflict involving Latinos and Asians as well as Muslims and Jews.

Education is only one important arena of conflict and competition. There have been large-scale Black–Asian and Black–Latino confrontations over economic resources and cultural differences in such cities as Miami; Washington, DC; New York; Chicago; and Los Angeles. Moreover, in prisons across the country, differences between Latino and Black inmates have often been a source of large-scale group disturbances.

In the years ahead, as Latinos and Asians increasingly bid to have their share of the American pie, the complexities of race relations are likely to grow rather than diminish.

Maintaining Political Power

Competition for scarce resources often contributes to hate and prejudice between ethnic and racial groups in a society. Even more likely to raise the hostility of the masses, various minorities throughout history have been selected by the dominant group as "servants of power" who assumed an important role working for the rulers of society in their efforts to maintain and consolidate their status at the pinnacle of power. The position of Jews in seventeenth- and eighteenth-century Germany provides a case in point. The Jews held only a marginal position in the social structure of the larger German society. They had no citizenship rights and were despised and persecuted by the German people. As a result, German Jews, taken from the squalor of the ghetto, found themselves at the mercy of the Germanic absolutist rulers who used them as instruments for maximizing their power in society. As servants of power to these rulers, court Jews became advisors, collaborators, bankers, and financiers. They supplied the armies, financed the wars, arranged for new loans, and settled debts. They came to monopolize the trade in silver, tobacco, and salt and built factories producing ribbon, cloth, silk, and velvet. In addition, they collected taxes and were diplomatic representatives, bankers, and financial administrators. Most importantly, Jews were confidants of the prince (Coser, 1972; Levin & Levin, 1982).

Renegade Christians were, like Jews, employed by fourteenth- and fifteenth-century Turkish sultans who sought to maintain and extend their power over their Muslim subjects. Taken as youth and converted to the Muslim faith, these foreign-born Christians became important human resources for the sultan's staff, serving in both civilian and military capacities as courtiers, administrators, and military officers. Renegade Christians provided Turkish rulers with a loyal and ambitious staff. Being the slaves of a single ruler as well as outsiders from the standpoint of the native-born population, they were totally dependent on the sultan, who, in turn, became freed from reliance on the support of his native Muslim population (Coser, 1972; Lybyer, 2007).

It should be noted that even where they are not chosen as servants of power, vulnerable and/or marginalized groups have frequently been targeted as the victims of collective displaced aggression. Instead of blaming the rulers of society for hard times, the masses redirect their hostility downward to such groups as welfare recipients, people of color, and Jews (Coser, 1972).

Conclusion

Much of the encouragement for hate attacks derives from the benefits that sympathizers and spectators secure from their verbal support or their passivity. On the psychological level, to the extent that they regard themselves as superior at the expense of others, individuals receive a boost to their self-esteem. Certain members of society, those who have a personality tendency to scapegoat outsiders, are especially likely to realize such gains. In addition, individuals who are intolerant of ambiguities benefit from the cultural images of various groups and depict these groups in stereotypical fashion. Even if such images are inaccurate, they structure the everyday experiences of a bigoted person, forming the impression that life is predictable and that dangerous people can be totally avoided.

Hate also has far-reaching economic and status benefits. Even the least bigoted members of the dominant group gain from the presence of despised individuals who are assigned the dirty work of society—the lowest-paying or most unpleasant tasks. In addition, hate justifies reducing or even eliminating the competition from less favored groups. Finally, the political leaders of society have taken advantage of outsiders who have little if any political clout and can be counted on to be loyal "servants of power." Certain minorities' supportive role in unpopular regimes, even if through no fault of their own, has engendered hostility among the masses.

In American society, many Whites continue to enjoy privileges that are simply not available to the members of racial minorities. White prerogatives are so deeply imbedded in our social structure that they may not be seen by those who enjoy them. Yet, not only do such racial advantages exist, but they continue to determine the support or lack of support that White Americans are willing to give to efforts toward eradicating racism (Feagin, 2000).

For society as a whole, hate may actually be thoroughly destructive. It robs its citizens of the possibility of unity and peace; it can easily escalate into full-scale ethnic warfare; it helps to create an entire range of costly social problems. Yet given the perceived and actual benefits of hate to particular individuals and groups in a society, the forces of resistance to change can be counted on to remain strong in the future.

Whether the forces of hate come from our history, social structure, culture, psychology, or elsewhere, they are experienced by us in the places where we live, work, and play. It is in these local situations that we feel the effects of bigotry, and it is here that we are most able to take a stand against it. In order to do so we will need to learn to recognize and overcome the local dynamics that often work to keep us compliant and quiet. This is the topic of the next chapter.

CHAPTER 6

The Production of Rebels, Deviants, and Other Decent People

We have attempted to make the case in previous chapters that the local situation (a neighborhood, business office, sports team, family, or other social group or organization to which a person belongs) is the place where most people experience the larger social, economic, cultural, and historical forces that affect their beliefs, attitudes, and behaviors. In addition, it is the dynamics of the local situation that can cause good people to stand by and do nothing while others are hurt, either physically or emotionally. Armed with knowledge of the dynamics of local situations, citizens are better able to overcome them in order to affect change for the better.

The Power of the Situation

Hate is a mundane, everyday phenomenon typically embraced and practiced by ordinary people for ordinary reasons in ordinary places. Research in social psychology suggests that it really doesn't take much to make bigotry operational. Normal individuals who are placed in situations with specific role requirements by credible authority figures tend, with frightening determination, to play the roles to which they have been assigned. Of course, individuals also have some control over their culture; they don't passively have to conform to it, although, unfortunately, many of them do just that.

When Normal People Do Abnormally Nasty Things

A classic study by Philip Zimbardo and his associates at Stanford University (1973, 2004) may help shed light on the phenomenon of normal people doing abnormal, even horrific, things to others. Zimbardo and his colleagues turned the basement of a building on campus into a mock prison. They created a number of cells by installing bars and locks on each room and then placing a cot in each one. Twenty student volunteers, all chosen for their mature and stable personalities, were selected to participate in the study. On a purely random basis (the flip of a coin), half of the students were assigned to play the role of guards and the other half were assigned to play the role of prisoners.

The experiment actually started at the homes of the 10 student prisoners. To increase the realism of the study, all of them were arrested, put in handcuffs, read their rights, and then driven to jail in police cars. They were then completely stripped, sprayed with disinfectants, issued prison uniforms, and placed into locked cells.

Everyone knew that the experiment was artificial and that it was supposed to end in two weeks. Nobody was really a prisoner; nobody was really a guard. It was pure make-believe decided by chance. Yet, after only a few days, both the prisoners and the guards were playing their roles to the hilt.

Guards were told only to keep order. Instead, they began to humiliate and embarrass the prisoners, coercing them to remain silent on command, to sing or laugh in front of the other inmates, and to clean up messes made by the guards. In some cases, the guards verbally and physically threatened and intimidated the prisoners, apparently for the purpose of asserting their authority.

The prisoners became more and more passive and compliant. In accord with the roles to which they had been assigned, the prisoners obeyed orders and accepted commands, no matter how unreasonable. They began to feel totally powerless to fight back. After only six days, four of the prisoners had to be excused from the study, having suffered serious episodes of anxiety, anger, or depression. In fact, the entire experiment was ended in less than a week when it became clear that the guards had become abusive and the prisoners were emotionally at risk.

Interviews conducted after the experiment ended were revealing. Both the prisoners and the guards told Zimbardo and his associates that they were both shocked and ashamed at how they had behaved. None of them would have predicted that they were capable of such cruelty, in the case of the guards, or obedience to authority, in the case of the prisoners. Remember that all of the student volunteers had been selected for their mature and stable personalities. Yet they all acted according to the roles created by the structure of prison life.

Zimbardo's prison experiment indicates the incredible power of situational factors to influence normal individuals, whatever their psychological makeup, to mistreat other human beings or to obey the cruelest sort of authority. The hopeful implication of Zimbardo's findings is that it is easier to change situations than to change individual predispositions. We can often structure the experiences of society's members in such a way that blind conformity to bigoted norms of behavior is minimized and respect for diversity is more likely to prevail.

Fighting Spectatorship

At the same time, it is important to emphasize that spectatorship is all too comfortable for many individuals. In accepting hate and prejudice, whether actively or passively, the members of society are typically rewarded in both a psychological and material sense. By contrast, those relatively rare individuals who choose to violate norms of separatism, respect diversity, and fight for the rights of exploited and victimized groups are likely to suffer losses of their own.

Moreover, even well-intentioned individuals who are willing to pay the price may not always act on behalf of vulnerable others who are in trouble. First, they must feel some sense of personal responsibility for the pain and suffering. It is all too easy to want to respond with help, but in light of the heavy personal cost, simply assume that someone else will surely come to the rescue (Latane & Darley, 1970).

Second, even if they are willing to risk their own security, they may still feel incompetent to proceed in any effective manner. Social scientists have discovered that those who intervene in a dangerous situation are likely to have had training in first aid, lifesaving, or police work. In addition, they tend to be exceptionally tall and heavy. These attributes give them the sense of efficacy (through training or strength) necessary to be injected into potentially hazardous situations. Good Samaritans also tend to be adventurous types who have taken other risks with their personal safety (London, 1970).

In addition, those who come to the rescue must realize that their help is actually appropriate to give. This means breaking through the cultural stereotypes and political propaganda to recognize that the members of a particular group are human beings who are worth saving. Education can be very effective here because it reduces stereotyped thinking (Chickering & Reisser, 1993; Selznick & Steinberg, 1969).

The difficulty of responding in the face of such ambiguities can be seen in Turkey's massacre of more than 1 million Armenians in 1915 (Staub, 1989). In a largely Muslim society, Armenians were part of a tiny Christian minority. Like other non-Muslims, including Greeks and Jews, Armenians tended to control Turkish commerce, trade, and finance. In addition, they were exempt from almost all taxes levied on the Islamic population. To make matters worse in a public relations sense, many of the industrious and intelligent Armenians had become quite successful; some were very wealthy. They soon became seen by the Turks as a devious, even parasitic, minority whose members had conspired with their enemy, Russia, against the majority Muslim population. By simply resisting repression and demanding their rights, Armenians were considered a threat. Not unlike other Christians in the region, they had been widely viewed as "cattle." But Armenians were also depicted as instruments of foreign intervention. Negative feelings toward the Armenian minority were exacerbated by a series of military losses that by 1913 had effectively eliminated the Ottoman Empire from Europe. During World War I, it suffered tremendous losses in a Russian invasion. By 1915, many of the country's Muslim majority held the Armenians responsible for Turkey's loss of power and its humiliating defeats (Staub, 1989).

The genocidal intentions of the Turkish leadership were not always clear-cut and unambiguously immoral to the general population of Muslims. As in Germany's response to the Nazi Holocaust, the mass murder of Armenians was justified as an effort to rid the homeland of an internal enemy that had long retarded the Empire's progress. Turkish writers of the day claimed that Armenian residents had committed acts of sabotage, subterfuge, espionage, and rioting. It was therefore necessary, they claimed, to deport the mutinous

Armenians to minimize the damage they were inflicting on the dominant population of the country. The deportation turned out to be a death march for thousands of women, children, and elders who starved along the way. Turks admitted that lives had been lost, but that the number of deaths was actually much smaller than that claimed by Armenians. To this day, more than a century later, Turkey has never recognized that an Armenian massacre occurred, let alone that the Turkish government or people had some responsibility for perpetrating it.

Intergroup Contact

There are some Americans—Black, White, and tan—who have given up on integration. They see efforts to bring together people of differing backgrounds as some sort of archaic strategy for assuaging liberal guilt rather than as an effective approach for reducing violence and other forms of discrimination. Those who are hopeless about getting groups together might find some kind of perverse comfort in the fact that major efforts at desegregating schools and neighborhoods over the past few decades have, in certain cases, ended in failure. In fact, there is even some evidence that desegregation sometimes actually supported and encouraged stereotyped thinking about the members of other races (Stephan, 1986).

The Impact of Competition

It is true that bringing groups together doesn't always reduce hate. As we have seen, various groups of Americans have been belittled, discredited, and harmed to the extent that they became widely considered a threat to the dominant group. Such historical accounts are supported by studies that show intergroup hostility escalating as a result of increasing intergroup contact, especially in the form of intense competition. In the area of employment, for example, White workers who compete directly with Blacks for jobs tend to express more bigoted racial attitudes than their counterparts in areas of the job market where there is little competition from Blacks (Cummings, 1980). The notion that hate depends for its motivation on the threat posed by another group of people may exaggerate the active and offensive position taken by the victim. Actually, it is the zero-sum contest that is threatening. Defensively, a group may resist when its land is taken by force, its women are sexually assaulted, and its people are enslaved or carted off to concentration camps. But it is the fact that one group possesses something that another group desires, not the resistance itself, that increases hate and prejudice.

In a classic study, Sherif and his collaborators (1961, 1988) demonstrated the link between competition and intergroup hostility in a series of experiments that took place at an isolated summer camp for 11- and 12-year-old boys. After a period of time together, the boys attending Sherif's camp were separated into two distinct groups and then placed in different cabins. When each group of boys had been given the time to develop a strong sense of group spirit and organization, Sherif arranged for a number of intergroup encounters—a tournament of competitive zero-sum games such as football, baseball, tug-of-war, and a treasure hunt—in which one group could fulfill its goals only at the expense of the other group. The tournament began in a spirit of friendliness and good-natured rivalry, but it soon became apparent that negative intergroup feelings were emerging in full force. The members of each group began to name-call their rivals, completely turning against members of the opposing group, even members whom they had selected as "best friends" upon first arriving at the camp. Sherif's findings suggest that when the maintenance or enhancement of the status of a group depends on the continued subordination of another group, then intergroup competition will turn ugly.

Reducing Hostility Between Groups

Yet, notwithstanding the nasty turn of events following his introduction of competitive games, Sherif also showed us how we might be able to reverse the movement toward intergroup hostility so that the participants begin to see one another more as allies than opponents. Just having more contact didn't foster good feelings between groups; in fact, it only served to reinforce the hatred that boys from the two groups felt toward their competitors. But in the final stage of his study, Sherif introduced a series of superordinate goals, a set of objectives greatly valued by the boys in both groups, that could not be achieved without everyone working together. Thanks to Sherif's behind-the-scenes manipulations, the boys were forced collectively to push a bus out of the mud; pool their money to rent a movie; and repair their water supply, which had been sabotaged by the researchers. The result was dramatic: Much of the intergroup hostility in the camp dissipated and new friendships flourished across group lines.

Sherif's concept of superordinate goals as a basis for improving intergroup relations has been applied to ethnically diverse elementary school classrooms in Texas and California (Aronson & Gonzalez, 1988). In these studies, students were interdependent in two ways: First, they were purposely structured around the goal of getting a good grade in the class so that when one student gained all of them gained. Second, their efforts were shared so that they worked together to achieve their goal (Brewer & Miller, 1996).

In a ground-breaking study, Aronson (Aronson & Patnoe, 1997) created what he called a jigsaw teaching technique, in which fifth-graders participated in a small experimental classroom. Each child was sorted into a racially integrated "learning group" and was given a piece of information she had to share with classmates in order to put the puzzle together. Not unlike Sherif's campers who worked together on shared goals, the key ingredient was that students in the learning group were forced to depend on one another to complete their group project and receive a grade. They taught one another; they shared information with one another. Cooperation rather than competition was the only way they could achieve a good grade in the course.

After using his jigsaw method for a period of six weeks, Aronson measured changes in the attitudes of students toward one another. As compared with children in traditional competitive classrooms, the fifth-graders in his jigsaw groups liked their classmates better, had more positive attitudes toward school, had better self-esteem, and performed just as well on their exams.

Pettigrew and Tropp (2000) concluded from their meta-analysis of 203 studies of intergroup contact that in the overwhelming majority (94%) of these studies, the investigators found an inverse relationship between contact and prejudice. Yet, as suggested in the findings of Sherif and Aronson, contact alone doesn't necessarily reduce hate. The effect of contact between groups depends on the quality of that contact.

Allport (1954) long ago suggested that intergroup contact would lead to a reduction in prejudice, but only under the following conditions: (1) when the groups in contact have equal status, (2) when group members engage in cooperative activity toward a shared goal, (3) when the interaction is personalized so that it breaks through stereotyped thinking, and (4) when the intergroup contact is supported by authorities or local norms. In more recent research, it has also been determined that the intergroup experience reduces prejudice to the extent that it provides participants with the opportunity to make friends with members of the other group (Pettigrew, 1998).

Most research into the impact of intergroup contact on prejudice has supported the notion that the good feeling that develops between cooperating friends from different groups actually generalizes in two ways. First, in many cases, it generalizes from the few immediate intimates to the entire group to which the few intimates belong. Second, individuals who come through contact to reduce their prejudice toward one outgroup seem to be more willing to interact with the members of outgroups generally. In other words, intergroup contact seems to reduce not only negative attitudes and feelings toward the cooperating group but also the general phenomenon known as ethnocentrism.

The Bulgarian experience provides an important illustration of the power of contact and cooperation in intergroup relations. In 1943, the citizens of this eastern European country, an ally of the Nazis, saved the lives of 50,000 Jewish citizens who awaited the trains that would have carried them to death camps. The Bulgarian king, Boris III, had already sent 11,000 Jews from occupied territories to their death, but his Bulgarian subjects would tolerate no more.

Unlike in many other European counties, Bulgarian Jews were dispersed throughout the social structure, playing important roles in a wide range of occupations apart from finance and commerce. Moreover, although maintaining their religious traditions and identity, many Jews were structurally assimilated into Bulgarian society, having intimate friends and acquaintances among their Christian and Muslim neighbors.

A grassroots community movement ensured that Bulgarian Jews would not be deported. There were protests from influential bishops in the Bulgarian Orthodox Church and from the professional organizations of doctors, lawyers, and authors. A bill was introduced in Parliament by its vice-president to ignore Hitler's decree. And many average Bulgarian citizens chose to wear the yellow Star of David, a symbol that the law required Jewish citizens to wear in order to identify them for deportation (Comforty, 2000; Levin & Rabrenovic, 2004).

Structuring Opportunities for Cooperation

Recognizing the power of intergroup contact to bring diverse segments of the population together in peace and harmony, we simply cannot afford to leave such occasions to chance. Piecemeal efforts to create optimal contact experiences will result in trivial improvements in the overall social climate. Instead, we need more deliberately created, structured opportunities for members of society to interact optimally on a cooperative and intimate basis with people who are different (Pettigrew & Tropp, 2000).

Notwithstanding incidents of intergroup conflict that have inevitably arisen over the past several decades, the U.S. Army provides a model for viewing what consequences can be expected when an institution makes large-scale structural changes to integrate Blacks and Whites under optimal circumstances. Racial animosities decreased when soldiers worked together as equal status partners who depended on one another for survival (Moscos & Butler, 1996).

Not unlike the experience of Black and White soldiers, children coming from diverse racial and socioeconomic backgrounds can be brought together in a spirit of cooperation and mutual respect. Modeling itself on the highly successful Chicago Children's Choir, the Boston Children's Chorus consists of diverse youngsters, grades 2 through 12, from city and suburban neighborhoods and schools. They sing, perform, and receive the applause of their audiences as a unified and cohesive group. According to Hubie Jones, the founder of the Boston Children's Chorus, many of the children develop friendships across racial and socioeconomic lines. Similarly, other communities in the United States have used sports such as soccer as opportunities to integrate refugees fleeing violence and oppression from Africa, among other places around the globe. In 2015 in Lewiston, Maine, for example, the local high school sent its soccer team to the state championship game, which they won. The team included players from Congo, Kenya, Turkey, Germany, and Somalia, who relied on one another to achieve their common objective. A recent documentary, *One Team: The Story of the Lewiston High School Blue Devils,* highlights the importance of soccer in helping longtime Lewiston residents embrace the refugees in their midst (Bass, 2015).

On college campuses around the country, resistance on the part of traditionally dominant students who feel threatened by the presence of new groups on campus has resulted in a revival of hate and bigotry. At one university on the east coast, for example, threatening hate mail was sent to numerous Black students on campus. At another, a student died after falling 60 feet when he and his friends attempted to affix a large hand-painted swastika to the roof of a campus building. At a small college in the mountain states, the gay and lesbian organization on campus was disbanded when all of its 12 members received threatening phone calls.

At least some of the influences working to separate students on campus by race, religion, national origin, sexual orientation, and disability status originate in the wider society and were present long before they matriculated. From an early age, for example, many children make their friendship choices within their own racial and religious groups. This pattern tends to continue through the college years. Still, the failure of such institutions of higher learning to adjust to the needs of a more diverse student body has also led many students on college campuses to resegregate themselves into special interest groups in which they might find the support and encouragement that are otherwise missing (Ehrlich, 1972, 1990, 2009).

Where separatism predominates on campus, it might be wise to create opportunities for leaders of segregated groups to come together, transcend their differences, and work in temporary alliances around common goals. Special-interest groups on campus—the gay and lesbian alliance, Latino center, international student association, Black student union, Vietnamese student alliance, and so on—are usually essential for providing minority students with what they require in order to stay in school but cannot seem to get from the wider campus community. At the same time, however, there should also be curricular and extracurricular opportunities for diverse students to put aside their differences temporarily and come together to cooperate in harmony and peace. At many colleges and universities, students from diverse backgrounds have organized rallies against violence, food and music festivals, and speaker series that defend or celebrate all of their group memberships.

With the same objective in mind, sociologist Will Holton and the first author teamed up to teach an experimental sociology course that took teams of undergraduate students out of the traditional classroom to provide service to the local community. Our primary objective was to broaden students' perspectives; to give them an opportunity to interact with people of different races, ethnicities, or religions; and to do so in a spirit of cooperation, civility, and goodwill.

Because of the quality of their personal essays and academic transcripts, 17 undergraduate students were selected to participate in our course. The majority was White, but Black, Asian, and Latino students were represented as well. Every week, each student in the course, as a member of a team, performed five hours of community service and then met together as a class for two hours to discuss related issues. In addition, students wrote logs summarizing their community service experiences for the week and a more inclusive paper at the end of the term. Our final class meeting together consisted of oral team presentations in which students summarized their community experiences and reflected on how those experiences had changed their own feelings and thinking about diversity.

The range of student reactions was as broad and varied as their agency placements, but typically they left a positive impression. Some reported initially feeling out of place when exposed to an unfamiliar situation in which they were, for the first time ever, the "racial minority." Others were fairly comfortable from the outset. Many students in our course discovered unexpected strengths among the community members they served. Richard, a young man from upstate New York, conducted empathy training as part of a conflict resolution program with racially diverse first-graders at an elementary school near Boston's Chinatown. Richard's experience changed his perspective. "Perhaps the biggest thing I noticed in working with these kids was just how little race differences matter to them," Richard said. "It is not that they don't understand that other people have different skin colors than they do; it's that they don't care. It made it so obvious to me that racial hatred is a learned thing."

Some of our students learned a good deal from being part of a project team whose members were diverse. For example, Marjorie, a biracial student who grew up in a part of Maine where there was only a tiny Jewish population, had been exposed to many anti-Jewish stereotypes. But through her partnership in a Cambridge agency with a Jewish woman from New York, she felt comfortable enough to speak with her about religion. Toward the end of the course, Marjorie remarked, "Now that I possess a better understanding of the Jewish faith and background, I am less likely to believe the stereotypes employed to discredit Jewish individuals."

Because they grew up shielded from those who are different, many of the students in our course were familiar with people from other racial and cultural groups only as the stereotypes they saw on television or in motion pictures. Their participation in community service learning provided an opportunity to interact cooperatively in a positive context with a wide range of individuals from other groups. At the same time, they were made aware of the existence of poverty and homelessness, flaws in the criminal justice system, prejudice and discrimination, and their own mortality. An unexpected advantage of our course for many of its students was to teach them that they are not at the center of the universe. As one of our students concluded after spending 10 weeks working with Boston teenagers: "The greatest content of learning in this course was about myself. I was forced to explore my own prejudices and those of others like me."

Follow the Leader

Researchers have discovered a common factor among German Christians who during World War II helped rescue the victims of their Nazi persecutors, civil rights activists of the 1950s and 1960s (called Freedom Riders), and altruistic children: The presence of someone to serve as a model of tolerance and empathy. For children, it is usually a parent who provides the strong moral leadership that leads them to accept a position of respect for diversity. In adults, this sort of leadership may derive from the work of politicians, entertainers, clergy, and journalists who use their platforms for the purpose of being exemplars for peace.

Sadly, our leaders—the people we count on to serve as role models for the rest of us—have not always provided the moral guidance necessary to inspire a reduction in hate and bigotry. Since the mid-1990s, for example, too many have espoused stereotyped views: Former representative Robert Armey referred to his colleague in the House as Barney Fag (not Barney Frank); talk show host Howard Stern spoke of Arabs as "towel heads"; the late Khalid Muhammad, then spokesperson for Farrakhan's Nation of Islam, told a group of college students in New Jersey that Jews were "bloodsuckers"; John Rocker, an Atlanta Braves pitcher, made negative stereotypic remarks in a *Sports*

Illustrated interview regarding immigrants, AIDS patients, welfare mothers, and New Yorkers; a CBS sportscaster referred to a Black basketball player as a "tough monkey"; ex-Senator Vincent C. Fumo called his Pennsylvania colleague in the state's senate a "faggot"; in an interview for Fox News Sunday, West Virginia senator Robert Byrd used the term "white nigger"; a major league baseball umpire was suspended for referring to a female administrator as a "stupid Jew bitch"; two Black bodybuilders accused California's former governor Arnold Schwarzenegger, who at the time was running for office, of a history of making racist remarks; the late Michael Jackson, popular singer and songwriter, left a message on the answering machine of his former advisor in which he suggests that "Jews suck. . . . They're like leeches"; talk show host Rush Limbaugh suggested that slavery "had its merits. For one thing, the streets were safer after dark." Then-Senator (later, Secretary of State) Hillary Clinton joked that Mahatma Gandhi used to run a gas station in St. Louis; speaking at a Strom Thurmond birthday party, former senator Trent Lott voiced his agreement with Thurmond's racist views; Alaska congressman Don Young used the term "wetbacks" to refer to Latino farmworkers; Senate Majority Leader Harry Reid called then-Senator Obama a "light-skinned" African American "with no Negro dialect." Texas governor Rick Perry's hunting compound was named "Niggerhead Ranch," and, while running for office, Donald Trump referred to women as "fat pigs, dogs, slobs and disgusting animals."

Obeying Orders

As we have seen, leadership can also help determine whether human beings are willing to do harm to others. Even before Zimbardo conducted his famous prison study, social scientists had already experimented with what it takes to get normal individuals to do hideous things to other human beings. The role played by strong leadership at home, in the community, or at the national level in fostering or reducing hate and prejudice can hardly be exaggerated. In a classic study, Stanley Milgram (1965, 1974; Blass, 2000) sought to determine whether a group of normal Americans could be persuaded to give a severe electrical shock to a total stranger just because a legitimate authority figure ordered them to do so. Actually, Milgram's original intention was to take his experiment to Germany to examine what he hypothesized to be the strong role of obedience to authority in German national character, a factor that Milgram saw as having contributed to the willingness of ordinary German citizens to go along with Hitler's final solution. Amazingly, Milgram found so much obedience to authority in Connecticut that he never got to Germany!

Milgram's subjects, all residents of New Haven and all volunteers, were told that they were participating in a study of memory and that they would play the role of teacher or student on a random basis. In reality, all of them were predetermined to be "teachers" who were seated before an electronic apparatus containing a panel of switches labeled with varying degrees of voltage from 15 to 450 V (labeled XXX). For every wrong answer offered by the "learner" (actually, a confederate of Milgram who pretended to get a shock by screaming or asking to be removed from the experiment), the "teacher" was told to punish him with a shock. As the study proceeded and the shock levels increased in intensity, the experimenter, dressed in a long white lab coat and holding a clipboard, urged reluctant subjects to comply by commanding them: "It is absolutely essential that you continue," and "You have no choice; you must go on." In this experiment, despite the screams of the learner and his appeal to be released from the study because of a heart condition, an incredible 60% of the volunteer subjects continued to administer a shock to the "learner" to the very end of the scale marked XXX at 450 V.

In Milgram's original experiment, the learner was seated in an adjoining room some distance from the subject. The remoteness of the victim served to provide psychological distance from the teacher, who could more easily deny any personal responsibility for delivering the punishing responses. In a subsequent study, however, the learner was brought right into the room with and was seated immediately next to the teacher so that they were touching.

When the teacher and learner were in proximity rather than distant, only 30%, about half as many volunteers, were willing to administer a maximum shock at the urging of an authority figure (Rochat & Modigliani, 1995).

The lesson for our purposes is that it is usually easier to harm a stranger than an intimate—usually more comfortable to injure someone when her misery is not visible. Many ordinary, even decent, people will obey the orders of a credible authority figure to do harm to others, but especially when they are able to distance themselves from the pain and suffering of their victims. When people who are different in significant ways come together, when they get to know one another as human beings, and when they touch one another's lives in important ways, it becomes much more difficult for them to do harm to one another. This is true about Turks and Bulgarians, Serbians and Kosovars, Israelis and Palestinians, Protestants and Catholics in Northern Ireland, or Blacks and Whites in the United States.

The cultural, structural, and psychological bases for inspiring harmful behavior give to hate a resistance to change that may be difficult (albeit not impossible) to overcome. To some extent, culture is self-perpetuating, especially when it serves important psychological functions for the individuals and groups in a society. At the individual level, however, it appears that the emotional component of intergroup hostility can be reduced when intimacy and friendship between the members of different groups are encouraged (Pettigrew, 1997).

The second major lesson to be learned from Milgram's studies of obedience involves the power of a leader to persuade ordinary people to do extraordinarily evil things. Many of Milgram's subjects who obeyed and administered painful shocks were afterwards deeply conflicted about what they had done. Following the study, many of them perspired and trembled badly, displaying all of the symptoms associated with anxiety and concern. They were hardly sociopaths lacking in empathy and conscience. On the contrary, they cared very much but they also felt a pressing obligation to comply with the dictates of legitimate authority.

The Role of Leadership

Milgram's study indicates dramatically just how important leadership can be to ordinary citizens who are accustomed to taking orders and going along with experts in their fields. We grow up learning to trust our leaders. Americans are no less vulnerable to the possibility of escalating intergroup tensions from hate to violence. Even a single event can be seen as intolerable and deserving of retaliation by members of the victim's group. An instructive example of the escalation effect can be found in New York City's Crown Heights neighborhood, which has long had a history of hostility between its Black and Jewish residents. In August 1991, seven-year-old Gavin Cato, a Black child who lived in Crown Heights, was accidentally killed when a car driven by an Orthodox Jewish motorist jumped the curb. Black youngsters sought to retaliate by racing through the streets of Crown Heights as they shouted anti-Semitic epithets and threats. A short time later, matters really got out of control when a 29-year-old rabbinical student from Australia, who was totally unconnected to the accident, was stabbed to death. For almost a week, Blacks and Jews exchanged insulting remarks, hurled rocks and bottles at one another, and broke windows in homes and cars. Dozens more were injured (Levin & McDevitt, 1993; Levin & Rabrenovic, 2001; Levin & Rabrenovic, 2004a).

Intergroup incidents do not always escalate into the sort of warfare that occurred in Crown Heights. Under certain conditions, a tragic event may even facilitate reconciliation and cooperation between groups. In the aftermath of the vicious 1998 murder of James Byrd in Jasper, Texas, community responses were much more reasonable and patient than they had been in Crown Heights.

It might seem that just the opposite would occur—that the brutal murder of a Black resident in Jasper would more likely precipitate a melee than would the accidental death of a Black resident in Crown Heights. Yet, instead of dividing the community on racial grounds, the murder of James Byrd actually served to bring the Black and White residents of Jasper together. In the aftermath of the slaying, townspeople reported going out of their way to cross racial lines in greeting residents and feeling a new street-level friendliness toward members of the other race.

Following the trial and conviction of the first defendant, the White supremacist's father phoned the local radio station not to hurl racial accusations but to urge townspeople to "fill the void made by this mess with love and tolerance" (Shlachter, 1999).

Just as in Crown Heights, Blacks and Whites in Jasper had not always been sympathetic toward one another. One issue that had long symbolized the community's struggle with race relations was the town's cemetery. A fence down the middle of the cemetery separated Whites buried on one side from Blacks buried on the other. After Byrd's murder, however, the town came to an agreement to integrate its cemetery. Many residents of Jasper, Black and White, joined together to pull out the posts and tear down the fence (Labalme, 1999).

In Crown Heights, mistrust and suspicion were palpable on both sides of the racial ledger. Many Black residents were convinced that the motorist who hit the Black child would get off scot-free due to the perception that Jewish residents enjoyed special treatment from city officials. At the same time, Jewish residents of Crown Heights were certain that the Black mayor of New York City would do little if anything to bring the murderer of the Australian rabbinical student to justice.

In contrast, the political leaders in Jasper had strong credibility among both its Black and its White residents. Local government had long been racially integrated. Black residents, who comprised some 45% of the town's population, occupied the position of mayor, two of the five city council positions, and the directorship of the Deep East Texas Council of Governments. In addition, school principals and the administrator of the largest hospital were Black.

Jasper's White sheriff went out of his way to inspire confidence among Black residents in the aftermath of Byrd's slaying. Within 24 hours, he had arrested two suspects and then immediately requested the assistance of the FBI. Moreover, Jasper's local 6,000-W radio station kept residents informed in an even-handed way about developments related to the murder and the trials, ensuring that racially dangerous rumors and anxieties never had an opportunity to spread (Shlachter, 1999).

Another important difference between the racial incidents in Crown Heights and Jasper, Texas, involves their residents' degree of community identification. In Crown Heights, identification seemed primarily to be based on race ("the Black community"), religion ("the Jewish community"), or a shared sense of being part of the much larger New York City population. In this regard, the Crown Heights neighborhood was almost irrelevant. By contrast, Jasper, Texas, represented a primary source of community identity for Black and White residents alike—all of them felt a common bond that transcended racial differences. Even extremists on both sides were genuinely embarrassed by the cruelty and sadism of James Byrd's murder. They seemed to unite across racial lines against the very strong stigma imposed on their community by members of the outside world (Levin & Rabrenovic, 2004b).

According to the U.S. Census Bureau, Latinos have officially replaced Blacks as America's largest minority (Wood, 2001). Latino politicians are expected to make significant gains in cities long dominated by Whites. What is more, in ethnically diverse cities such as Los Angeles, Latinos now fight for political offices held by other minorities, especially Blacks.

The relationships possible between Blacks and Latinos provide a model for understanding the choices that minority groups are likely to face in the future. The growing numbers of Latino voters in major cities across the country will ensure that they gain greater clout at least at the local level. Their increasing presence in cities and towns also places them in competition with other groups, ensuring that intergroup tensions at workplaces and in schools will occasionally flare.

The most important question for the future involves in which direction groups such as Latinos, Blacks, and Asians will decide to go. Will they choose to remain apart and in conflict? Or will they work together in a spirit of cooperation toward the fulfillment of a set of objectives important to all groups?

The Impact of Deviance

In an early examination of conformity, Solomon Asch (1952) studied a group of eight people in a classroom situation who were asked to match the length of a line drawn on the blackboard with one of three comparison lines drawn on an index card. All judgments were made out loud and in order of seating in the room. Actually, only one participant in the Asch study was a naive subject; and he voiced his judgment after hearing several other students state theirs first. (These others were confederates of Asch who had been instructed to respond incorrectly when asked to match the length of the lines.)

Over a number of trials with different groups, approximately one-third of the naive subjects made incorrect estimates in the direction of the inaccurate majority; in other words, about one in three conformed. But when a lone dissenter, a deviant, gave support to the naive subject by going against the majority judgment, the rate of conformity dropped dramatically to less than 6%. Thus, if even one spectator decides to break away from the inertia of the masses and become a rebel, she might serve as a role model for many other bystanders to imitate.

Because of the surprisingly large number of subjects in Milgram's experiment who obeyed a leader's order to punish a stranger, we might forget that about 40% of the volunteers in his original study did not comply. These were the rebels, the deviants, and the incredibly decent and independently motivated people who, even under trying circumstances, simply (or not so simply) refused to follow the dictates of legitimate authority.

When Rebels Rebel

Very few Nazi or Schutzstaffel (SS) officers were known to have been rebels who defied authority by refusing to cooperate with anti-Jewish policies. Yet even limited opposition by rebellious German officials and citizens, especially during the early years of the Nazi regime when Hitler was still concerned about gaining popular support, might have effectively saved Jewish lives. For example, an important Nazi official in Denmark allowed the escape of more than 6,000 Jews to Sweden by warning Danish leaders of the looming deportation of Jews and then delaying the execution of the order. Such noncompliance was as rare as it was dangerous. Instead, most citizens took the path of least resistance and conformed to the demands of the prevailing regime. German employers often went along with anti-Jewish policies, firing Jewish workers even before they were required to do so (Staub, 1989).

There are at least a few rebels on every campus in the United States. Refusing to be spectators or conformists in the area of intergroup relations, they organize rallies, demonstrations, festivals, or clubs on campus to bring students together or to protest the forces of division. In their exceptional zeal, they may also feel alone and unrecognized.

Some years ago, the Brudnick Center on Conflict and Violence at Northeastern University collaborated with Steve Wessler's Center for the Prevention of Hate Violence then located at the University of Southern Maine to bring hundreds of college students to Boston for the purpose of attending a National Student Symposium where they received awards for their efforts at combating hate and prejudice on their campuses. Three hundred students representing more than 70 colleges and universities from more than 22 states plus the District of Columbia and the province of Quebec attended. All had been nominated for their good work by the dean of students on their campuses. The symposium was funded by the Safe and Drug-Free Schools Program of the U.S. Department of Education and the Bureau of Justice Assistance of the U.S. Department of Justice.

Student attendees were nominated on the basis of their work on an antihate project, for example, hate crimes awareness week at the University of California at Berkeley, an annual diversity festival at the University of Alabama, a community forum to end hate at the University of Southern Maine, a diversity action council at Ohio State University, and diversity peer education programs at State University of New York at Stonybrook and at Texas A&M University.

The symposium agenda included roundtable discussions in which students shared their successes and frustrations working on their campuses with issues around the objective of reducing hate and prejudice. In addition, they attended skill-building workshops that addressed such concerns and policies as confronting dating violence through student-led programs; improvising peacemaking through dance; addressing degrading language, slurs, and jokes; promoting tolerance through understanding; creating an antihate website; facing history and ourselves; reducing hate on campus through community service learning; and so on.

The many benefits of bringing together college students who work to combat hate and prejudice were overshadowed by the important twofold objective of the symposium: first, to recognize and reward such efforts, and second, to let students discover they are not alone. Even rebels like to know they have company and are appreciated by others.

The Importance of Empathy Across Groups

Self-interest continues too frequently to determine our most important concerns and issues. What do the late Christopher Reeve, Michael J. Fox, Doug Flutie, and Katie Couric have in common besides the fact that they are well-known media personalities? All four became champions of a cause only after they or a member of their family had been struck down by a catastrophic accident or illness. Each suffers or suffered—Reeve from a spinal cord injury, Fox from Parkinson's disease, Flutie from his son's autism, and Couric from her husband's death as a result of colon cancer. Each deserves a good deal of credit for channeling concern and energy into a worthy cause. But none became involved as a spokesperson for the cause until it had affected him or her in some very personal way. It is much more difficult to think of celebrities who have become thoroughly immersed in a disease that has not afflicted their own families.

In the same way, a missing ingredient in much of intergroup relations is empathy that cuts across group lines: the ability of an individual to feel the pain and suffering of groups to which she does not belong. A compelling but exceptional example of this sort of feeling for the victimization of another group of people is provided in the book *White Men Challenging Racism* (2003), a collection of 35 personal stories chronicling the experiences of White men who sought to combat racism and fight for social justice. More typically, however, when a Latino is victimized, hundreds of Latinos protest. When someone who is Jewish is bashed, hundreds of Jews demonstrate. When a gay person is attacked, hundreds of gays and lesbians march. Because they are viewed as having a vested interest, protestors who belong to a victim's group simply lack the credibility that a protestor from some other group, especially from the perpetrator's group, would have.

Sadly, it is more common for the people in one group to willingly accept the basic validity of stereotypes of other groups while they totally reject the nasty stereotypes of their own group. Thus, someone who is Black might be incensed to find that she is labeled lazy or intellectually inferior but find no difficulty in completely buying into the stereotype that all Jews are mercenary and devious. Someone who is Jewish might be outraged to learn he is stereotyped as evil and money-grubbing but might wholeheartedly agree with the image of Blacks as being stupid and lacking in motivation.

Individuals too frequently have great compassion for the plight of victims within their own group but not much left over for outsiders. Thus, Blacks might chastise Jews who continue to remember the Nazi Holocaust and its victims. It is amazing, they argue. Jews must think they have some kind of monopoly on suffering. More than 70 years have passed and they still dwell on the atrocities committed against Jews in Europe. It's time to stop living in the past and get on with their lives. By the same token, Jews might be critical of Blacks who continue to recall the evils of slavery and Jim Crow segregation. It is amazing, they argue. Blacks must think they have some kind of monopoly on suffering. More than a century has gone by, and they still dwell on the atrocities of slavery. Even Jim Crow laws have been dead for more than 40 years. It's time to stop blaming history for their lack of success and get on with their lives.

Even the brightest and most distinguished observers can have tunnel vision when it comes to the suffering of their own group. David Horowitz (1994), who, according to his fascinating autobiography, grew up in a Jewish home where Yiddish was spoken, placed advertisements in college newspapers around the country condemning the idea of paying reparations to Black Americans whose ancestors were enslaved. Sadly, his ads inspired not a discussion of the issue but divisiveness and hostility between various groups on a number of campuses. Students protested, demonstrated, stole newspapers, and demanded that the student editors who permitted the printing of the ads be fired. At one university, on the day that Black students protested Horowitz's ad, a message referring to the mass murder at Columbine High and threatening to kill Blacks and Jews was found written on a men's room wall.

Putting aside the question of whether reparations for slavery are a good idea, it is clear that Horowitz's (2001) arguments are not totally without bias. To justify his view that Black Americans have done very well in this country, he unfairly compares the per capita income of Black Americans with Blacks living in African countries, when he should have compared the incomes of Black

Americans today with what they would have earned if they had come to this country as a free people and hadn't experienced institutionalized oppression. He tries to minimize the prevalence of slavery by observing that only one White in five was a slaveholder. And he focuses on slavery as having occurred 150 years ago, but he fails to acknowledge the many decades of Jim Crow segregation (our version of Apartheid) that followed the abolition. Ironically, very few Americans were talking seriously about the possibility of reparations for slavery until Horowitz brought the issue to public scrutiny through his college advertisements (Associated Press, 2001).

On the Black side of the ledger, Derrick Bell (1992) has written a powerful analysis in which he convincingly argues the permanence of racism in American life. But when it comes to explaining the negative reaction of many Whites, including Jews, to Nation of Islam minister Louis Farrakhan's anti-Semitic, anti-Catholic, and anti-White statements, Bell argues that Farrakhan "is perhaps the best living example of a black man ready, willing, and able to 'tell it like it is' regarding who is responsible for racism in this country" (p. 118). Indeed, in comparison with his rather weak attempt to justify Farrakhan's bigoted rhetoric, Bell is more critical of Jews who "leap with a vengeance on inflammatory comments by Blacks" (p. 121).

We have seen that spectators find greater gains in embracing the bigotry of others than they do in respecting those who are different. In going along with hate and prejudice, spectators may believe that they benefit in terms of finances, friendships, or status. In many cases, they may be right. Conversely, opposition to bigotry may also be influenced by the perceived and actual benefits and costs. This gives us a clue that respect for differences also depends in some part on costs and benefits. In Nazi Germany, although admittedly few in number, there were pockets of resistance to the anti-Semitic measures instituted by Hitler's regime. Even as late as 1938, the leaders of two Bavarian villages risked paying the ultimate sacrifice by protecting local synagogues from being destroyed. Economic factors seemed to play a significant role in such decisions. Throughout southern Germany, local farmers depended on Jews who were actively involved in livestock trading and so they were largely opposed to barring Jewish traders from operating in their area. Until the end of 1937 when the Gestapo became actively involved, in only one district were Jews excluded from the livestock trade. Instead, Jewish traders in Bavaria continued to work and to maintain their friendships with local Christian farmers (Barnett, 1999).

The possibility of a coalition involving more than one vulnerable group seems to depend on their members' locating common ground. At the turn of the twentieth century, for example, White ethnic groups—Irish Americans, Italian Americans, and Jewish Americans—put aside their differences in favor of joining together in the labor movement. Shared economic interests became a basis for forming an alliance in the workforce.

During the 1950s and 1960s, Black Americans and Jewish Americans who recognized their shared vulnerability initially worked together in the civil rights movement. The coalition to a considerable extent dissipated as the interests of Blacks and Jews grew apart in response to significant social changes occurring through the 1970s and 1980s. First, Black Americans, especially those who emphasized "Black power," no longer felt it was desirable for Whites to assume leadership roles in the movement.[1] Second, Jewish Americans became predominantly middle- and upper-middle-class in their socioeconomic status, whereas large numbers of Black Americans remained mired in poverty. In addition, affirmative action goals and quotas that were seen by many Black Americans as advantageous to members of their group had been used historically as a weapon with which to deny Jewish Americans admission to colleges, law schools, and medical schools (Lerner & West, 1996).

Even those groups whose economic objectives do not seem to overlap might find common ground as the actual or potential victims of violence. Differences in socioeconomic status seem much less important when groups share a concern with survival in the face of hate. During the early years of the 1990s, for example, a disproportionate number of Black churches in southern states were burned to the ground, some by members of organized hate groups (e.g., the Ku Klux Klan) and others by teenagers and young adults who hated both Blacks and Jews and were looking for a thrill. Many Jewish organizations got involved in lending their assistance, giving their support, and making contributions for the purpose of repairing and restoring church buildings in the south.

Empathy across groups may be too rare, but it is far from nonexistent. In 1992, filmmaker Jelena Silajdzic fled Bosnia-Herzegovina after watching her homeland deteriorate into a battlefield of ethnic violence and bloodshed. Settling into her new home in the Czech Republic, Silajdzic was appalled when she saw her adopted country's 200,000 Roma facing constant discrimination and humiliation. As in most central European nations, Roma in the Czech Republic have been restricted in restaurants, denied permission to swim in public pools, treated like shoplifters in stores and shops, segregated into inferior schools, and attacked by skinheads. In a recent survey of the residents of the Czech Republic, 79% of respondents said they would not want Roma as neighbors (Marklein, 2005).

Seeing this situation as intolerable, Silajdzic founded an organization to publicize the plight of European Gypsies. In 2000, she was honored by the UN High Commissioner for Refugees with the Nansen Medal, an award given to one refugee from each continent who employs his or her skills in the service of others (Whitmore, 2001).

Human Agency: The Ability to Create "Good" Situations

As social scientists, we are both keenly aware of the impact the social structure has on the presence of crime and violence in neighborhoods. For example, in many urban areas across the country there are places where rates of poverty

---

[1] The cofounder of the NAACP was White and Jewish. To understand the emerging negative reaction to this fact among Black Americans, simply imagine how feminists might have responded if leaders of the women's movement had been men.

and unemployment are high; where racial minorities are segregated into substandard public housing projects; where lots of single parents, particularly females, must raise their children on their own; where school districts leave "many children behind"; where gangs of unsupervised teens and young adults sell illicit drugs on the streets in broad daylight and throughout the night; and where physical and social disorder is present all around. In places like these, the schools fail miserably, families are lacking in resources, trash and graffiti decorate the streets and the parks, crime and violence flourish, and residents have little hope for a bright and prosperous future.

It is often the case, moreover, that matters get worse when the fear of crime keeps good people indoors under lock and key, so they don't get to know their neighbors or the young people on the streets. In addition, many of the young men who live in these places become criminal offenders when they participate in the lucrative illegal drug trade rather than work minimum-wage jobs in fast-food restaurants or convenience stores. Once arrested and sent to jail for long periods of time, a consequence of the war on drugs, they leave their wives or girlfriends and children alone to fend for themselves. Often lacking supervision at home and in the neighborhood, children with an incarcerated parent may be more likely to use drugs, commit crimes, drop out of school, and engage in risky sexual behaviors. Far too often, they have their own children while still very young. The institutions of law, criminal justice, and education among many others are unwitting collaborators in a social structure that maintains this downward spiraling cycle that continues to reproduce itself generation after generation.

The Agentic Perspective

It is clear that social structural conditions experienced in neighborhoods affect the people who live there. What is less clear is how this happens. How does the social context interact with individual psychological processes, ultimately affecting how residents in neighborhoods think and behave? For those of us who have experienced living and working in neighborhoods like the one described above, it might appear that generations of people are doomed to the cycle of poverty and crime once it takes hold. This is supported by a popular view that people process information from the environment much like a computer system does. The environment provides data as inputs, the person processes these data through a neurological network in the body, and then an output is generated in the form of behavior. The individual becomes like a mathematical function whereby a particular input (environmental condition) will generate a predictable output. In other words, the behavior of people in the situation is, for the most part, determined by the environmental conditions that exist there.

In contrast to this viewpoint, the agentic perspective holds that people are not just passive recipients of environmental conditions, but they are conscious of and interact with their environments, and are capable of shaping them as desired (Joas, 1997). According to Albert Bandura (2001), human beings have agency, meaning they can intentionally make things happen to improve their life situations or to achieve future goals. Broadly, agency refers to the ability of individuals (and groups) to plan into the future, set action strategies in accordance to the plan, and to reflect on the action taken and make modifications when necessary.

According to social psychologist G. H. Mead, the most important aspect of human agency (at least for the points we want to make here) is that it involves self-reflectiveness, meaning the ability of each of us to evaluate our own thoughts and behaviors to determine their adequacy (Joas, 1997). This includes the ability to verify that our thoughts about our future plans are correct and that our behaviors are likely to result in the desired outcomes. The beliefs in our own efficacy, or the ability to produce desired results with our intentional actions, are central to human agency. Efficacy beliefs affect the way people think about the world, either optimistically or pessimistically, and provide the basis for the power to alter the courses of action people take throughout their lives. This is important because situations that produce bad behaviors, like those in the Stanford prison experiment described earlier in this chapter, or the inner-city neighborhood described at the beginning of this section, are likely to remain as they are unless efficacy beliefs are positive. When self-efficacy is high individuals remain motivated toward more action and optimistic about their future; when self-efficacy is low, they tend to lose motivation and become more pessimistic about their future.

According to Bandura, there are three types of human agency: personal, proxy, and collective. Personal agency is what we described above, the ability of a person to reflect on his or her environment and change it for the better. However, there are many aspects of modern life over which we really have no direct control, but whose decisions, policies, and practices directly affect our lives. For example, when state or federal legislatures pass laws on such topics as immigration, education, health care, or social security, they have the power to impact our lives significantly. Often, people do not have the time, energy, or resources to deal directly with all of these things, so they rely on legislative representatives, government officials, and lobbying groups, among others, to take action for them. This type of agency is referred to as proxy agency. In social situations like the neighborhood described at the beginning of this section, people often turn to police officers and government officials to fix the neighborhood problems.

Similar to our beliefs in our own efficacy, our beliefs in the efficacy of these proxy agents can and do affect our worldviews. When the proxy agents are effective, perceived efficacy is high and people are likely to be optimistic about their futures and their abilities to control these important, albeit distal, aspects of their lives. When proxy agents fail repeatedly, efficacy beliefs decrease, optimism can turn to pessimism, and individuals and whole communities can become apathetic. Collective pessimism and apathy are significant forces against change and are inextricably linked to the downward spiraling conditions in neighborhoods and communities. We believe it is the case that when people cannot achieve results alone or through proxy agents, then the third form of agency, collective agency, is the only way left to proceed.

According to Bandura, the key elements of personal and proxy agency extend to groups, organizations, neighborhoods, communities, and whole societies. This makes sense because we know that collective entities like those mentioned above have unique characteristics of their own that are different from those of their individual members. Kurt Lewin (1939/1997) explained it this way:

> Groups are sociological wholes; the unity of these sociological wholes can be defined operationally in the same way as a unity of any other dynamic whole, namely, by the interdependence of its parts. . . . [I]t means a full recognition of the fact that properties of a social group, such as its organization, its stability, its goals, are something different from the organization, the stability, and the goals of the individuals in it. (p. 60)

We would add to Lewin's statement that the efficacy beliefs of the individual may also be different from the efficacy beliefs of the group as a whole and vice versa. Although the efficacy beliefs of a person and a group may be correlated to some degree, it would be wrong to say they are the same. For instance, it is clear that a group of high achievers on an "All Star" sports team might have plenty of self-efficacy in regard to their own individual athletic abilities, but this does not mean that together they automatically possess a collective belief that their team will come out on top. Collective efficacy, as we will discuss next, has a developmental sequence of its own; and although it is related to personal or proxy efficacy, it is at the same time very different. Collective efficacy affects the outlook and functioning of the group and is a major predictor of desirable outcomes in such diverse settings as athletic teams, business groups, professional associations, and neighborhoods.

Collective Efficacy in Neighborhoods

In a groundbreaking study of neighborhood crime in the city of Chicago, Robert Sampson and his colleagues (Sampson, Raudenbush, & Earl, 1997) discovered that even in poor, segregated inner-city neighborhoods like the one we described earlier, residents can work against the macro-sociological forces by acting locally with their neighbors. These researchers found that in the neighborhoods that recorded high levels of collective efficacy on survey instruments, crime and disorder were minimal. The researchers defined the term "collective efficacy" as "cohesion among residents combined with shared expectations for the social control of public space" (Sampson & Raudenbush, 1999, p. 603).

In a practical sense, collective efficacy means that residents watch out for each other and will intervene if a problem arises, such as the appearance of dangerous gangs and drugs. Their collective function is similar to the function of a body's immune system—stopping disease as soon as it is introduced into the body (neighborhood). The people who live in these neighborhoods are interdependent in the sense that their interactions help one another maintain the identity and safety of the neighborhood. As we have mentioned previously about the concept of interdependence, it arises when groups of people work toward a goal or fate that they hold in common. As Sampson suggests, we can assume that people share the goal of living in a safe place (Sampson & Raudenbush, 1999). They also share a common fate; if the neighborhood deteriorates all residents suffer the same negative consequences. So, in the same way that Zimbardo intentionally created the bad situation at his university building in the form of a mock prison, neighborhood residents can join together to create good situations.

Neighborhood agency, like personal agency, requires intentional action, future planning, the implementation of an action strategy, and a reflection on the values, ideas, and actions being taken, making modifications when needed. Whether residents participate in the neighborhood activities is a function of their beliefs about their collective ability to transform their neighborhood, that is, collective efficacy.

Neighborhood Agency and Collective Efficacy

Since the publication of the findings from the Chicago neighborhood study (Sampson & Raudenbush, 1999), many researchers and practitioners have been searching for ways to understand and promote the development of collective efficacy in neighborhoods. During the past several years, the second author has been investigating the impact of policing styles on neighborhood-level collective efficacy. In many neighborhoods, residents hand over the responsibility for public safety to the police. They engage in proxy agency whereby the police stand in as experts to deal with crime and disorder. By giving the police this authority, citizens expect that they will be successful. However, the police are often not equipped to deal with the complex social issues that produce so much crime. As a result, neighborhood residents become angry, frustrated, and apathetic. When confronted about their shortcomings in this regard, the police generally claim to be understaffed, but often agree to try different strategies, such as community policing, walking patrols, drug sweeps, undercover operations, and more. The result is that crime may be suppressed while the police are still present, but once they move on to different neighborhoods the problems return, and the cycle continues.

We think it is important to note that the police are frustrated by this situation too. Unfortunately, when some officers begin to think their efforts don't make a difference, they may become less committed to lawful ways of acting and more prone to "street justice," since the criminal justice system, of which they are part, does not seem to work. In other officers, apathy may appear in the form of a general unwillingness to conduct proper investigations; prolonged time spent on calls for service in order to run personal errands; or speaking with citizens in hurried, degrading, and otherwise unprofessional ways. As long as the police see their role as "protecting" communities (i.e., as professional proxies for neighborhood residents), and residents fail to join a collective effort to transform the neighborhood, then situations in many neighborhoods will continue to decline.

In Figure 6.1 we depict a process of building neighborhood-level collective efficacy in a developmental sequence along a horizontal continuum. At point

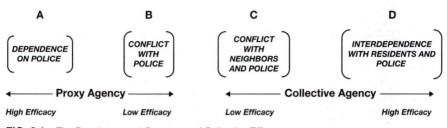

FIG. 6.1   The Developmental Sequence of Collective Efficacy.

A community residents use proxy agency and the police comply. At point A proxy efficacy is high because the police are able to respond effectively to the crimes that are reported. We think it is fair to say that neighborhoods at point A are probably low-crime communities. At this point neighborhood residents, collectively, are psychologically and emotionally dependent on police when crime and disorder appear. The actual developmental sequence begins as the level of crime and disorder grows beyond what the police can handle as proxies for the community. At this point the police become less effective in dealing with crime and disorder and officers become defensive in their interactions with the community because they are blamed for this failure (point B). At this stage of development residents are frustrated and complain that the police must do better; the police take a defensive posture and tend to become insular in their relations with "outsiders." In their public response, police administrators may offer to try different tactics, such as foot and bike patrols or zero-tolerance strategies like the enforcement of loitering laws and other public nuisance ordinances. These activities when implemented may appease residents for a short time, or until crime rises to the point the police are again unable to control it. This seems to be the place in the developmental cycle where the police and community get stuck, going back and forth for decades from point A to point B. Only by giving up on proxy agency and shifting to collective agency will the police and community improve their chances of success.

At point C of Figure 6.1 the police and community together have realized that the police cannot solve the problems alone (proxy agency) and that everyone must join the effort (collective agency). This often occurs when police–community conflict reaches a fever pitch, and the parties agree to engage in dialogue about the problem. At this point they must come to accept the shared reality that working together interdependently is the only way out. In the beginning of this stage (point C), collective efficacy is low and conflict remains high until members of the core group can reach consensus on a shared vision for the future of the neighborhood, concrete goals or milestones that will serve as markers of progress and may motivate the members to continue their efforts, and an interactive, coordinated plan of action. Although the interactions between police and residents might be difficult at this point, the participants will soon realize that through the conflict, trust will develop. This trust continues to grow as members create plans of action with clear roles and responsibilities of all parties. When the energy and activities of the group shift away from planning and are more focused on action and attaining the goals of the group, then perceptions of collective efficacy within the group are likely to rise (point D).

The importance of this example is not only to demonstrate a way of changing local situations for the purpose of crime control and public safety generally, but it is also to demonstrate a way to think about combating prejudice, discrimination, and hate-motivated violence. Simply expecting someone else to do this for us (proxy agency) will not work. We depend on our legislators to pass laws that protect us from discrimination and related violence, but these laws must be enforced, and we must work together to create local situations where intolerance and bigotry can be prevented long before they occur. Working together collectively (collective agency) is really the only way to ensure the creation of a social atmosphere that supports the integration of diverse groups and the elimination of prejudice and discrimination from our world.

Conclusion

As we saw in chapter 4, certain hate-filled individuals have been able to turn their lives around. Tom Leyden, for example, had been deeply entrenched in the Nazi skinhead movement and eventually renounced his bigoted views to become an activist for the cause of intergroup harmony. Working for the Simon Wiesenthal Center, he plays an important role in warning parents about the dangers of being exposed to organized hate groups through the Internet. Leyden's ability to make the transformation gives us clues as to how hatemongers and dabblers can be disabused of hate and prejudice. Leyden is an articulate and intelligent spokesperson. Everything that he gained by his membership in a racist skinhead group (the sense of belonging and the feeling of importance) Leyden continues to enjoy now by representing the other side of the issue. He is in great demand as a speaker and is frequently asked to air his views on national radio and television. Leyden's views find an audience of parents eager to learn from him how it is possible for their children to avoid making the same mistakes that he did.

Leyden's experiences suggest that we can reduce bigotry only to the extent that we give our youngsters healthy alternatives to hate and violence. Prejudice can be expected to decline to the extent that hatemongers, dabblers, sympathizers, and spectators are given structured opportunities to feel good about themselves, to have hope for the future, and to gain a sense of belonging without hating and hurting people who are different. Anything less than a major structural change will probably miss the mark.

The evidence from history and social science research suggests that intergroup harmony largely depends on the members of one group seeing members of another group as valuable human beings rather than as subhuman opponents. The roots of violent hatred are typically grounded in a tradition of intergroup aloofness and separatism in which the relations between groups have turned cold, bitter, and empty of empathy. One group comes to believe sincerely that its members would be better off by eliminating the members of another group.

Conversely, the violence of hate is unlikely when diverse people have developed a tradition of friendship, cooperation, and mutual respect, when the members of one group are not seen as a threat or a challenge to the opportunities enjoyed by another, and when the individuals in a group are widely regarded as making an important contribution to the well-being of society.

Creating a world like this may seem impossible, but it isn't; others have accomplished it by working together to transform their neighborhoods, organizations, and whole communities. Human beings are hardwired with the faculties to intentionally take action, to plan into the future, to reach out to experts and to others, and to work interdependently toward common goals and toward a shared vision of a desirable future situation like the one described. This is the only way hate and violence can be dismantled and a peaceful coexistence achieved.

It would be tragic if, for the sake of short-term objectives, we were to allow the course of history to unfold without effectively intervening in a process otherwise destined for intergroup conflict and violence. For the purpose of reaching sympathizers and spectators, it may be necessary to create structured opportunities for increasing friendship and cooperation between groups whose members have traditionally been at serious odds. In the context of intergroup relations, it is distance, not familiarity, that breeds contempt.

Appendix A

Anti-Hate Websites

Anti-Defamation League
http://www.adl.org

Asian American Justice Center
http://www.napalc.org

Brudnick Center on Violence and Conflict
http://www.violence.neu.edu

California Association of Human Relations Organizations
http://www.cahro.org

Center for the Study of Hate & Extremism, California State University San Bernardino
http://hatemonitor.csusb.edu

Community Relations Service of the Department of Justice
http://www.usdoj.gov/crs

Facing History and Ourselves
http://www.facing.org

FBI/Uniform Crime Reports
http://www.fbi.gov/ucr/ucr.htm#hate

Gay and Lesbian Alliance Against Defamation
http://www.glaad.org/about

Gay, Lesbian and Straight Education Network
http://www.glsen.org

Human Rights Campaign
http://www.hrc.org

Institute on Race and Justice, Northeastern University
http://www.northeastern.edu/irj

Leadership Conference on Civil Rights
http://www.civilrights.org

Leadership Education for Asian Pacifics
http://www.leap.org

National Association for Multicultural Education
http://www.nameorg.org

National Council of La Raza
http://www.nclr.org

National Gay and Lesbian Task Force
http://www.ngltf.org

National Italian American Foundation
http://www.niaf.org

National Urban League
http://www.nul.org

Native American Rights Fund
http://www.narf.org

Northeastern University's Center for the Study of Sport in Society
http://www.sportinsociety.org

Not in Our Town
http://www.pbs.org/niot

Parents, Family and Friends of Lesbians and Gays
http://www.pflag.org

Partners Against Hate
http://www.partnersagainsthate.org

Political Research Associates
http://www.politicalresearch.org

Research Center on Violence, West Virginia University
https://violenceresearch.wvu.edu

Research Institute for Human Security & Cooperation
http://www.ushatecrimes.com

Simon Wiesenthal Center
http://www.wiesenthal.com

Southern Poverty Law Center
http://www.splcenter.org

Tolerance and Non-Discrimination Information System
http://www.tandis.odihr.pl

Appendix B

Division E—Matthew Shepard and James Byrd, Jr. Hate Crimes Prevention Act

Sec. 4701. Short Title

This division may be cited as the "Matthew Shepard and James Byrd, Jr. Hate Crimes Prevention Act".

Sec. 4702. Findings

Congress makes the following findings:

1. The incidence of violence motivated by the actual or perceived race, color, religion, national origin, gender, sexual orientation, gender identity, or disability of the victim poses a serious national problem.
2. Such violence disrupts the tranquility and safety of communities and is deeply divisive.
3. State and local authorities are now and will continue to be responsible for prosecuting the over-whelming majority of violent crimes in the United States, including violent crimes motivated by bias. These authorities can carry out their responsibilities more effectively with greater Federal assistance.
4. Existing Federal law is inadequate to address this problem.
5. A prominent characteristic of a violent crime motivated by bias is that it devastates not just the actual victim and the family and friends of the victim, but frequently savages the community sharing the traits that caused the victim to be selected.

6. Such violence substantially affects interstate commerce in many ways, including the following:

   A. The movement of members of targeted groups is impeded, and members of such groups are forced to move across State lines to escape the incidence or risk of such violence.

   B. Members of targeted groups are prevented from purchasing goods and services, obtaining or sustaining employment, or participating in other commercial activity.

   C. Perpetrators cross State lines to commit such violence.

   D. Channels, facilities, and instrumentalities of interstate commerce are used to facilitate the commission of such violence.

   E. Such violence is committed using articles that have traveled in interstate commerce.

7. For generations, the institutions of slavery and involuntary servitude were defined by the race, color, and ancestry of those held in bondage. Slavery and involuntary servitude were enforced, both prior to and after the adoption of the 13th amendment to the Constitution of the United States, through wide-spread public and private violence directed at persons because of their race, color, or ancestry, or perceived race, color, or ancestry. Accordingly, eliminating racially motivated violence is an important means of eliminating, to the extent possible, the badges, incidents, and relics of slavery and involuntary servitude.

8. Both at the time when the 13th, 14th, and 15th amendments to the Constitution of the United States were adopted, and continuing to date, members of certain religious and national origin groups were and are perceived to be distinct "races". Thus, in order to eliminate, to the extent possible, the badges, incidents, and relics of slavery, it is necessary to prohibit assaults on the basis of real or perceived religions or national origins, at least to the extent such religions or national origins were regarded as races at the time of the adoption of the 13th, 14th, and 15th amendments to the Constitution of the United States.

9. Federal jurisdiction over certain violent crimes motivated by bias enables Federal, State, and local authorities to work together as partners in the investigation and prosecution of such crimes.

10. The problem of crimes motivated by bias is sufficiently serious, widespread, and interstate in nature as to warrant Federal assistance to States, local jurisdictions, and Indian tribes.

Sec. 4703. Definitions

a. AMENDMENT.—Section 280003 (a) of the Violent Crime Control and Law Enforcement Act of 1994 (Public Law 103-322; 108 Stat. 2096) is amended by inserting "gender identity," after "gender,".

b. THIS DIVISION.—In this division—

   1. the term "crime of violence" has the meaning given that term in section 16 of title 18, United States Code;

2. the term "hate crime" has the meaning given that term in section 280003(a) of the Violent Crime Control and Law Enforcement Act of 1994 (Public Law 103-322; 108 Stat. 2096), as amended by this Act;
3. the term "local" means a county, city, town, township, parish, village, or other general purpose political subdivision of a State; and
4. the term "State" includes the District of Columbia, Puerto Rico, and any other territory or possession of the United States.

Sec. 4704. Support for Criminal Investigations and Prosecutions by State, Local, and Tribal Law Enforcement Officials

a. ASSISTANCE OTHER THAN FINANCIAL ASSISTANCE.—
   1. IN GENERAL.—At the request of a State, local, or tribal law enforcement agency, the Attorney General may provide technical, forensic, prosecutorial, or any other form of assistance in the criminal investigation or prosecution of any crime that—
      A. constitutes a crime of violence;
      B. constitutes a felony under the State, local, or tribal laws; and
      C. is motivated by prejudice based on the actual or perceived race, color, religion, national origin, gender, sexual orientation, gender identity, or disability of the victim, or is a violation of the State, local, or tribal hate crime laws.
   2. PRIORITY.—In providing assistance under paragraph (1), the Attorney General shall give priority to crimes committed by offenders who have committed crimes in more than one State and to rural jurisdictions that have difficulty covering the extraordinary expenses relating to the investigation or prosecution of the crime.
b. GRANTS.—
   1. IN GENERAL.—The Attorney General may award grants to State, local, and tribal law enforcement agencies for extraordinary expenses associated with the investigation and prosecution of hate crimes.
   2. OFFICE OF JUSTICE PROGRAMS.—In implementing the grant program under this subsection, the Office of Justice Programs shall work closely with grantees to ensure that the concerns and needs of all affected parties, including community groups and schools, colleges, and universities, are addressed through the local infrastructure developed under the grants.
   3. APPLICATION.—
      A. IN GENERAL.—Each State, local, and tribal law enforcement agency that desires a grant under this subsection shall submit an application to the Attorney General at such time, in such manner, and accompanied by or containing such information as the Attorney General shall reasonably require.
      B. DATE FOR SUBMISSION.—Applications submitted pursuant to subparagraph (A) shall be submitted during the 60-day period beginning on a date that the Attorney General shall prescribe.

    C. Requirements.—A State, local, and tribal law enforcement agency applying for a grant under this subsection shall—

      i. describe the extraordinary purposes for which the grant is needed;

      ii. certify that the State, local government, or Indian tribe lacks the resources necessary to investigate or prosecute the hate crime;

      iii. demonstrate that, in developing a plan to implement the grant, the State, local, and tribal law enforcement agency has consulted and coordinated with nonprofit, nongovernmental victim services programs that have experience in providing services to victims of hate crimes; and

      iv. certify that any Federal funds received under this subsection will be used to supplement, not supplant, non-Federal funds that would otherwise be available for activities funded under this subsection.

4. Deadline.—An application for a grant under this subsection shall be approved or denied by the Attorney General not later than 180 business days after the date on which the Attorney General receives the application.

5. Grant amount.—A grant under this subsection shall not exceed $100,000 for any single jurisdiction in any 1-year period.

6. Report.—Not later than December 31, 2011, the Attorney General shall submit to Congress a report describing the applications submitted for grants under this subsection, the award of such grants, and the purposes for which the grant amounts were expended.

7. Authorization op appropriations.—There is authorized to be appropriated to carry out this subsection $5,000,000 for each of fiscal years 2010, 2011, and 2012.

Sec. 4705. Grant Program

a. Authority to Award Grants.—The Office of Justice Programs of the Department of Justice may award grants, in accordance with such regulations as the Attorney General may prescribe, to State, local, or tribal programs designed to combat hate crimes committed by juveniles, including programs to train local law enforcement officers in identifying, investigating, prosecuting, and preventing hate crimes.

b. Authorization of Appropriations.—There are authorized to be appropriated such sums as may be necessary to carry out this section.

Sec. 4706. Authorization for Additional Personnel to Assist State, Local, and Tribal Law Enforcement

There are authorized to be appropriated to the Department of Justice, including the Community Relations Service, for fiscal years 2010, 2011, and 2012 such sums as are necessary to increase the number of personnel to prevent and respond to alleged violations of section 249 of title 18, United States Code, as added by section 4707 of this division.

Sec. 4707. Prohibition of Certain Hate Crime Acts

a. In General.—Chapter 13 of title 18, United States Code, is amended by adding at the end the following:

"§ 249. Hate crime acts

"a. In General.—

"1. Offenses involving actual or percerved race, color, religion, or national origin.—Whoever, whether or not acting under color of law, willfully causes bodily injury to any person or, through the use of fire, a firearm, a dangerous weapon, or an explosive or incendiary device, attempts to cause bodily injury to any person, because of the actual or perceived race, color, religion, or national origin of any person—

"A. shall be imprisoned not more than 10 years, fined in accordance with this title, or both; and

"B. shall be imprisoned for any term of years or for life, fined in accordance with this title, or both, if—

"i. death results from the offense; or

"ii. the offense includes kidnapping or an attempt to kidnap, aggravated sexual abuse or an attempt to commit aggravated sexual abuse, or an attempt to kill.

"2. Offenses involving actual or perceived religion, national origin, gender, sexual orientation, gender identity, or disability.—

"A. In general.—Whoever, whether or not acting under color of law, in any circumstance described in subparagraph (B) or paragraph (3), willfully causes bodily injury to any person or, through the use of fire, a firearm, a dangerous weapon, or an explosive or incendiary device, attempts to cause bodily injury to any person, because of the actual or perceived religion, national origin, gender, sexual orientation, gender identity, or disability of any person—

"i. shall be imprisoned not more than 10 years, fined in accordance with this title, or both; and

"ii. shall be imprisoned for any term of years or for life, fined in accordance with this title, or both, if—

"I. death results from the offense; or

"II. the offense includes kidnapping or an attempt to kidnap, aggravated sexual abuse or an attempt to commit aggravated sexual abuse, or an attempt to kill.

"B. Circumstances described.—For purposes of subparagraph (A), the circumstances described in this subparagraph are that—

"i. the conduct described in subparagraph (A) occurs during the course of, or as the result of, the travel of the defendant or the victim—

"I. across a State line or national border; or

"**II.** using a channel, facility, or instrumentality of interstate or foreign commerce;

"**ii.** the defendant uses a channel, facility, or instrumentality of interstate or foreign commerce in connection with the conduct described in subparagraph (A);

"**iii.** in connection with the conduct described in subparagraph (A), the defendant employs a firearm, dangerous weapon, explosive or incendiary device, or other weapon that has traveled in interstate or foreign commerce; or

"**iv.** the conduct described in subparagraph (A)—

"**I.** interferes with commercial or other economic activity in which the victim is engaged at the time of the conduct; or

"**II.** otherwise affects interstate or foreign commerce.

"**3.** OFFENSES OCCURRING IN THE SPECIAL MARITIME OR TERRITORIAL JURISDICTION OF THE UNITED STATES.—Whoever, within the special maritime or territorial jurisdiction of the United States, engages in conduct described in paragraph (1) or in paragraph (2) (A) (without regard to whether that conduct occurred in a circumstance described in paragraph (2)(B)) shall be subject to the same penalties as prescribed in those paragraphs.

"**b.** CERTIFICATION REQUIREMENT.—

"**1.** IN GENERAL.—No prosecution of any offense described in this subsection may be undertaken by the United States, except under the certification in writing of the Attorney General, or a designee, that—

"**A.** the State does not have jurisdiction;

"**B.** the State has requested that the Federal Government assume jurisdiction;

"**C.** the verdict or sentence obtained pursuant to State charges left demonstratively unvindicated the Federal interest in eradicating bias-motivated violence; or

"**D.** a prosecution by the United States is in the public interest and necessary to secure substantial justice.

"**2.** RULE OF CONSTRUCTION.—Nothing in this subsection shall be construed to limit the authority of Federal officers, or a Federal grand jury, to investigate possible violations of this section.

"**c.** DEFINITIONS.—In this section—

"**1.** the term 'bodily injury' has the meaning given such term in section 1365(h) (4) of this title, but does not include solely emotional or psychological harm to the victim;

"**2.** the term 'explosive or incendiary device' has the meaning given such term in section 232 of this title;

"**3.** the term 'firearm' has the meaning given such term in section 921 (a) of this title;

"**4.** the term 'gender identity' means actual or perceived gender-related characteristics; and

"**5.** the term 'State' includes the District of Columbia, Puerto Rico, and any other territory or possession of the United States.

"**d.** STATUTE OF LIMITATIONS.—

"**1.** OFFENSES NOT RESULTING IN DEATH.—Except as provided in paragraph (2), no person shall be prosecuted, tried, or punished for any offense under this section unless the indictment for such offense is found, or the information for such offense is instituted, not later than 7 years after the date on which the offense was committed.

"**2.** DEATH RESULTING OFFENSES.—An indictment or information alleging that an offense under this section resulted in death may be found or instituted at any time without limitation."

"**b.** TECHNICAL AND CONFORMING AMENDMENT.—The table of sections for chapter 13 of title 18, United States Code, is amended by adding at the end the following:

"249. Hate crime acts."

Sec. 4708. Statistics

a. IN GENERAL.—Subsection (b)(l) of the first section of the Hate Crime Statistics Act (28 U.S.C. 534 note) is amended by inserting "gender and gender identity," after "race,".

b. DATA.—Subsection (b)(5) of the first section of the Hate Crime Statistics Act (28 U.S.C. 534 note) is amended by inserting, "including data about crimes committed by, and crimes directed against, juveniles" after "data acquired under this section".

Sec. 4709. Severability

If any provision of this division, an amendment made by this division, or the application of such provision or amendment to any person or circumstance is held to be unconstitutional, the remainder of this division, the amendments made by this division, and the application of the provisions of such to any person or circumstance shall not be affected thereby.

Sec. 4710. Rule of Construction

For purposes of construing this division and the amendments made by this division the following shall apply:

1. IN GENERAL.—Nothing in this division shall be construed to allow a court, in any criminal trial for an offense described under this division or an amendment made by this division, in the absence of a stipulation by the parties, to admit evidence of speech, beliefs, association, group membership, or expressive conduct unless that evidence is relevant and admissible under the Federal Rules of Evidence. Nothing in this division is intended to affect the existing rules of evidence.

2. VIOLENT ACTS.—This division applies to violent acts motivated by actual or perceived race, color, religion, national origin, gender, sexual orientation, gender identity, or disability of a victim.

3. CONSTRUCTION AND APPLICATION.—Nothing in this division, or an amendment made by this division, shall be construed or applied in a manner that infringes any rights under the first amendment to the Constitution of the United States. Nor shall anything in this division, or an amendment made by this division, be construed or applied in a manner that substantially burdens a person's exercise of religion (regardless of whether compelled by, or central to, a system of religious belief), speech, expression, or association, unless the Government demonstrates that application of the burden to the person is in furtherance of a compelling governmental interest and is the least restrictive means of furthering that compelling governmental interest, if such exercise of religion, speech, expression, or association was not intended to—
   A. plan or prepare for an act of physical violence; or
   B. incite an imminent act of physical violence against another.
4. FREE EXPRESSION.—Nothing in this division shall be construed to allow prosecution based solely upon an individual's expression of racial, religious, political, or other beliefs or solely upon an individual's membership in a group advocating or espousing such beliefs.
5. FIRST AMENDMENT.—Nothing in this division, or an amendment made by this division, shall be construed to diminish any rights under the first amendment to the Constitution of the United States.
6. CONSTITUTIONAL PROTECTIONS.—Nothing in this division shall be construed to prohibit any constitutionally protected speech, expressive conduct or activities (regardless of whether compelled by, or central to, a system of religious belief), including the exercise of religion protected by the first amendment to the Constitution of the United States and peaceful picketing or demonstration. The Constitution of the United States does not protect speech, conduct or activities consisting of planning for, conspiring to commit, or committing an act of violence.

Sec. 4711. Guidelines for Hate-Crimes Offenses

Section 249(a) of title 18, United States Code, as added by section 4707 of this Act, is amended by adding at the end the following:

"(4) GUIDELINES.—All prosecutions conducted by the United States under this section shall be undertaken pursuant to guidelines issued by the Attorney General, or the designee of the Attorney General, to be included in the United States Attorneys' Manual that shall establish neutral and objective criteria for determining whether a crime was committed because of the actual or perceived status of any person."

Sec. 4712. Attacks on United States Servicemen

a. IN GENERAL.—Chapter 67 of title 18, United States Code, is amended by adding at the end the following:

"§ 1389. Prohibition on attacks on United States servicemen on account of service

"a. IN GENERAL.—Whoever knowingly assaults or batters a United States serviceman or an immediate family member of a United States serviceman, or who knowingly destroys or injures the property of such serviceman or immediate family member, on account of the military service of that serviceman or status of that individual as a United States serviceman, or who attempts or conspires to do so, shall—

"1. in the case of a simple assault, or destruction or injury to property in which the damage or attempted damage to such property is not more than $500, be fined under this title in an amount not less than $500 nor more than $10,000 and imprisoned not more than 2 years;

"2. in the case of destruction or injury to property in which the damage or attempted damage to such property is more than $500, be fined under this title in an amount not less than $1000 nor more than $100,000 and imprisoned not more than 5 years; and

"3. in the case of a battery, or an assault resulting in bodily injury, be fined under this title in an amount not less than $2500 and imprisoned not less than 6 months nor more than 10 years.

"b. EXCEPTION.—This section shall not apply to conduct by a person who is subject to the Uniform Code of Military Justice.

"c. DEFINITIONS.—In this section—

"1. the term 'Armed Forces' has the meaning given that term in section 1388;

"2. the term 'immediate family member' has the meaning given that term in section 115; and

"3. the term 'United States serviceman'—

"A. means a member of the Armed Forces; and

"B. includes a former member of the Armed Forces during the 5-year period beginning on the date of the discharge from the Armed Forces of that member of the Armed Forces."

"b. TECHNICAL AND CONFORMING AMENDMENT.—The table of sections for chapter 67 of title 18, United States Code, is amended by adding at the end the following:

"1389. Prohibition on attacks on United States servicemen on account of service."

Sec. 4713. Report on Mandatory Minimum Sentencing Provisions

a. REPORT.—Not later than 1 year after the date of enactment of this Act, the United States Sentencing Commission shall submit to the Committee on the Judiciary of the Senate and the Committee on the Judiciary of the House of Representatives a report on mandatory minimum sentencing provisions under Federal law.

b. CONTENTS OF REPORT.—The report submitted under subsection (a) shall include—

1. a compilation of all mandatory minimum sentencing provisions under Federal law;
2. an assessment of the effect of mandatory minimum sentencing provisions under Federal law on the goal of eliminating unwarranted sentencing disparity and other goals of sentencing;
3. an assessment of the impact of mandatory minimum sentencing provisions on the Federal prison population;
4. an assessment of the compatibility of mandatory minimum sentencing provisions under Federal law and the sentencing guidelines system established under the Sentencing Reform Act of 1984 (Public Law 98-473; 98 Stat. 1987) and the sentencing guidelines system in place after Booker v. United States, 543 U.S. 220 (2005);
5. a description of the interaction between mandatory minimum sentencing provisions under Federal law and plea agreements;
6. a detailed empirical research study of the effect of mandatory minimum penalties under Federal law;
7. a discussion of mechanisms other than mandatory minimum sentencing laws by which Congress can take action with respect to sentencing policy; and
8. any other information that the Commission determines would contribute to a thorough assessment of mandatory minimum sentencing provisions under Federal law.

Source: https://www.gpo.gov/fdsys/pkg/CHRG-111shrg56684/pdf/CHRG-111 shrg56684.pdf.

References

Abelmann, N., & Lie, J. (1995). *Blue dreams: Korean Americans and the Los Angeles riots.* Cambridge, MA: Harvard University Press.

Adorno, T. W., Frankel-Brunswick, E., Levinson, D. J., & Sanford, R. N. (1950). *The authoritarian personality.* New York: Harper and Row.

Akers, R. L. (2000). Social learning theory. *Criminological theories: Introduction, evaluation, and application* (pp.71–97). Los Angeles: Roxbury Publishing Company.

Allport, G. W. (1954). *The nature of prejudice.* Reading, MA: Addison-Wesley.

American Academy of Child and Adolescent Psychiatry. (2005). *Multiracial-children.* Retrieved April 20, 2006, from http://www.aacap.org/publications/factsfam/71.htm.

Ancheta, A. N. (1998). *Race, rights, and the Asian American experience.* New Brunswick, NJ: Rutgers University Press.

Anti-Defamation League. (2000). *ADL Backgrounder on anti-semitism in the United States.* New York: ADL.

Anti-Defamation League. (2001). *Anti-semitism and prejudice in America.* New York: ADL.

Anti-Defamation League. (2005, April 4). Anti-semitic incidents at highest level in nine years. *ADL Audit.* New York: ADL.

Anti-Defamation League. (2006, April 24). Extremists declare "Open Season on Immigrants; Hispanics Target of Incitement and Violence." *ADL Report.* New York: ADL.

Anti-Defamation League. (2009). *Confronting the new faces of Hate: Hate Crimes in America.* New York: ADL

Anti-Defamation League (2015). The ADL Global 100. http://global100.adl.org.

Armas, G. C. (2001, March 11). Asian-American population surges. *Boston Globe*, p. A2.

Aronson, E., & Gonzalez, A. (1988). Desegregation, jigsaw, and the Mexican-American experience. In P. Katz & D. Taylor (Eds.), *Eliminating racism: Profiles in controversy.* New York: Plenum Publishing.

Aronson, E., & Patnoe, S. (1997). *The jigsaw classroom.* New York: Longman.

Asch, S. (1952). Effects of group pressures upon the modification and distortion of judgment. In G. E. Swanson, T. M. Newcomb, & E. L. Hartley (Eds.), *Readings in social psychology.* New York: Holt, Rinehart, and Winston.

Associated Press. (1994, September 16). *Man convicted of Hate crime killing.* Retrieved April 22, 2006, from http://www.nexis.com.

Associated Press. (2001, April 21). *U Conn students protest reparations ad.* Retrieved April 22, 2006, from http://www.nexis.com.

Associated Press. (2005, February 7). *Iran leader denounces prophet cartoons.* Retrieved April 22, 2006, from http://www.nexis.com.

Associated Press. (2007, October 4). *Police arrest convicted New Hampshire tax evaders barricaded in home since January.* Retrieved November 18, 2007, from http://www.foxnews.com/story/0,2933,299517,00.html.

Associated Press. (2009, January 21). *Inauguration day survey.* Retrieved July 14, 2009, from http://surveys.ap.org.

Association of American Medical Colleges. (2007–2008). *Women in U.S. Academic Medicine Statistics and Medical School Benchmarking, 2007–2008.* Retrieved July 14, 2009, from http://www.aamc.org.

Australia Immigration Visa Services. (2000, July). *Immigration laws.* Retrieved August 1, 2000, from http://www.migrationint.com.au/news/gabraltar/jul_2000-12mn.asp.

Australian Broadcasting Corporation. (2005, December 14). *Iranian president denies Holocaust*. Retrieved January 25, 2006, from http://www.abc.net.au/news/news-items/200512/s1531177.htm.

Barker, K. & Baker, A. (2014, December 21) New York officers' killer, adrift and ill, had a plan. *New York Times*. Retrieved November 1, 2015 from http://www.nytimes.com/2014/12/22/nyregion/new-york-police-officers-killer-was-adrift-ill-and-vengeful.html?_r=0.

Barnard, A. (2010, June 22). A novel twist for prosecution of hate crimes. *New York Times*. Retrieved March 29, 2016, from http://www.nytimes.com/2010/06/23/nyregion/23hate.html.

Barnett, V. J. (1999). *Bystanders: Conscience and complicity during the Holocaust*. Westport, CT: Praeger.

Bandura, A. (2001). Social cognitive theory: An agentic perspective. *Annual Review of Psychology, 52*, 1–26.

Bass, A. (2015, November 19). How soccer made refugees Americans. CNN. Retrieved March 29, 2016, from http://www.cnn.com/2015/11/19/opinions/bass-immigrants-soccer-maine.

Beck, A. T. (1999). *Prisoners of Hate: The cognitive basis of anger, hostility, and violence*. New York: HarperCollins.

Belkin, D. (2001, January 7). Anti-Semitic beliefs revealed in death. *Boston Globe*, p. B7.

Bell, D. (1992). *Faces at the bottom of the well: The permanence of racism*. New York: Basic Books.

Bell, J. (2002). *Policing hatred: Law enforcement, civil rights, and hate crime*. New York: New York University Press.

Beller, S. (1997). "Pride and prejudice" or "sense and sensibility"? In D. Chirot & A. Reid (Eds.), *Essential outsiders*. Seattle, WA: University of Washington Press.

Bellisfield, G. (1972–1973). White attitudes toward racial integration and the urban riots of the 1960s. *Public Opinion Quarterly, 36*, 579–584.

Bem, D. J. (1970). *Beliefs, attitudes, and human affairs*. Belmont, CA: Brooks/Cole.

Bem, D. J. (1992). On the uncommon wisdom of our lay personality theory. *Psychological Inquiry, 3*, 82–84.

Bennett, S., Nolan, J. J., & Conti, N. (2009). Defining and measuring hate crime: A potpourri of issues. In B. Perry & B. Levin (Eds.), *Hate crimes: Vol. 1, Understanding and defining Hate crime* (pp. 163–182). Westport, CT: Praeger Publishers.

Berkowitz, L. (1993). *Aggression: Its causes, consequences, and control*. New York: McGraw-Hill.

Berrill, K. (1992). Anti-gay violence and victimization in the United States: An overview. In G. Herek & K. Berrill (Eds.), *Hate crimes: Confronting violence against lesbians and gay men*. Newbury Park, CA: Sage Publications.

Berry, B. (1965). *Race and ethnic relations*. Boston, MA: Houghton Mifflin.

Billig, M., & Tajfel, H. (1973). Social categorization and similarity in intergroup behavior. *European Journal of Social Psychology, 3*, 27–52.

Blanton, D. (2007). Fox News Poll: Majority says O. J. Simpson guilty of robbery. Retrieved June 25, 2009, from http://www.foxnews.com/story/2007/09/27/fox-news-poll-majority-says-oj-simpson-guilty-of-robbery.html.

Blascovich, J., Wyer, N. A., Swart, L. A., & Kibler, J. L. (1997). Racism and racial categorization. *Journal of Personality and Social Psychology, 72*, 1364–1372.

Blass, T. (2000). *Obedience to authority: Current perspectives on the Milgram paradigm*. Mahwah, NJ: Erlbaum.

Blee, K. (2003). *Inside organized racism: Women in the hate movement*. Berkeley, CA: University of California Press.

Boeckmann, R. J., Turpin-Petrosino, C., & Levin, B. (2002). Understanding the harm of hate crime. *Journal of Social Issues, 58*(2), 207–410.

Bonacich, E. (1972, October). A theory of ethnic antagonism: The split labor market. *American Sociological Review, 37*(5), 547–559.

Bonds, M., & Stoker, S. (2000). *Bully-proofing your school.* Longmont, CO: Sopris West.

Bonilla-Silva, E. (2014). *Racism without racists.* Lanham: Rowman and Littlefield.

Borgeson, K., & Valeri, R. M. (2007). The enemy of my enemy is my friend. *American Behavioral Scientist, 51*(2), 182–195.

Brewer, M. B., & Miller, N. (1996). *Intergroup relations.* Ann Arbor, MI: Brooks/Cole.

Brigham, C. (1923). *A study of American intelligence.* Princeton, NJ: Princeton University Press.

Brink, W., & Harris, L. (1964). *The Negro revolution in America.* New York: Simon and Schuster.

Brink, W., & Harris, L. (1967). *Black and white.* New York: Simon and Schuster.

Brook, K. A. (1999). *The Jews of Khazaria.* Northvale, NJ: Jason Aronson.

Brown, R. (1986). *Social psychology: The second edition.* New York: The Free Press.

Brown, T. (1995). *Black lies, white lies.* New York: William Morrow.

Browning, C. R. (1992). *Ordinary men.* New York: HarperPerennial.

Brustein, W. (1996). *The logic of evil.* New Haven, CT: Yale University Press.

Brustein, W., & King, R. D. (2004). Anti-semitism in Europe before the Holocaust. *International Political Science Review, 25*(1), 35–53.

Burkey, R. M. (1971). *Racial discrimination and public policy in the United States.* Lexington, MA: Heath.

Campbell, A. (1971). *White attitudes toward black people.* Ann Arbor, MI: University of Michigan Press.

Canedy, D. (2001, March 13). Florida likely to accelerate boy's request for clemency. *The New York Times.*

Carr, P. L. (2000). Faculty perceptions of gender discrimination and sexual harassment in academic medicine. *Annals of Internal Medicine, 132*(11), 889–896.

CBS. (2007). *No hate crime charges in torture case.* Retrieved March 24, 2008, from http://www.cbsnews.com/stories/2007/09/12/national/main3253257.shtml.

CBS/AP. (2015, January 7). *Manhunt after deadly attack on Paris newspaper.* Retrieved March 29, 2016 from http://www.cbsnews.com/news/charlie-hebdo-french-satirical-magazine-paris-office-attack-leaves-casualties.

CBS4Boston. (2006, February 2). *Manhunt continues for New Bedford shooting suspect.* Retrieved May 1, 2006, from http://cbs4boston.com/topstories/local_story_033062737.html.

Chesler, P. (2003). *The new anti-semitism.* San Francisco, CA: Jossey-Bass.

Chickering, A. W., & Reisser, L. (1993). *Education and identity.* San Francisco, CA: Jossey-Bass.

Clark, R. & Lett, C. (2014, November 11). What happened when Michael Brown met Officer Darren Wilson. CNN. Retrieved November 1, 2015, from http://www.cnn.com/interactive/2014/08/us/ferguson-brown-timeline.

CNN. (2000, August 6). *True believers; hot rocks; breach of faith.* Retrieved August 22, 2000, from http://www.nexis.com

CNN. (2001, September 17). *Hate crime reports up in wake of terrorist attacks.* Retrieved September 20, 2001, from http://www.nexis.com.

CNN. (2008). *No murder conviction in Mexican immigrant's beating death.* http://www.cnn.com/2009/CRIME/05/01/pa.immigrant.beating/index.html.

Comer, J. P. (1972). *Beyond black and white.* Chicago, IL: Quadrangle.

Comforty, J. (2000). *The optimists.* Evanston, IL: Comforty Media Concepts.

Cook, L. (2015, November 20). Data show links between fear of terrorist attacks, anti-Muslim bias. *US News and World Report*. Retrieved November 25, 2015, from http://www.usnews.com/news/blogs/data-mine/2015/11/20/data-show-links-between-fear-of-terrorist-attacks-anti-muslim-bias.

Cosby, B., & Poussaint, A. F. (2007). *Come on, people*. Nashville, TN: Thomas Nelson.

Coser, L. A. (1972). The alien as a servant of power: Court Jews and Christian renegades. *American Sociological Review, 37*(5), 574–581.

Cracknell, D., and Gadher, D. (2003). Labour is warned of asylum backlash. *Sunday Times,* January 26, 2003, p. 8.

Crocker, J., & Major, B. (1989). Social stigma and self esteem: The self protective properties of stigma. *Psychological Review, 96*, 608–630.

Cronin, S., McDevitt, J., Farrell, A., & Nolan, J. J. (2007). Bias-crime reporting: Organizational responses to ambiguity, uncertainty, and infrequency in eight police departments. *American Behavioral Scientist, 51*(2), 213–231.

Cummings, S. (1980). White ethnics, racial prejudice and labor market segmentation. *American Sociological Review, 85*, 938–950.

Dalesio, E. P. (2006, March 4). Was ex-student's SUV attack a hate crime? Associated Press.

Daniels, J. (2009). *Cyber racism*. New York: Rowman and Littlefield.

Daniels, R. (2002). *Coming to America: A history of immigration and ethnicity in American life*. New York: Harper Perennial.

Davis, S. (2009, July 29). WSJ/NBC Poll: Who's at fault in Gates arrest? *Wall Street Journal.*

Deane, C., & Fears, D. (2006, March 9). Negative perception of Islam increasing. *Washington Post*, p. 1.

DeMillo, A. (2000, August 5). Student says harassment haunted her. *Seattle Times*, p. A11.

Deutsche Presse-Agentur, "Four German Youths Sentenced for Anti-Foreigner Attacks," January 24, 2003; Retrieved from http://www.nexis.com.

Dewey, J. (1910/1997). *How we think*. Mineola, NY: Dover Publications, Inc.

Dimont, M. I. (1962). *Jews, god, and history*. New York: Signet.

Dunbar, E. (2006). Race, gender, and sexual orientation in hate crime victimization: Identity politics or identity risk? *Violence and Victims, 21*(3), 323–337.

Ehrlich, H. (1972). *The social psychology of prejudice*. New York: Wiley.

Ehrlich, H. (1990). *Ethnoviolence on college campuses*. Baltimore, MD: National Institute Against Prejudice and Violence.

Ehrlich, H. (2009). *Hate crimes and ethnoviolence*. Boulder, CO: Westview Press.

Elder, L. (2000). *The ten things you can't say in America*. New York: St. Martin's Press.

Emery, T., & Robbins, L. (2009, June 12). Holocaust museum shooter James von Brunn had history of hate. *The Seattle Times*, p. 1.

Esposito, J. L. (2006, February 13). Muslims and the West: A culture war? Gallup News Service.

European Parliament, Policy Department. (2008, October). *The social situation of the Roma and their improved access to the labour market in the EU*. Brussels: Author. Retrieved November 22, 2009, from http://www.europarl.europa.eu/activities/committees/studies/download.do?file=23375.

Ezekiel, R. S. (1995). *The racist mind: Portraits of American Neonazis and Klansmen*. New York: Viking.

Farley, J. E. (2004). *Majority–minority relations* (5th ed.). Upper Saddle River, NJ: Prentice Hall.

Farrell, K. (2015, March 10). Straight man gay-bashed on college campus. *Unicorn Booty*. Retrieved November 30, 2015 from https://unicornbooty.com/straight-man-gay-bashed-on-college-campus.

Feagin, J. R. (2000). *Racist America: Roots, current realities, and future reparations.* New York: Routledge.

Feagin, J. R., & Vera, H. (1995). *White racism.* New York: Routledge.

Federal Bureau of Investigations. (1997). *Hate crime date collection guidelines.* Washington, DC: U.S. Government Printing Office.

Federal Bureau of Investigations. (2004). *Hate crime statistics 2003.* Washington, DC: U.S. Government Printing Office.

Federal Bureau of Investigations. (2008). *Hate crime statistics.* Washington, DC: U.S. Government Printing Office.

Federal Bureau of Investigations. (2008). *Crime in the United States.* Washington, DC: U.S. Government Printing Office.

Fein, H. (1979). *Accounting for genocide: National responses and Jewish victimization during the Holocaust.* New York: The Free Press.

Fernandez, M. (2015, April 30). Freddie Gray's injury and the police "rough ride." *New York Times*. Retrieved November 1, 2015 from http://www.nytimes.com/2015/05/01/us/freddie-grays-injury-and-the-police-rough-ride.html.

Finn, P. (2000, December 22). Neonazis spreading hate chat from U.S. *Boston Globe*, p. A19.

Finn, P. (2002, March 29). A turn from tolerance: Anti-immigrant movement in Europe reflects post–September 11 views on Muslims. *Washington Post*, p. A1.

Fishbein, H. D. (1996). *Peer prejudice and discrimination.* Boulder, CO: Westview Press.

Fischer, K. (2000, July 20). Parents request action: Washington vigil set to remember slain Marion man. *Charleston Daily Mail*.

Fiske, S. T., & Neuberg, S. L. (1990). A continuum of impression formation, from category-based to individuating processes. In M. P. Zanna (Ed.), *Advances in experimental social psychology* (Vol. 23). New York: Academic Press.

Flannery, N. P. (2015, October 26). Why are so many women being killed on the outskirts of Mexico City? *Forbes*. Retrieved October 27, 2015 from http://www.forbes.com/sites/nathanielparishflannery/2015/10/26/why-are-so-many-women-being-killed-on-the-outskirts-of-mexico-city.

FNC. (2000, August 9). *Special report.* Retrieved August 25, 2000, from http://www.nexis.com.

Fox, J., & Levin, J. (2006). *The will to kill: Explaining senseless murder.* Boston, MA: Allyn and Bacon.

Frankel, G. (2003, July 16). For Jews in France, a "kind of intifada"; Escalation in hate crimes leads to soul-searching, new vigilance. *Washington Post*, p. A1.

Franklin, J. H., & Starr, I. (1967). *The Negro in 20th century America.* New York: Vintage.

Franklin, K. (2002). Good intentions: The enforcement of hate crime penalty-enhancement statutes. *American Behavioral Scientist*, 46(1), 154.

Fraternal Order of Police (2015, January). Enough is enough: FOP president calls on Congress to expand hate crimes law to protect police. Retrieved November 1, 2015, from http://www.fop.net/servlet/display/news_article?id=6015&XSL=xsl_pages/public_news_individual.xsl&nocache=449270.

Gallup Organization. (2009, January 26). Obama's initial approval ratings in historical context. Retrieved July 14, 2009, from http://www.gallup.com/poll/113968/obama-initial-approval-ratings-historical-context.aspx.

Gallup Organization (2016). Race relations. Retrieved January 2, 2016, from http://www.gallup.com/poll/1687/race-relations.aspx?version=print.

Galton, F. (1883). *Inquiries into human faculty and its development.* London: Macmillan.

Gambino, R. (1977). *Vendetta.* New York: Doubleday.

Genovese, E. D. (1969). *The world the slaveholders made.* New York: Pantheon.

Gerstenfeld, P. B. (2004). *Hate crimes: Causes, controls, and controversies.* Thousand Oaks, CA: Sage.

Gillman, O. (2015, September 10). Woman who chained mentally disabled adults to boiler in basement so she could steal $212,000 in social security checks over 10 years pleads guilty to 196 counts including murder to avoid death sentence. *Daily Mail.* Retrieved September 20, 2015 from http://www.dailymail.co.uk/news/article-3228848/Woman-chained-mentally-disabled-adults-boiler-basement-steal-212-000-social-se-curity-checks-10-years-pleads-guilty-196-counts-including-murder-avoid-death-sentence.html#ixzz435ZuaVl5.

Goldhagen, D. J. (1996). *Hitler's willing executioners: Ordinary Germans and the Holocaust.* New York: Basic Books.

Goodstein, L. (1996, April 20). Report cites harassment of Muslims. *Washington Post,* p. A3.

Goodwin, C. (1994). Professional vision. *American Anthropologist, 96*(3), 606–633.

Gordon, D., & Pardo, N. (1997, September). Hate crimes strike changing suburbs. *Chicago Reporter,* p. 1.

Grattet, R., & Jenness, V. (2001). The birth and maturation of hate crime policy in the United States. *American Behavioral Scientist, 45,* 668–696.

Grattet, R., & Jenness, V. (2008). Transforming symbolic law into organizational action: Hate crime policy and law enforcement practice. *Social Forces, 87*(1), 1–28.

Green, D. P., Strolovitch, D. Z., & Wong, J. S. (1997). *Defended neighborhoods, integration, and hate crime.* Unpublished manuscript, Institution for Social and Policy Studies, Yale University at New Haven.

Gullo, K. (2001, March 11). US report links race, force used by police. *Boston Globe,* p. A3.

Halpern, T., & Levin, B. (1996). *The limits of dissent: The constitutional status of armed civilian militias.* Amherst, MA: Aletheia Press.

Hamm, M. S. (1994). *Hate crime: International perspectives on causes and control.* Cincinnati, OH: Anderson.

Hanh, N. T. (2006). *Understanding our mind.* Berkley, CA: Parallax Press.

Harlow, C. W. (2005, November). *Hate crime reported by victims and police* (Bureau of Justice Statistics special report). Washington, DC: Bureau of Justice Statistics.

Harris Interactive (2005, May 2). *Labour enjoys a 13-point lead in party identification, but Tories more likely to vote.* Retrieved May 22, 2005, from http://www.nexis.com.

Harris, H. R., & Farhi, P. (2004, July 3). Debate continues as Cosby again criticizes black youths. *Washington Post,* p. A1.

Harris, M. (1964). *Patterns of race in the Americas.* New York: Walker.

Helm, T. (2001, February 8). Young Germans see "good side" to Nazis. *Daily Telegraph,* p. 17.

Herek, G. M., Gillis, J. R., Cogan, J. C., & Glunt, E. K. (1997). Hate crime victimization among lesbian, gay, and bisexual adults: Prevalence, psychological correlates, and methodological issues. *Journal of Interpersonal Violence, 12*(2), 195–215.

Herrnstein, R. J. (1971, September). I.Q. *The Atlantic,* pp. 43–64.

Herrnstein, R. J., & Murray, C. (1994). *The bell curve: Intelligence and class structure in American life.* New York: The Free Press.

Hilberg, R. (1992). *Perpetrators, victims, bystanders: The Jewish catastrophe 1933–1945.* New York: HarperCollins.

Holian, T. J. (1998). *The German Americans and World War II*. New York: Peter Lang.

Horowitz, D. (1994). *Radical son*. New York: Touchstone Books.

Horowitz, D. (2001, January 3). Ten reasons why reparations for blacks is a bad idea for blacks—and racist too. *FrontPageMagazine.com*. Retrieved February 1, 2002, from http://www.nexis.com.

Horton, J. O., & Horton, L. E. (2006). *Slavery and the making of America*. New York: Oxford University Press.

Human Rights First. (2008). *2008 Hate Crime Survey*. New York: Author. Retrieved September 1, 2009, from http://www.humanrightsfirst.org/discrimination/pages.aspx?id=157.

Hummel, J. (1987, Fall). Not just Japanese Americans. *The Journal of Historical Review*, 7(3), 285.

Hutchinson, E. O. (2007, October 15). *Bill Cosby's new book full of racial stereotypes*. Retrieved November 1, 2007, from http://www.alternet.org/story/65306.

Hyman, H. H., & Sheatsley, P. B. (1956). Attitudes toward desegregation. *Scientific American, 195*, 35–39.

Hyman, H. H., & Sheatsley, P. B. (1964). Attitudes toward desegregation. *Scientific American, 211*, 16–23.

Iganski, P. (2008). *"Hate crime" and the city*. Bristol, U.K.: The Policy Press

Iganski, P., & Kosmin, B. (2003). *A new anti-semitism? Debating Judeophobia in 21st-century Britain*. London: Profile Books and the Institute for Jewish Policy Research.

Iganski, P., Kielinger, V., & Paterson, S. (2005). *Hate crimes against London's Jews*. London: Institute for Jewish Policy Research.

Iganski, P., & Levin, J. (2015). *Hate crime: A global perspective*. New York: Routledge.

Infostormer. (2015, June 11). Jewish vermin cry after reporter asks Bernie Sanders if he has dual Israeli citizenship. Retrieved June 20, 2015 from http://www.infostormer.com/jewish-vermin-cry-after-reporter-asks-bernie-sanders-if-he-has-dual-israeli-citizenship.

Jacobs, J. B., & Potter, K. A. (1997). Hate crimes: A critical perspective. In M. Tonry (Ed.), *Crime and justice: A review of research*. Chicago, IL: University of Chicago Press.

Jacobs, J. B., & Potter, K. (1998). *Hate crimes: Criminal law and identity politics*. New York: Oxford University Press.

Jacobs, P., Landau, S., & Pell, E. (1971). *To serve the devil* (Vol. 1). New York: Vintage.

Janofsky, M. (1997, April 10). Under siege, Philadelphia's criminal justice system suffers another blow. *New York Times*, p. A14.

Jenness, V., & Broad, K. (1997). *Hate crimes: New social movements and the politics of violence*. New York: Aldine De Gruyter.

Jenness, V., & Grattet, R. (2004). *Making hate a crime: From social movement to law enforcement*. New York: Russell Sage Foundation.

Jensen, A. (1969). How much can we boost IQ and scholastic achievement? *Harvard Educational Review*.

Joas, H. (1997). *G. H. Mead: A contemporary reexamination of his thought*. Cambridge, MA: MIT Press. 1997.

Kamin, L. (1973, December). War of IQ: Indecisive genes. *Intellectual Digest*, pp. 22–23.

Karl, J. (1995). *The right to bear arms*. New York: Harper.

Katz, F. E. (1993). *Ordinary people and extraordinary evil*. Albany, NY: State University of New York Press.

Kauzlarich, M. (2015, June 15). Beyond the chokehold: The path to Eric Garner's death. *New York Times*.

Keen, S. (1988). *Faces of the enemy*. New York: Harper and Row.

Kim, K. C. (1999). *Koreans in the hood*. Baltimore, MD: Johns Hopkins University Press.

Kochiyama, Y. (2001). Then came the war. In J. Ferrante & P. Browne Jr. (Eds.), *The social construction of race and ethnicity in the United States* (2nd ed.). Upper Saddle River, NJ: Prentice Hall.

Kolchin, P. (2003). *American slavery 1619–1877*. New York: Hill and Wang.

Kovel, J. (1971). *White racism: A psychohistory*. New York: Vintage Books.

Labalme, J. (1999, November 17). Discussion focuses on hate crimes. *Indianapolis Star*, p. B1.

LaGumina, S. J. (1973). *Wop!* San Francisco, CA: Straight Arrow.

Lane, R. (1997). *Murder in America: A history*. Columbus, OH: Ohio State University Press.

Langer, E. (1990, July 16/23). The American NeoNazi movement today. *The Nation*, pp. 82–107.

Langman, P. (2009). *Why kids kill: Inside the minds of school shooters*. New York: St. Martin's Griffin.

Larson, S. (2000, August 26). Essays explore, illuminate Creole culture. *Times-Picayune*, p. 3.

Latane, B., & Darley, J. M. (1970). *The unresponsive bystander*. New York: Appleton-Century-Crofts.

Laue, C. (2000, May 7). A wave of student activities in suburban Omaha and nationwide seeks harassment protections. *Omaha World Herald*, p. 1.

Lawrence, C. (1987). The id, the ego and equal protection: Reckoning with unconscious racism. *Stanford Law Review, 39*, 317–323.

Lawrence, F. M. (1999). *Punishing hate: Bias crimes under American law*. Cambridge, MA: Harvard University Press.

Lazare, B. (1894). *Anti Semitism: Its history and causes*. Lincoln: University of Nebraska Press, English translation, 1995.

Lee, E. (2015). *The making of Asian America*. New York: Simon and Schuster.

Lee, Y.-T., Jussim, L., & McCauley, C. (1995). *Stereotype accuracy: Toward appreciating group differences*. Washington, DC: American Psychological Association.

Leovy, J. (2015). *Ghettoside*. New York: Spiegel and Grau.

Leparmentier, A. (2000, September 13). German racist killers get long jail terms. *Manchester Guardian Weekly*, p. 33.

Lerner, M., & West, C. (1996). *Jews and blacks*. New York: Plume Books.

Levin, B. (1992–1993, Winter). Bias crimes: A theoretical and practical overview. *Stanford Law and Policy Review*, pp. 165–171.

Levin, B. (1999). Hate crimes: Worse by definition. *Journal of Contemporary Criminal Justice, 15*, 1–21.

Levin, B. (2009). The long arc of justice: Race, violence, and the emergence of hate crime law. In B. Levin (Ed.), *Understanding and defining hate crime* (pp. 1–22). Westport, CT: Praeger.

Levin, J. (1997a, March 1). Visit to a patriot potluck. *USA Today*, p. A6.

Levin, J. (1997b, July 13). N. Irish racialize "The Troubles." *Boston Herald*, p. 22.

Levin, J. (2011, March 1). The invisible hate crime. *Pacific Standard*. Retrieved March 16, 2016, from http://www.psmag.com/politics-and-law/the-invisible-hate-crime-27984.

Levin, J., & Fox, J. A. (1991). *Mass murder: America's growing menace*. New York: Berkley Books.

Levin, J., & Levin, W. J. (1982). *The functions of discrimination and prejudice*. New York: Harper and Row.

Levin, J., & Levin, W. J. (1988). *The human puzzle*. Belmont, CA: Wadsworth.

Levin, J., & McDevitt, J. (1993). *Hate crimes: The rising tide of bigotry and bloodshed*. New York: Plenum.

Levin, J., & McDevitt, J. (1995a, August 4). The research needed to understand hate crime. *Chronicle of Higher Education*, p. B12.

Levin, J., & McDevitt, J. (1995b, August). Landmark study reveals hate crimes vary significantly by offender motivation. *Klanwatch Intelligence Report*, p. 79.

Levin, J., & McDevitt, J. (2002). *Hate crimes revisited: America's war against those who are different*. Boulder, CO: Westview Press.

Levin, J., & Paulsen, M. (1999). *Encyclopedia of human emotions* (Vol. 1). New York: Macmillan Reference.

Levin, J., & Rabrenovic, G. (2001). Hate crimes and ethnic conflict: An introduction. *American Behavioral Scientist, 45*(4), 574–588.

Levin, J., & Rabrenovic, G. (2004a). Preventing ethnic violence: The role of interdependence. In Y.-T. Lee (Ed.), *The psychology of ethnic conflict*. Westport, CT: Greenwood Press.

Levin, J., & Rabrenovic, G. (2004b). *Why we hate*. Amherst, NY: Prometheus Books.

Levin, J., & Rabrenovic, G. (2006, April 7). Give us still your masses. *Boston Herald*, p. 25.

Levin, J., & Rabrenovic, G. (2009). Hate as cultural justification for violence. In B. Levin (Ed.), *Understanding and defining hate crime* (pp. 41–54). Westport, CT: Praeger.

Levin, J. & Reichelmann, A. (2015). From thrill to defensive motivation: The role of group threat in the changing nature of hate-motivated assaults," *American Behavioral Scientist, 19* (12); 1546–1561.

Levin, J., & Thomas, A. R. (1997, September). Experimentally manipulating race: Perceptions of police brutality in an arrest. *Justice Quarterly, 14*(3), 577–585.

Lewin, K. (1939/1997). *Resolving social conflicts & field theory in social science*. Washington, DC: American Psychological Association.

Lewin, K. (1951). *Field theory in social science* (D. Cartwright, Ed., pp. 188–237). New York: Harper & Bros.

Lewis, O. (1968). The culture of poverty. In D. P. Moynihan (Ed.), *On understanding poverty*. New York: Basic Books.

Leyden, T. J. (2008). *Skinhead confessions, Springville*. Utah: Sweetwater Books.

Lieberman, M., & Freeman, S. M. (2009). Confronting violent bigotry: Hate crime laws and legislation. In B. Perry & F. Lawrence (Eds.), *Hate crimes. Vol. 5, Responding to Hate Crime* (pp. 1–30). Westport, CT: Praeger Publishers.

Lifton, R. (1961). *Thought reform and the psychology of totalism*. New York: W. W. Norton.

Livingston, I. (2008, February 28). 800G rip-off of 93-yr.-old is hate crime. *New York Post*.

Locksley, A., Ortiz, V., & Hepburn, C. (1980). Social categorization and discriminatory behavior: Extinguishing the minimal intergroup discrimination effect. *Journal of Personality and Social Psychology, 39*(7), 73–83.

Logan, R. (1954). *The betrayal of the Negro*. New York: Collier.

London, P. (1970). The rescuers: Motivational hypotheses about Christians who saved Jews from the Nazis. In J. Macauley & L. Berkowitz (Eds.), *Altruism and helping behavior*. New York: Academic Press.

Ludwig, J. (2000, February 28). Perceptions of black and white Americans continue to diverge widely on issues of race relations in the U.S. Gallup News Service.

Lybyer, A. H. (2007). *The government of the Ottoman Empire in the time of Suleiman the Magnificent*. Whitefish, MT: Kessinger Publishing.

Macdonald, A. (1978). *The Turner diaries*. New York: Barricade Books.

Malkin, M. (2006, March 4). Muslim terrorist attacks UNC–Chapel Hill. *Southchild*. Retrieved from http://southchild.com/?p=312.

Marklein, M. B. (2005, February 2). European effort spotlights plight of the Roma. *USA Today*, p. A6.

McCarthy, J. (2015). In U.S., socialist presidential candidates least appealing. Gallup Organization. Retrieved June 22, 2015, from http://www.gallup.com/poll/183713/socialist-presidential-candidates-least-appealing.aspx.

McClintock, M. (2005). *Everyday fears: A survey of violent hate crimes in Europe and North America.* New York: Human Rights First.

McDevitt, J., Balboni, J., Garcia, L., & Gu, J. (2001). Consequences for victims: A comparison of bias- and non-bias-motivated assaults. *American Behavioral Scientist, 45*(4), 697–713.

McDevitt, J., Cronin, S., Balboni, J., Farrell, A., Nolan, J. J., & Weiss, J. (2003). *Bridging the information disconnect in national bias crime reporting.* Washington, DC: U.S. Department of Justice.

McDevitt, J., Levin, J., & Bennett, S. (2002). An updated typology of hate crime motivations. *Journal of Social Issues, 58,* 303–317.

McWhorter, J. H. (2000). *Losing the race: Self sabotage in black America.* New York: The Free Press.

McWhorter, J. H. (2005). *Winning the race: Beyond the crisis in black America.* New York: Gotham Books.

Merton, R. K. (1957). *Social theory and social structure.* New York: The Free Press.

Milgram, S. (1965). Some conditions of obedience and disobedience to authority. *Human Relations, 18,* 57–75.

Milgram, S. (1974). *Obedience to authority: An experimental view.* New York: Harper and Row.

Moskos, P. (2008). *Cop in the hood: My year policing Baltimore's eastern district.* Princeton, N.J.: Princeton University Press.

Moscos, C., & Butler, J. (1996). *All that we can be: Black leadership and racial integration in the army way.* New York: Basic Books.

Moynihan, D. P. (1965). *The Negro family: The case for national action.* Washington, DC: U.S. Government Printing Office.

Myers, M. (2015, September 21). Race relations in U.S. at a low point in recent history, new poll suggests. *PBS NewsHour.*

Myrdal, G. (1944). *An American dilemma.* New York: Harper and Row.

National Law Enforcement Officers Memorial Fund. Officer deaths by year (1791–2014). Retrieved November 24, 2015 from http://www.nleomf.org/facts/officer-fatalities-data/year.html.

National Coalition for the Homeless. (2009, August). *Hate, Violence, and Death on Main Street USA, 2008.* Retrieved September 15, 2009, from http://www.national-homeless.org/publications/hatecrimes/index.html.

National Conference for Community and Justice. (2000). *Taking America's pulse II: Survey of intergroup relations in the United States.* New York: NCCJ.

National Journal Group, Inc. (2000, August 10). *Lieberman: Dallas NAACP chapter pres. gone after "Jew" comment.* Retrieved August 11, 2000, from http://www.nexis.com.

Newport, F. (1999, December 9). Racial profiling is seen as widespread, particularly among young black men. Gallup News Service.

Nickerson, C. (2006, April 24). Racial attacks in Germany stir World Cup fear. *Boston Globe,* pp. 1, 8.

Noel, D. L. (1968, Fall). A theory of the origin of ethnic stratification. *Social Problems, 16*(2), 157–172.

Nolan, J. J., & Akiyama, Y. (2002). Assessing the climate for hate crime reporting in law enforcement organizations. *The Justice Professional, 15*(2), 87–103.

Nolan, J. J., Bennet, S., & Rodrigues, E. (2008). *The nature of relgious hate crimes in the United States pre and post 9/11*. Presented at the 13th International Metropolis Conference, October, 27–31, Bonn, Germany.

Nolan, J. J., McDevitt, J., Cronin, S., & Farrell, A. (2004). Learning to see hate crime: A framework for understanding and clarifying ambiguities in bias crime classification. *Criminal Justice Studies, 17*(1), 91–105.

Olzak, S., Shanahan, S., & McEneaney, E. H. (1996, August). Poverty, segregation, and race riots: 1960 to 1993. *American Sociological Review, 61*, 590–613.

Organization for Security and Cooperation in Europe (OSCE), Office of Democratic Institutions and Human Rights (ODIHR). (2008). *Hate crimes in the OSCE region— incidents and responses: Annual report for 2007*. Warsaw: Author. Retrieved June 26, 2009, from http://www.osce.org/publications/odihr/2008/10/33850_1196_en.pdf.

Osborne, J. (1995). Academics, self esteem, and race: A look at the underlying assumptions of the disidentification hypothesis. *Personality and Social Psychology Bulletin, 21*, 449–455.

Parillo, V. N. (2005). *Strangers to these shores*. Boston, MA: Allyn and Bacon.

Patriot Fax Network. (1996). *Origin of Khazarians*. From author's private collection.

Patterson, O. (1998). *Rituals of blood*. New York: Basic Civitas.

Peacock, T. (2015, October 15). 2 Philadelphia gay bashing suspects plead out. *LGBT News*. Retrieved October 15, 2015 from http://www.peacock-panache.com/2015/10/philadelphia-gay-bashing-plead-kathryn-knott-rejects-deal-19821.html.

Pearce, D. M. (1979, February). Gatekeepers and homeseekers: Institutional patterns in racial steering. *Journal of Social Problems, 26*(3), 325–342.

Perry, B. (2003). Where do we go from here? Researching hate crime. *Internet Journal of Criminology*. Retrieved July 1, 2009, from http://www.internetjournalofcriminology.com.

Petroni, F. A. (1972, Summer). Adolescent liberalism—The myth of a generation gap. *Adolescence*, pp. 221–232.

Pettigrew, T. F. (1964). *A profile of the Negro American*. New York: Van Nostrand Reinhold.

Pettigrew, T. F. (1997). The affective component of prejudice: Empirical support for the new view. In S. A. Tuch & J. K. Martin (Eds.), *Racial attitudes in the 1990s: Continuity and change*. Westport, CT: Praeger.

Pettigrew, T. F. (1998). Intergroup contact theory. *Annual Review of Psychology, 49*, 65–85.

Pettigrew, T. F., & Tropp, L. R. (2000). Does intergroup contact reduce prejudice? Recent meta analytic findings. In S. Oskamp (Ed.), *Reducing prejudice and discrimination*. Mahwah, NJ: Lawrence Erlbaum Associates.

Potok, M. (2013, March 26). DOJ study: More than 250,000 hate crimes a year, most unreported. Southern Poverty Law Center. Retrieved March 27, 2013 from http://www.splcenter.org/hatewatch/2013/03/26/doj-study-more-250000-hate-crimes-year-most-unreported.

Potok, M. (2015, March 9). The year in hate and extremism. Southern Poverty Law Center. Retrieved March 9, 2015 from http://www.splcenter.org/fighting-hate/intelligence-report/2015/year-hate-and-extremism-0.

Pratto, F., Sidanius, J., Stallworth, L. M., & Malle, B. F. (1994). Social dominance orientation: A personality variable predicting social and political attitudes. *Journal of Personality and Social Psychology, 67*, 741–763.

Public Broadcasting System. (1996). *Not in Our Town II*. Retrieved June 2, 2009, from http://www.pbs.org/niot.

Quanty, M. B., Keats, J. A., & Harkins, S. G. (1972). Prejudice and criteria for identification of ethnic photographs. *Journal of Personality and Social Psychology, 32*, 449–454.

Quillian, L. (1995). Prejudice as a response to perceived group threat: Population composition and anti-immigrant and racial prejudice in Europe. *American Sociological Review, 60*(4), 586–611.

Radler, M. (2001, March 22). ADL: Antisemitism up 49% in NYC. *Jerusalem Post*, p. 5.

Rayburn, J. (1999, September 1). Cross burner found guilty. *Deseret News*, p. B1.

Regoli, R., & Hewitt, J. (2000). *Delinquency in society*. Boston, MA: McGraw Hill.

Religion News Service. (2005, November 19). In brief. *Washington Post*, p. B9.

Riffkin, R. (2014, May 30). New record highs in moral acceptability. Gallup Organization. Retrieved May 30, 2014 from http://www.gallup.com/poll/170789/new-record-highs-moral-acceptability.aspx.

Reuters. (2001, March 9). Feud with bully eyed in Pa. shooting. *Boston Globe*, p. A5.

Robertson, T., & Kerber, R. (2000, August 6). History unchained. *Boston Sunday Globe*, p. B12.

Rochat, F., & Modigliani, A. (1995). The ordinary quality of resistance: From Milgram's laboratory to the village of Le Chambon. *Journal of Social Issues, 5*, 195–210.

Rodriguez, C. (2001, March 8). Latinos surge in census count. *Boston Globe*, p. 1.

Rokeach, M. (1952). Attitude as a determinant of recall. *Journal of Abnormal and Social Psychology, 47*, 482–488.

Rosenblum, M. (2003, December 14). Unease grows among Europe's Jews. *Washington Post*, p. A29.

Rosenwald, M. (2002, January 28). Many teens silent on hate crimes, study finds. *Boston Globe*, p. B2.

Rosnow, R. L. (1972, March). Poultry and prejudice. *Psychology Today*, pp. 53–56.

Ross, H. J. (2014). *Everyday bias*. Boulder: Rowman and Littlefield.

Roth, A. (2001, February 1). Teenager charged in rampage speaks out. *San Diego Union Tribune*, p. B1.

Rothbard, M., Evans, M., & Fulero, S. (1979). Recall for confirming events: Memory processes and the maintenance of social stereotyping. *Journal of Experimental Social Psychology, 15*, 343–355.

Rothenberg, P. S. (2015). *White privilege* (5th ed.). Duffield: Worth Publishing.

Rushton, J. P. (2001). *Race, evolution, and behavior: A life history perspective*. Port Huron, MI: Charles Darwin Research Institute.

Russell, K. K. (1998). *The color of crime*. New York: New York University Press.

Ryan, W. (1971). *Blaming the victim*. New York: Vintage.

Saad, L. (2005, May 20). Gay rights attitudes a mixed bag. The Gallup Organization. Retrieved August 1, 2006, from http://www.gallup.com/poll/16402/gay-rights-attitudes-mixed-bag.aspx.

Saad, L. (2008, November 24). *Nurses shine, bankers slump in ethics ratings*. http://www.gallup.com/poll/112264/Nurses-Shine-While-Bankers-Slump-Ethics-Ratings.aspx?version=print.

Sampson, R. J., & Raudenbush, S. W. (1999). Systematic social observation of public spaces: A new look at disorder in urban neighborhoods. *American Journal of Sociology, 105*(3), 603–651.

Sampson, R. J., Raudenbush, S. W., & Earls, F. (1997). Neighborhoods and violent crime: A multilevel study of collective efficacy. *Science, 277*, 918–924.

Santana, A., & Lengel, A. (2001, March 29). DC officers upbraided over e-mails. *Washington Post*, p. B1.

Schevitz, T. (2002, November 26). FBI sees leap in anti-Muslim hate crimes. *San Francisco Chronicle*, p. 1.

Schmalleger, F. (1999) *Criminal justice today*. Upper Saddle River, NJ: Prentice Hall.

Schmidt, M. S. & Apuzzo, M. (2015, April 7). South Carolina officer is charged with murder of Walter Scott. *New York Times*. Retrieved November 1, 2015, from http://www.nytimes.com/2015/04/08/us/south-carolina-officer-is-charged-with-murder-in-black-mans-death.html.

Schneider, D. (2006). *Slavery in America*. New York: Checkmark Books.

Schulhofer, S. J., Tyler, T. R., & Huq, A. Z. (2011). American policing at a crossroads: Unsustainable policies and the procedural justice alternative. *The Journal of Criminal Law & Criminology, 101* (2) 335–374.

Schuman, H., Steeh, C., Bobo, L., & Krysan, M. (1997). *Racial attitudes in America*. Cambridge, MA: Harvard University Press.

Selznick, G. J., & Steinberg, S. (1969). *The tenacity of prejudice*. New York: Harper Torchbooks.

Serico, C. (2015, November 2). Former NAACP leader Rachel Dolezal: "I was biologically born white." Today.com: http://www.today.com/news/former-naacp-leader-rachel-dolezal-i-was-biologically-born-white-t53636.

Shandley, R. R. (1998). *Unwilling Germans? The Goldhagen debate*. Minneapolis, MN: University of Minnesota Press.

Shapiro, T., Meschede, T., & Charo, S. (2013, February). The roots of the widening racial wealth gap: Explaining the black-white economic divide. Institute on Assets and Social Policy, Brandeis University.

Sheff, R. (2015, November 17). Far-right backlash in France after Paris attacks. Human Rights First. Retrieved November 30, 2015, from http://www.humanrightsfirst.org/blog/far-right-backlash-france-after-paris-attacks.

Sherif, M., & Sherif, C. W. (1961). *Intergroup conflict and cooperation: The robbers cave experiment*. Norman, OK: University of Oklahoma Press.

Sherif, M., Harvey, O. J., White, B. J., Hood, W. R., & Sherif, C. W. (1988). *The robbers cave experiment*. Middletown, CT: Wesleyan University Press.

Shively, M., Cronin, S., & McDevitt, J. (2001). *Understanding the characteristics of bias crime in Massachusetts high schools*. Boston, MA: Center for Criminal Justice Policy Research.

Shlachter, B. (1999, February 28). Jasper residents relieved trial's over. *Fort Worth Star-Telegram*, p. 1.

Sidanius, J., Pratto, F., & Bobo, L. (1994). Social dominance orientation and the political psychology of gender: A case of invariance. *Journal of Personality and Social Psychology, 67*, 998–1011.

Sidduque, H. (2009, August 28). Madonna booed at Romania concert. *The Guardian*. Retrieved September 1, 2009, from http://www.guardian.co.uk/music/2009/aug/28/madonna-booed-at-romania-concert.

Sigall, H., & Page, R. (1971). Current stereotypes: A little fading, a little faking. *Journal of Personality and Social Psychology, 18*, 247–255.

Smith, R. C. (1995). *Racism in the post civil rights era*. Albany, NY: State University of New York Press.

Smith, T. (2007). *The Crescent City lynchings: The murder of chief Hennessy, the New Orleans "Mafia" trials, and the Parish prison mob*. Guilford, CT: Lyons Press.

Smith, V. (2000, July 8). Groups want answers on death: Gay-rights activists demand to know if case is hate crime. *Charleston Daily Mail*.

Smith, V. (2001, August 21). Teen receives 20 years in slaying. *Charleston Gazette*.

Smith, V. (2002, November 25). Warren family settles wrongful death case before trial. Associated Press.

Sniderman, P. M., & Piazza, T. (1993). *The scar of race*. Cambridge, MA: The Belknap Press.

Southern Poverty Law Center. (2016). Teaching Teachers: Professional Development to Improve Student Achievement. Retrieved March 28, 2016 from http://www.tolerance.org/article/teaching-teachers-professional-development-improve-student-a.

Southern Poverty Law Center. (2006, Spring). Inspired by Neo-Nazi tracts, youth's rampage ends in death. *Intelligence Report*, p. 4.

Southern Poverty Law Center. (2009, July 1). *Terror from the right*. Retrieved July 14, 2009, from https://www.splcenter.org/20100126/terror-right.

Stampp, K. M. (1956). *The peculiar institution*. New York: Vintage Books.

Staub, E. (1989). *The roots of evil: The origins of genocide and other group violence*. Cambridge, MA: Cambridge University Press.

Steele, C. (1992, April). Race and the schooling of black Americans. *The Atlantic Monthly*, 68–78.

Steele, C., & Aronson, J. (1995). Stereotype threat and the intellectual test performance of African Americans. *Journal of Personality and Social Psychology, 69*, 797–811.

Steiner, I. D., & Johnson, H. H. (1963, March). Authoritarianism and conformity. *Sociometry*, pp. 21–34.

Stephan, W. G. (1986). The effects of school desegregation. In R. Kidd, L. Saxe, & M. Saxe (Eds.), *Advances in applied social psychology*. New York: Erlbaum.

Stevick, E. (2000, August 5). Student describes years of taunting. *Everett Herald*, p. 1.

Stone, W. F. (1993). *Strength and weakness: The authoritarian personality today*. New York: Springer.

Stylinski, A. (2001, March 16). Polish role is admitted in 1941 massacre. *Boston Globe*, p. 15.

Sullaway, M. (2004). Psychological perspectives on hate crime laws. *Psychology, Public Policy, and Law, 10*(3), 250–292.

Sung, B. L. (1961). *The mountain of gold: The story of the Chinese in America*. New York: Macmillan.

Tabor, J., & Gallagher, E. (1995). *Why Waco? Cults and the battle for religious freedom in America*. Berkley, MA: University of California Press.

Tajfel, H., Billig, M., Bundy, R. P., & Flament, C. (1971). Social categorization and intergroup behavior. *European Journal of Social Psychology, 1*, 149–178.

Takagi, D. Y. (1992). *The retreat from race*. New Brunswick, NJ: Rutgers University Press.

Tatum, B. D. (1997). *Why are all the black kids sitting together in the cafeteria?* New York: Basic Books.

Thomas, W. I., & Thomas, D. S. (1928). *The child in America*. New York: Knopf.

Thompson, C., Schaefer, E., & Brod, H. (2003). *White men challenging racism: 35 personal stories*. Durham, NC: Duke University Press.

Tonry, M. (1995). *Malign neglect: Race, crime, and punishment in America*. New York: Oxford University Press.

Towle, A. (2007, March 9). UMass students respond to campus gay bashing. Towleroad. Retrieved March 9, 2007, from http://www.towleroad.com/2007/03/umass_students.

Triandis, H. C., and Triandis, L. M. (1972). Some studies of social distance. In J. Brigham & T. Weissbach (Eds.), *Racial attitudes in America*. New York: Harper and Row.

Tuckman, J. (2003, May 11). After 10 years of fears, a new theory. *The Houston Chronicle*, p. 21A.

Turner, M. A., & Mikelsons, M. (1992). Patterns of racial steering in four metropolitan areas. *Journal of Housing Economics*, 2, pp. 199–234.

Turner, P. A. (1993). *I heard it through the grapevine*. Berkley, MA: University of California Press.

U.S. Bureau of the Census. (2010). Census Briefs and Reports. Retrieved from http://www.census.gov/2010census.

U.S. Department of Justice. (1998). *Hate crime training: Core curriculum for patrol officers, detectives, and command officers*. Washington, DC: Bureau of Justice Assistance.

U. S. Department of Justice. (2015). *Investigation of the Ferguson Police Department*. Washington, DC.

Wachtel, P. L. (2001). *Race in the mind of America*. New York: Routledge.

Wagner, L. & Peralta, E. (2015, November 24). 3 people in custody in shooting of 5 Black Lives Matter protesters in Minneapolis. National Public Radio. Retrieved November 29, 2015, from http://www.npr.org/sections/thetwo-way/2015/11/24/457214142/5-people-are-shot-at-site-of-black-lives-matter-protest-in-minneapolis.

Watts, M. (1997). *Xenophobia in United Germany*. New York: St. Martin's Press.

Weiss, J. (1996). *Ideology of death: Why the Holocaust happened in Germany*. Chicago, IL: Ivan R. Dee.

Welch, L. (1999, June). Uppity women. *Ms. Magazine*. Retrieved March 30, 2016 from http://www.msmagazine.com/jun99/uppitywomen-jun.asp.

Westie, F. R. (1964). Race and ethnic relations. In R. E. L. Faris (Ed.), *Handbook of modern sociology*. Skokie, IL: Rand McNally.

White, J. E. (1996, November 25). Texaco's high-octane racism problems. *Time*, p. 23.

White, J. E. (1999, March 8). Prejudice? Perish the thought. *Time*, p. 36.

Whitmore, B. (2001, April 1). Bosnia refugee a hero to Czech Gypsies. *Boston Globe*, p. A9.

Wiesel, E. (1977). Freedom of conscience: A Jewish commentary. *Journal of Ecumenical Studies, 14*, 638–649.

Wilhelm, S. M. (1970). *Who needs the Negro?* Cambridge, MA: Schenkman.

Willie, C. V. (1996). Dominant and subdominant people of power: A new way of conceptualizing minority and majority populations. *Sociological Forum, 11*(1), 135–152.

Williams, H., & Murphy, P. V. (1990). The evolving strategy of police: A minority view. *Perspectives on Policing, 13*. Washington, DC: National Institute of Justice.

Wilson, J. Q. (1992, November/December). Crime, race, and values. *Society, 91*, 90–93.

Wisconsin v. Mitchell, 508 U.S. 476 (1993).

Woldoff, R. A., & Weiss, K. (2010). "Stop snitchin": Exploring definitions of the snitch and implications for urban black communities. *Journal of Criminal Justice and Popular Culture, 17*(1), 184–223.

Wood, D. B. (2001, March 16). As their numbers rise, so does political pull. *Christian Science Monitor*, p. 3.

Woodward, C. V. (1955). *The strange career of Jim Crow*. New York: Oxford University Press.

Word, C., Zanna, M., & Cooper, J. (1974). The nonverbal mediation of self-fulfilling prophecies in interracial interaction. *Journal of Experimental Social Psychology, 10*, 109–120.

Worland, J. (2015, January 4). Police turn their backs on mayor during the second NYPD officer funeral. *Time*. Retrieved November 1, 2015, from http://time.com/3652979/deblasio-nypd-funeral.

Wyer, R. S., Jr., & Srull, T. K. (1994). *Handbook of social cognition*. Hillsdale, NJ: Erlbaum.

Zimbardo, P. G. (2004). A situationist perspective on the psychology of evil: Understanding how good people are transformed into perpetrators. In A. Miller (Ed.), *The social psychology of good and evil: Understanding our capacity for kindness and cruelty.* New York: Guilford.

Zimbardo, P. C., Haney, C., & Banks, W. C. (1973, April 8). A Pirandellian prison. *New York Times Magazine*, p. 7.

Index